My Love Affair
with England

Also by Susan Allen Toth

My
Love Affair
== *with* ==
England

Susan Allen Toth

BALLANTINE BOOKS • *NEW YORK*

The following chapters have appeared, in slightly different form, in The
New York Times: "Watching for Badgers"; "Bugles over Bodmin";
"Walk Softly and Carry a Hickory Stick"; and "A Pilgrimage to
Culbone." "My Voyage on the Queen Mary" appeared in The
Washington Post.

Library of Congress Cataloging-in-Publication Data
Toth, Susan Allen.
    My love affair with England / Susan Allen Toth.—1st ed.
        p.   cm.
    ISBN 0-345-37725-7
    I. Title.
DA632.T67   1992
914.204'858—dc20   91-58329
                                                         CIP

Designed by Ann Gold
Manufactured in the United States of America
First Edition: October 1992
10 9 8 7 6 5 4 3

High on a hill above Padstow, an old fishing village on the North Cornwall coast, a footpath leads along the estuary toward the cliffs edging the sea. Several benches have been placed on this path, and on mild days, villagers sit here, alone or chatting together, and look out across the water to the green hills beyond. On the back of one bench is a small plaque, inscribed "One Day, Henry! Luv, Ida."

The past lives on, in art and memory, but it is not static: it shifts and changes as the present throws its shadows backwards. The landscape also changes, but far more slowly; it is a living link between what we were and what we have become.

—Margaret Drabble, *A Writer's Britain*

Contents

ix

Preface

My travels in England have never followed a straight line, and neither does this memoir. The chronological chapters begin with my first trip to England ("1960: Thumbs Up!") and end in the present ("1984–1992: On the Sunny [If Wrong] Side of the Street"). Interspersed are chapters moving back and forth that reflect particular aspects of my travels or recent experiences in England.

Acknowledgments

This memoir is one to which many friends have contributed, often in ways they did not realize. My travels in England have been made much easier by Terry Malcheski, who helped arrange many trips; Jim Foran, who unfailingly tended the home front; Carl Stewart, a genius at finding cottages wherever James and I wanted to stay; Philip and Hilary Chapman, who welcomed and refreshed us. Joyce Skaggs Brewster shared my first love of the English countryside, and Faithe King Davis and Anne Balderston later guided me through many a shady patch.

In preparing this book, I have been grateful for the encouragement and advice of Carolyn Anthony, Marcia Appel, Nancy Baltins, John Coughlan, Helen Gilbert, Léonie Gombrich, Valerie Monroe, Felicity Thoet, and Pat West. As always, Julie Friedman Gaff was there when I needed her.

Molly Friedrich is the kind of acute and supportive agent every writer wants, and I have been lucky enough to work with her for many congenial years. With his unfailing warmth, intelligent criticism, and enthusiasm, Joe Blades, my editor, not only made the miles between Minnesota and New York disappear but also managed to convince me that we were imaginatively traveling in England together.

Both at home and abroad, James Stageberg, my husband, always does his best to keep me on the sunny side of the street. He is an integral part of the title and texture of this book.

My Love Affair
with England

The Enchanted Island:
An Introduction

W

e will be landing at Gatwick Airport shortly.
Please make sure your seat belts are securely
fastened and your carry-on luggage is stowed
beneath the seat in front of you." As the instructions drone
on, like a reassuring chant from a night nurse, I look eagerly
out the small scratched window. Yes, I can see it below
me. England! Still there. Waiting. As we swoop lower, over
hedgerows, dark clusters of trees, and tiny white dots of
sheep against a shimmering green background, I find myself muttering an incantation.

Every English major of my generation probably once
knew the famous speech given by the dying Duke of
Gaunt in Shakespeare's *Richard II*. It was an invocation not
only to England but to the gods of English literature:

> *This royal throne of kings, this sceptred isle,*
> *This earth of majesty, this seat of Mars,*
> *This other Eden, demi-paradise,*
> *This fortress built by Nature for herself*
> *Against infection and the hand of war,*
> *This happy breed of men, this little world,*

This precious stone set in the silver sea,
Which serves it in the office of a wall
Or as a moat defensive to a house
Against the envy of less happier lands,
This blessed plot, this earth, this realm, this England,
This nurse, this teeming womb of royal kings . . .

When I saw for the first time England taking shape through the clouds like an enchanted island, those lines floated into my mind. Whenever I return, they still waft back—although, with passing years, the speech has dissolved into a blur of disconnected images.

In the summer of 1960, before my senior year of college, my new stepfather made it possible for me to go abroad. That was how I thought about foreign travel: "going abroad," a phrase evoking castles, sidewalk cafés, peasant aprons and lace mantillas, mountain villages and fishing ports, thatched cottages and marble museums. It echoed with mellifluous foreign accents, goat bells, cathedral chimes, ships' horns, train whistles, and the songs of Venetian gondoliers and Volga boatmen. Growing up during the 1950s in Ames, Iowa, where few people ever went abroad, I heard that phrase like the song of the Sirens.

When I embarked on that first trip, I had only been in an airplane twice before. Once aloft, I sat up all night, too excited even to try to sleep, savoring every meal and peanut, drinking endless cups of coffee, and listening to the captivating accents of the British Airways crew. Fascinated, I studied the foreign money they held up, with names from Austen and Dickens: shilling, half a crown, bob, tenner. They told us about the guinea, a coin that didn't exist, exactly, although we would have to know what it was worth.

In those days airplane travel had style. Our Smith College charter flight featured champagne, linen napkins, wet finger towels, and filet mignon—all conveyed with an air of elegance that seems incredible to me now as I sink my plastic fork into a soggy piece of anonymous sole. Since airplane travel was so formal, I carefully dressed for my journey in a neat drip-dry shirtwaist, coordinating sweater, high heels, and nylon stockings. The belt on the dress pinched, but I felt properly put together. (Thirty years later, I pad onto the plane in well-worn running shoes, wearing baggy slacks and sloppy sweater, and carrying earplugs, eye mask, and sleeping pill.) I had to look just right. After all, I was on my way to England.

Is it possible to see a country clearly when, at first sight of it, a passage from Shakespeare comes into one's mind? Perhaps not. I cannot remember when I did not have an imaginary picture of England. When I was young, my mother had on her bookshelves a large blue volume called *A Literary Tour of England.* Its title did not intrigue me. In fact, I was mainly drawn to it because it was just the right size and weight to press leaves for science projects. But as I turned the pages, looking for one not yet damp and wrinkled, I could not help but notice the full-page photographs. I remember a sepia-toned meadow of daffodils bending under a breeze, with Wordsworth's lines on the opposite page. The artful extravagance of those daffodils astonished me.

Like many readers before me who lisped and lilted along with Mother Goose, I entered the English landscape at an early age. While my mother read me the classic rhymes, I jogged on my horse to Banbury Cross, swung to the insistent rhythms of London Bridge (*falling* down, *falling* down), and listened to the chiming bells of Whitechapel. As I burrowed in the Ames Public Library, I grew increasingly at home in England. I enviously watched Peter Pan soar in a Kensington nursery, stood invisibly with Christopher Robin to watch the changing of the guard at Buckingham Palace, and drank tea with Alice at the Mad Hatter's tea party.

Make-believe seemed easier in England. I larked about with Toad and Badger on the river, and I was mesmerized by Charles Kingsley's tales of Water Babies. A spidery Arthur Rackham illustration warned me that drowned fairies lurked at the bottom of the Serpentine, wherever that was. Fairies! I never would have dreamed of encountering one near Ames's muddy and man-made Lake La Verne.

As the years went by I of course read American as well as English literature. I shook to the hoofbeats of the headless horseman in Sleepy Hollow, I rode at midnight with Paul Revere, and I wandered with Betsy, Tacy, and Tib through Deep Valley, Minnesota. But I realized, without being told, that English literature was grander. In my junior year of high school, we had a required course in American literature, a sort of patriotic inoculation, like our required year of Iowa history in sixth grade. Although I sighed at Sara Teasdale's plaintive love lyrics, I knew she was not in the same league as Shakespeare, whose *Julius Caesar* we had read the year before.

At Smith, one majored in English. One did not major in

something called American. The standard prerequisite was a course that began with *Beowulf*, moved ponderously through Chaucer, Shakespeare, Spenser, and Pope, and then picked up a little speed as it rolled into Byron. American literature was a sort of detour, a thinly wooded patch of scrubby foothills on the broad and neatly cobbled path that led from Grendel's mother to Tennyson's Kraken and finally to Yeats's great beast slouching toward Bethlehem. If someone got snared by surprise into an interest in Hawthorne or Melville, she could always change to a major in American Studies. There Benjamin Franklin and James Fenimore Cooper were thoroughly mixed with history, sociology, art, economics, and political science, forming a respectable intellectual mortar to hold up what my English professors intimated was an academic house of straw.

Later, when I delved into American Studies as a graduate student, I found a thick and dappled native forest. But by this time I was already so devoted to Donne, Austen, George Eliot, Browning, and most of the other English pantheon that even the impressive weight of Henry James or William Faulkner could not entirely shift the balance of my allegiance. I wrote a dissertation on New England women local colorists, but when I eventually became a professor, I chose to teach my advanced seminar on the Bloomsbury Group instead.

Somewhere during my growing up, a vision of England began to take shape in my mind. This England was a nation with a complicated history, full of Tudors, Stuarts, and Georges and punctuated by endless wars involving roses, Cromwell, and the French. It was a lingering feudal world of castles and country estates, inhabited by dukes and baronets, chambermaids and butlers, tenant farmers and shepherds, militia and tinkers. Its heart, of course, was London, where Dick Whittington's cat prowled among Dickens's miasmic fogs, Sherlock Holmes still played the violin in Baker Street, Bunter opened the door of Lord Peter Wimsey's Piccadilly flat, and Clarissa Dalloway window-shopped on Bond Street. But it extended far beyond London, past the Brontës' Yorkshire moors, through D. H. Lawrence's Midlands, and deep into Hardy's Wessex. Its music was a symphonic chorus of bugles sounding the Charge of the Light Brigade, nightingales singing in Berkeley Square, and Frank Sinatra crooning about a foggy day in London Town.

For more than thirty years, this England has filled a special place in my life. It has meant different things to me at different times. When I longed as a college student to go to Europe, abroad, with all its allure, first meant England. Over the years I kept coming back. During a difficult first marriage, I twice left my husband for trips to England, which I somehow thought might help. A few years after my divorce, recovering from a failed love affair, I went to London for two weeks, imagining the city would distract me. At thirty-six, trying to galvanize my life, I took my little daughter to London for seven months while I directed a semester's program for American college students.

When I fell in love again, and James and I began thinking about marriage, I wanted to take him to England to see if he would love it, too. Perhaps it was some sort of test. He had been there many times before, but he promised to view it with new eyes, and he did. We were married a few months after our return.

A year after our wedding, my closest friend lay dying of cancer. All through a long Minnesota winter, I sat by her bedside and talked with her about the coming summer and a trip James and I were planning to the West Country. We pretended I could tell her about it when I returned, but we both knew better. A few weeks after she died, James and I boarded a plane. I remember shivering under a cloudy sky on Exmoor that June, walking and listening to the wind, trying to confront my grief.

Despite more than a dozen trips to England, I have never wanted to live there permanently. After my seven-month stay I was glad to return to a plumber I knew, a one-stop supermarket, sun-washed skies, roads with shoulders, a telephone that always worked, and friends on the other end of the line. If I were ever to move to England, I suspect it would take me a long time to make close friends. Although I have found the English pleasant and helpful, I do not feel I know any of them very well.

I do not blame the English. If they keep to themselves, I also keep to myself. At home in America, I guard my privacy, cherishing the easy and congenial company of my husband or quiet time alone. When I am in England, I need even more meditative space. Since I travel quite intensely, looking and listening and walking hard, at night I am ready to stop. I have to absorb what I experience and gather my energies for the next day. I want to sink into bed with a book, not traipse down to the pub to talk about politics or football. So I do not usually make social overtures.

I do not think of myself as an authority on contemporary English life. My only guides to society, politics, or economics are what I observe, read, or gather from casual conversations in gardens, on walking trails, in the greengrocer's, or at bed-and-breakfast tables. What I read is mainly what I gather from the *Times* or *Observer* or a copy of the *Daily Mail* I sometimes sneak underneath the *Times* when I bring back the morning papers. I have also absorbed something from the BBC, both radio and television.

When I come home, I continue to follow with interest what is going on in England, but American newspapers and magazines don't tell me much more about England than English journalists tell me about America. I admire political and sociological experts, but I'll never be one. When I read Richard Critchfield's account of several hundred interviews he conducted for his 1990 study, *An American Looks at Britain*, I realized I would not even have known what relevant questions to ask Barbara Cartland, Jeremy Irons, or Douglas Hurd. The title of Critchfield's book also reminded me that the country I know is England, not really the whole of Great Britain, that complex and uneasy union that includes Ireland, Scotland, and Wales. Although I have traveled briefly in Wales and lowland Scotland, I was only once in Ireland, long ago and then for a mere handful of days.

Nor am I a scholar of English history. How could I pose as one when I shamefacedly doze over almost any definitive volume of economic, social, military, or political commentary? I even bogged down in Winston Churchill's popular *A History of the English-Speaking Peoples*. My reading is eclectic and eccentric. Although I avidly collect English travel books, which help me plan my own trips, I prefer very specific ones, on the history of cottage architecture, for example, or gardens not open to the public, or

Wainright's favorite walks in the Lake District.

I also like to read gifted writers on English landscape they love, such as Daphne du Maurier on Cornwall, or Nigel Nicolson on Kent, or Richard Johnson on East Anglia. I am easily enticed, as well, by contemporary novels that work carefully on English backgrounds; P. D. James's *Devices and Desires* sent me to North Norfolk, and A. S. Byatt's *Possession* has made me want to return to the Yorkshire coast.

Although I admire their tenacity and cleverness, I confess I have not learned much from the English travel writers who practice what I think of as Bleak Chic. In their England, depressed and still class-ridden, the sun never shines, except perhaps to illuminate an ugly power station, shopping center, or crowded caravan site. England for them has become a theme park, but without Disney's standards of careful planning and polished cleanliness.

Of course, their England may be the true one. My view of England, largely based on central London and the English countryside, usually does not incorporate the slums of Manchester or the smoky skies of Stoke-on-Trent. I have not probed into the discontents of small shopowners in unfashionable resorts or the anger of displaced farmers or the limited horizons of an office assistant in a cold bedsitter in a dreary London street. Nor have I personally confronted the constraints of rigid class distinctions or endured the sometime failures of socialism or suffered the rigors of a profiteering conservatism.

My personal and perhaps antiquated image of England was brought home to me several years ago, when my teenage daughter, Jenny, spent a semester in England.

Jenny's study-abroad program was part of a large American commercial operation that contracted with English families to house and feed American students who were placed in participating local schools. Jenny lived with a host family in a tidy suburb just outside London in the Green Belt. Her England was a very different imaginative creation from mine, a curious and often unpleasant blend of Dickens, John Osborne, and Paul Theroux.

Although the Putnams, Jenny's family, seemed fairly financially secure—the father was an engineer, the mother a secretary—Jenny found that they clung to their position in life as if it might disintegrate beneath them at any moment and plunge them into an indescribable abyss. They scrimped and saved, never going once during the four months Jenny lived with them to a movie or a restaurant—and certainly never into nearby London for a play or concert. Nor did they entertain friends; Jenny never heard either one of them speak of friends or take telephone calls from any.

Lunches for the Putnams' three children were carefully planned and budgeted, down to the last cookie. Jenny, thin and athletic but with an insatiable teenage appetite, once asked for a cookie after dinner. Margery, her "host mom," told her sharply, "Absolutely not. Those are for the girls' school lunches. Every single one of those cookies is accounted for." Although Jenny's program paid the Putnams to prepare her lunches, she soon realized that her allotment did not include cookies.

As part of her family chores, Jenny cleared the table after supper. The youngest girl, a timid eight-year-old, often followed her into the kitchen and stood and watched while Jenny scraped and stacked the dishes. Finally Jenny asked her why. The girl diffidently confided, "My mom sent me out here to make sure you don't nick any extra food." Strange things happened in that closely guarded household. When Jenny developed an evident fondness for a certain breakfast cereal, the carton disappeared from the kitchen counter. Putting pots and pans away a few days later, she eventually discovered the cereal hidden in a dark corner of a lower shelf.

Although the Putnams' budget extended to occasional desserts of canned puddings or packaged cakes, it did not cover fresh fruits or many vegetables. Mainly everyone ate a recurring menu of chicken, stewed beef, or mutton, served alternately with potatoes, parsnips, or rutabagas, and supplemented by mounds of heavily cooked cabbage. "I think I'm developing a food obsession, Mom," she said to me one week when I called. "You know, not about anything particular, just about *food.*"

To save on heat, the Putnams shut off all radiators in the bedrooms at night and closed off much of the house during the day. Toward the end of her visit, when a flu epidemic was sweeping through London along with bone-chilling December winds, Jenny called us collect unexpectedly in the middle of our night. She was home from school, sick and alone. "Margery has hidden the thermometer and locked the medicine cabinet," she said, "because she thinks I'm shamming and don't want to go to school. When I took my temperature last night, it was a hundred and three. Margery got cross and told me not to make a fuss, just to take all my clothes off and get into bed without any blankets, and then my fever would go down. This morning when she left for work, she unplugged the phone and hid it, because she thinks I've lied about the number of times I've used it and paid for local calls, but I've found it, and I just felt I had to call you. I'm sure I'll be okay, but I feel really hot and funny and kind of light-headed. I'm not sure what to do. Actually, I feel a little scared." The flu had already killed dozens of people in England, and I was scared, too. Within an hour I had called an old friend in London who arranged to pick up my seventeen-year-old and house her for the remaining ten days of her stay.

For Jenny, being part of this limited, regulated, and frugal life was undoubtedly an invaluable, though certainly unappreciated, education. One friend of mine, who has spent sabbatical years in England, commented acidly on Jenny's reported discomfort, "Well, maybe it's time she learned what it's like not to live in an affluent, throwaway society. We Americans are so critical of those who don't have our resources. We have no idea how strapped many English supposedly middle-class families are. They can't afford to waste." She may have been right. But she also admitted that she herself had no intention of ever return-ing to England for anything more than a brief visit.

Neither does Jenny. She does retain happy memories about London, which she was able to explore on occa-sional weekends, and about the English countryside. Her main solace during her four months' stay was a footpath that began at the edge of the Putnams' housing estate or development. The unfrequented path led through fields, pastures, and a small wood. Early in the morning and sometimes at dusk, Jenny jogged there through fog, mist, rain, and even occasional sunshine. She loved the greenness of it, she said, the sound of birds, the wildflowers at the edge of the path, and the feeling of being alone in the thick white mist. When Jenny talks a little wistfully about that path, she comes close to the spirit with which I have traveled in England.

But she still does not understand why James and I continue to return there, year after year. An avid would-be explorer, who at seventeen had already been to England, Germany, the Netherlands, Japan, and many parts of America, Jenny has long been disgusted by the sameness of my ambitions. "You're going back to England *again?*" she asks querulously, pitying herself for having such a fuddy-duddy for a mother. "Why?"

Why indeed? I often ask myself the same question. I browse through travel magazines and think idly about the caves of Gibraltar, Gaudi's architecture in Spain, the canals of Venice, and the islands outside Stockholm. For years I have been fascinated by the remote beauty of the Arctic and Antarctic. Browsing in a book of aerial photographs, I transport myself to the Himalayas, where I used to think of trekking. Why England? Why not Crete, for example, where James and I spent ten glorious days on our first major vacation together? Crete has ruins, mountains, sea, and sun. I cannot swim nude from a hot sand beach any-where I know in England. Why not France, where we feasted on Provençal olives, Brie, and baguettes, or Nor-way, whose fjords were once home to both James's and my great-grandparents? Why not a number of other places, all with fine food and weather?

Why England? What does it offer that I lack in my life? What in my background, both geographic and personal, has made England my country of choice for pilgrimage? What have I found there, what have I learned, what has nourished me? The last time she asked, I did not have the answers for Jenny. I wrote this memoir partly so I could find them out for myself.

Ghost-Hunting

*T*he last time I was in London, I lay awake in the dark of the upstairs bedroom of our rented Cloth Fair flat, wondering whether I would see the ghost. On our first night there, as I flipped through the visitors' book, I had been riveted by one entry: "As we were having sherry in the front room last night, George and I think we heard the ghost in the upstairs bedroom." Heard what? What ghost? The entry did not say. But it had said enough. During our ten nights in the flat, I waited uneasily for the closet door to open or the murky folds of the curtains to begin to move.

I have never seen a ghost. I can't say that I believe in them, but I can't say that I don't. My life has been full of enough coincidence, unexpected meetings, and moments of astonishment that I hesitate to decide something cannot happen because it has not yet happened to me. Yet when I am home, in Minnesota or anywhere else in America, I do not think much about ghosts. I am only alert to them in England.

One of the reasons I go to England has to do with ghosts—or, more precisely, with my belief that England is the kind of place to find ghosts. The Midwest, where I have lived most of my life, is not. Although I love the Iowa prairie country where I grew up, the lake-sprinkled low-lands of Minnesota where I have spent my last twenty-eight years, and the river bluffs of western Wisconsin, where I often retreat on weekends, I know that I am drawn to England partly because it offers me many things the Midwest does not.

We Midwesterners do have our reputed hauntings. At local bookstores I have seen a few thinnish titles like *Minnesota Mysteries* or *Wisconsin Ghost Stories*. I've never been tempted to do more than glance through them. Yet tucked among my shelves devoted to England, between bed-and-breakfast directories and National Trust hand-books, are several well-thumbed guides to purported ghosts in England. I am a little embarrassed about owning these ghost guides. I rationalize that browsing through these books probably puts me in the proper frame of mind for travel: open, receptive, and ready for anything.

My latest addiction is Simon Marsden's *The Haunted Realm*, a ghost guide whose brooding black-and-white photographs perfectly evoke the sites where spirits might wish to linger: a yew-shaded churchyard, mist-shrouded ruins, and dark tors looming on Dartmoor. Marsden also photographs ghostly artifacts, like the Screaming Skull of Bettiscombe, which he shows being fondly cradled by its owner. In an introduction to Marsden's book, novelist Colin Wilson outlines his case for ghosts, some of whom he perceives as images in electromagnetic fields. These images, he explains, can be impressed upon the atmo-sphere by intense passion or by inexplicable chance, and remain suspended in time and space, waiting to be picked up by certain sensitivities.

When I was growing up, I would never have had to be convinced that ghosts really existed. Like many young readers, I devoured ghost stories indiscriminately, from horror comic books to Henry James's *The Turn of the Screw*. Ghost stories were a common heritage. At Camp Fire Girls' Camp, our counselor mesmerized us with frightening stories as the flames on the campfire flickered into darkness. Some of the ghosts she described were absolutely real, she assured us. Friends of hers had known people who had seen them.

At slumber parties, in the shivery predawn hours, everyone competed with tales of terror that slowly drove us, shuddering, deeper into our blanket rolls. My favorite was "The Monkey's Paw," a story my dramatic aunt Millee, a librarian, had once told me. In this classic chiller by W. W. Jacobs, an old couple is given a shriveled monkey's paw that can grant three wishes. Their first wish is for a large sum of money. Next day, their only son is caught, mangled, and killed in the machinery at the local mill. The management offers them that exact sum as recompense.

Frantic with grief when she hears the news, the wife seizes the monkey's paw from her husband and wishes for their dead son to be brought back to life. When, late at night, a furious knock sounds at their door, undoubtedly the horribly mutilated son returned from the grave, I always paused for effect. What was waiting on the other side of that door? Everyone shrieked obligingly. Of course, we never found out. The old woman opens the door to an empty night. Her husband has used their last wish, just in time, to send the apparition back to the grave.

If I had tried to fix a locale for "The Monkey's Paw," I would have unhesitatingly picked England, a country I already knew from my omnivorous reading. The old man and his wife didn't seem American. Their story was too bleak, too grotesque, too gruesome. The America I knew was determinedly optimistic. No, for me "The Monkey's Paw" could not have taken place in Iowa.

Simon Marsden would have understood. In his book he openly confessed: "I chose Britain and Ireland as 'The Haunted Realm' because they are the traditional home of ghosts, with so many historic houses and castles in remote settings, and because of the eccentricity of many of their inhabitants and the mythology of the ghost story that still persists. I did not include any 'modern day' hauntings, such as council houses or bingo halls, as mine is an unashamedly romantic approach to the genre and such places do not exist in my own particular 'fantasy world.' "

We did have haunted houses in Iowa. At least, any old, run-down and uninhabited house quickly acquired a lurid reputation. Even a house three blocks down the hill on our eminently respectable street had a certain atmosphere that, in the right light and mood, might be considered frightening. Set on a knoll back from the street in a grove of tangled elms, the long-unpainted house had faded lace curtains that were always closed. Although I biked up and down Oakland Hill many times a week, I never saw any sign of life in that darkened house. After dusk I walked on the other side of the street.

When my mother took my sister and me for drives in the country around Ames, we sometimes saw abandoned farmhouses that looked as if they might be satisfactorily haunted. With their windows knocked in and doors hanging askew, they seemed so jarring in an otherwise neatly ordered landscape that they demanded investigation. But when my older sister and I managed to explore one such farmhouse, I was cured forever of wanting to know more about them. It was a day when my mother must not have known where we were going or what we were doing, for I know we had been warned that deserted houses were dangerous. Their broken floors could send us cascading into a cellar, we might get tetanus from a rusty nail, we might even find lurking tramps with foul intentions.

I remember clambering with difficulty that afternoon through a muddy field over broken cornstalks—it was late fall, a more suitable season for ghost-hunting than the hot midsummer sun—until we finally scrambled up a broken-down porch and entered the ruined house. Small and dirty, it was half-filled with broken furniture and dotted with mouse droppings. In one corner were a few empty cans and some crumpled newspaper, perhaps signs of long-gone tramps. Banal graffiti, scribbled on the walls, assured us that Kilroy had been there. Nothing in that depressing environment suggested ghosts.

So if I wanted to believe in ghosts, I knew I had better think of them somewhere far removed from such ordinary and tawdry surroundings. Like Simon Marsden, I decided to locate my fantasy world in England. I had identified England as a fairy-tale country ever since I had seen my first Map of Fairyland hung in the Children's Room of the Ames Public Library. The compass on this poster-size map pointed East of the Sun and West of the Moon. From a turreted tower in one corner, Rapunzel let down her golden hair. Not far away, Sleeping Beauty lay surrounded by briars, waiting for her young knight on his white horse. He was proudly riding from another section of the map. Jack was climbing his beanstalk only inches from Cinderella, who sat in her pumpkin coach. Cloud-capped, jagged peaks, labeled The Misty Mountains, rose in another corner, near an enchanted lake, watched over by a fire-breathing dragon.

I have not seen this Map of Fairyland for a very long time, and perhaps it is no longer published. Worse, it may now be dotted with Disney characters or Teenage Mutant Ninja Turtles. But it certainly lives in my own mind, because when I was young, it seemed to me a tangible proof—what is more certifiable than a map?—that the imaginative world I had discovered through my love of books really did exist. When I looked at that map, I could see myself riding on my own caparisoned white horse toward the Misty Mountains.

That imaginative world was synonymous with England. Not only Mother Goose but most familiar fairy tales, which I knew mainly through collections like *The Blue Fairy Book* and *The Green Fairy Book*, were English. So were tales of King Arthur and other heroes, who all seemed to have lived in England. St. George battled a dragon in its mountainous rocky lair. Deep in Sherwood Forest, Robin Hood lived a life of saucy freedom with his Merry Men. Everything got romantically mixed up together. For England and St. George! For St. George and the Dragon! For dragons, castles, and ghosts!

When I grew older, I convinced myself I no longer

believed in fairy tales, myths, and legends. Then, when I decided to major in English literature at college, I arranged to spend a summer studying in England. What happened to me at twenty that summer has surely happened to hundreds of thousands, probably millions, of American tourists before and since. I discovered the romance of history.

As I wandered through London and then hitchhiked from Stratford to Stonehenge, Warwick Castle to Loch Lomond, I found myself not just dipping my toe into the current of the past but almost sinking into it over my head. When I walked down Whitehall, where Charles I, flawed but gallant, had been executed, or stood in the shadow of Donne's shrouded effigy in St. Paul's, or strolled the pleasure grounds at Hampton Court where Anne Boleyn had dallied with Henry VIII, I felt historical ghosts thick around me.

Perhaps no one is as vulnerable to the lure of England's many-layered past as a young American reader who has grown up under the wide empty skies of the Midwest. To me, the Midwest was almost featureless, compared, for instance, with New England, home of the House of the Seven Gables, or to the myth-ridden Far West. Nothing in Ames seemed historic or even very old. If a building did age, it was eventually renovated beyond recognition or else torn down. If I had known where to stand and how to listen, somewhere in Ames I might have been able to catch an echo from the past of the heavy rumble of wagon wheels on a prairie schooner heading west. But history seemed to have vanished from Iowa. In England, it was still alive.

The entire country vibrated with spirits, who glided through intervening years, decades, centuries, and even recorded history itself with an ease that astonished me. When I saw Stonehenge, it made me feel that England was a spiritual tuning fork, humming to all those distant vibrations. I remember my gasp of surprise as the car I was in came over a hill and I saw the stones rise on Salisbury Plain. No matter how many pictures a visitor has seen of Stonehenge, it remains profoundly disturbing, a tumbled circle of huge hewn shapes rising out of nowhere on a treeless barren plain. Even now, thirty years later, as James and I drive over the rushing A303, I still catch my breath when Stonehenge appears in front of me with the suddenness of a dream.

In 1960, the site was not as heavily visited as it is today, and it had not yet been fenced off. It was a cool summer day, with a rainy mist blowing over Salisbury Plain. I wandered among the stones, touching them, feeling the wind ruffle my hair, looking out over the sweeping fields and meadows beyond the circle. Then and now, the high plateau stretches out in all directions, with no sign of human habitation anywhere. Although a few other tourists circled around me, they were dwarfed by the overwhelming sky and silenced by the whistling wind.

I thought of Hardy's Tess, lying exhausted on one of these stones; of Druids, whom I pictured as strange austere priests in flowing robes; of midsummer solstice and sacrificial rites. No one in 1960 had yet produced a convincing explanation of how or why these gigantic stones had been dragged and erected to this hilltop, so far from where they had been quarried. So I felt I was standing in the midst of a mystery, thinking of mysteries. (I was, however, also an excited young tourist. I still have a snapshot taken of me that day: I am perched on a sacred stone, my ankles neatly crossed, and, not noticeably haunted, I am smiling at the camera.)

Although I sensed ghosts everywhere that summer when I was twenty, I do not think I found them at all alarming. If I read in a guidebook at a stately home about its notorious White Lady, I was intrigued and titillated by the idea that I might see her floating above a marble staircase—even though I never did. Ghosts caused only a delightful shiver. Who would feel afraid in the sunlit rosy-brick ruins of Kenilworth, which seem almost to have been invented by Sir Walter Scott? Even on bloody Tower Green, it was hard to envision any nightmarish spirits that would not be discomfited by the tidy green grass, sleek black ravens, and murmuring groups of tourists.

Perhaps, too, ghosts did not seem a pressing issue at the age of twenty. Somewhere after my early teenage years, probably about the time I stopped going to slumber parties, I was no longer so fascinated by spirits, hauntings, and supernatural tales. I thought of ghost stories, if at all, as something rather childish, like believing in Santa Claus or tree fairies. When we are young, ghost stories offer extended possibilities, a universe that exists beyond the so-called real world, a world of dreams that can come true—if sometimes with alarming results. As we grow older, the everyday world consumes us.

The time line for believing in ghosts is a delicate one. Several years ago, when my daughter was fifteen, she begged to accompany James and me on our next trip to

England. We agreed and arranged for her best friend, Annelise, to come, too. Perhaps because she had seen Simon Marsden's *The Haunted Realm* lying open on our coffee table, or because she, like me, had somehow imbibed the notion of England as a country that was inhabited by ghosts, she asked if we could please see some haunted houses. Consulting Marsden, I picked Athelhampton in Dorset, only an hour's drive from a hotel where we'd be staying.

But by the time summer came, Jennifer had turned sixteen, and ghosts no longer seemed to hold much appeal. In fact, when we got there, England itself did not inspire great enthusiasm. Our countryside itinerary did not include any bright lights, and the quiet and leisurely attractions of great houses and gardens were not high on a teenager's list of allurements. Jenny and Annelise rode drowsily in the backseat of our rented car, plugged into their pacifying Walkmans, and spoke only to exchange tapes with each other. Much of the time their eyes were closed.

But I still held out hope for haunted Athelhampton. Trying to scratch up some excitement, I insisted upon reading aloud Marsden's entry, describing several ghosts who regularly appeared at the manor. One of Athelhampton's more unusual spirits was a pet monkey, mistakenly immured in a secret passageway several centuries ago, who now could sometimes be heard vainly scratching behind a wall. The Martyn family crest subsequently featured a chained ape, holding in its paw a mirror, with the disconcerting inscribed warning: "He who looks at Martyn's ape, Martyn's ape shall look at him." Athelhampton sounded promising.

It looked promising, too. Marsden had photographed Athelhampton's topiary gardens from a disconcerting angle, surrounded by black sky and deep shadows. Blank geometric forms, guarding the distant house, loomed in the foreboding foreground. Another equally unnerving photograph showed a garden statue of Queen Victoria. Short, plump, and grandmotherly, Queen Victoria would not ordinarily scare anybody. But Marsden had managed to photograph the statue quite close and had bathed it in a deadening white light. It looked as if it were staring with blinded eyes right at the onlooker.

On the bright sunny afternoon we drove to Athelhampton, the English countryside did not look in the least haunted. We had had no rain for two weeks, and the unusual heat made us all a little lethargic. Instead of lingering in the Athelhampton gardens, whose topiary might eventually have worked a spell on us, we went almost directly into the house. I glanced at the carved yews as I passed; in sunlight, they no longer seemed ominous. Part of the garden held palm trees. It is hard to picture ghosts among palms.

The house itself was satisfactorily ancient. Along with many other visitors—for Athelhampton is an established tourist attraction—we trooped up and down narrow stairs, under low archways, and beneath dark Tudor paneling and carved moldings. If I had been alone, I think I could have easily imagined a haunting, for, like most Tudor houses, Athelhampton seemed both convoluted and oppressive. But thudding feet and muttered comments dispelled any possibility of daydreaming.

As they walked behind James and me, Jenny and Annelise were unenthralled. Athelhampton was not their first historic house, and understandably, it could animate no Tudor ghosts for girls who had only the vaguest notions who the Tudors had been.

As we were leaving Athelhampton I stopped at the entry desk and, in a moment of desperation, leaned close to the elderly gentleman who presided over the roll of tickets. "Such an old house," I said with forced geniality. "I don't suppose you have any ghosts? I think I've read somewhere that Athelhampton is haunted." Jennifer, embarrassed, looked away and tried to pretend I wasn't her mother.

The elderly gentleman smiled pleasantly. "Oh yes," he said. "Now, I haven't seen one myself, but a colleague of mine ran into a serving wench near the stables and then realized later who she was. Dressed in the style of the times, you know."

I oohed appreciatively.

He glanced about to see if, among the steady flow of those who were leaving, any nonpaying tourists were slipping in. "In a house like this, you can see them in full daylight," he continued. "You walk into a sunny room, and there they are. But they're gone in a flash. Only later do you realize who it was." He smiled again and turned away to two waiting customers.

With Jenny tugging at my arm, I walked out to the courtyard. The sun was so bright it would have dissolved even the most determined ghost.

On the way home from Athelhampton, I thought about my brief conversation with the guide. I wished I had been able to ask him more. I was pleased and a little thrilled that ghosts (even if I'd missed them) still hovered about the halls of that ancient country house. Jenny and Annelise, sleepily murmuring to each other in the backseat, didn't want to talk. James, holding a firm course on the treacherous A35, fiddled with the dial of the car radio. Looking out the window, I watched the green Dorset hills rise and fall and clouds move over the fading sun.

That ghost-chasing afternoon in Athelhampton, I began to realize that I was the one—not our teenager—who was (somewhat shamefacedly) interested in haunted houses. Since my first visit to England, my feelings about ghosts had slowly undergone a subtle change. For most of my twenties and thirties, I had seen England rather like a living literary museum, full of specters from the past who had little to say to me personally. Then, in my forties, I had begun to search in England for something else.

Like many people in middle age, I could no longer avoid asking hard, perhaps unanswerable, questions. I have always brooded about death much more than most of my friends. Losing my father when I was seven has conditioned me to an awareness of the possible imminence of death that would not have been unusual in medieval times. I didn't need to keep a skull by the bedside. I *knew* death was nearby. Eventually, those I loved learned to call to say, "I've missed the bus . . . I'm staying late at the office . . . I'm going to stop for groceries . . . I'm staying overnight at Annelise's. Not to worry." They knew I might otherwise sit and wait for the sound of a patrol car pulling up in front of the house.

By the time I entered my forties, I had to confront more than imaginings. My dearest friend contracted cancer; after several years, she died an excruciatingly slow death. A book editor I had come to know and love died not long before, an old high-school friend suddenly succumbed to AIDS not long after. My favorite uncle suffered several strokes; he, too, was soon gone. Time seemed to grow increasingly short.

As a result of all this brooding, I found myself embarked on an unsteady, halting, and unpredictable spiritual journey. As my journey continues, it has sometimes led me to England. This might seem surprising, for England is not a country sought by most twentieth-century spiritual pilgrims. Today's overseas visitors to the shrine at Canterbury are probably most interested in colorful postcards, and the English themselves are not notably religious. As many studies point out, the Church of England has suffered a long decline. A startlingly small percentage of Britons attend Sunday services regularly—according to Richard Critchfield in *An American Looks at Britain*, perhaps only three percent. Once, when James attended a Sunday service in the Anglican church at Lynmouth, a thriving tourist-oriented town in North Devon, he was one of seven worshipers.

And yet the physical presence of the Anglican church provides a profoundly spiritual dimension to the English landscape. Medieval stone churches dot the countryside, their spires often visible from miles away. An ancient church stands at the center of almost every village. Even when villages are clustered within a mile or two, each is apt to have its own church. The enormous cost of maintaining these churches is mind-boggling, but somehow, so far, the English have done it. Almost every church seems to have shining brass, fresh flowers, and needlepointed kneeling cushions. We have often been greeted on our visits by an older woman who is busy polishing or arranging flowers.

Most churches, even if partially restored, are still magnificent buildings, and whenever possible, James and I stop to see them. This is very different from our travel habit at home. Touring America, we seldom feel compelled to drive out of our way to investigate churches. Most are architecturally uninteresting, and if we did want to see them, we would be likely to find them closed. In England, churches are usually open during the day to casual visitors, who can pick up an informative handboard for a self-guided tour, glance briefly around, and leave—or decide instead to sit quietly for a time and meditate.

English churches are wonderful places for meditation. The thick stone walls and muted light create an atmosphere of silence and peace. Even the great cathedrals, with their relentless flow of tourists, not only are large enough to absorb a multitude of whispers and shuffling footsteps, but they always reserve a separate chapel for private prayer. This is usually a partitioned-off segment of the cathedral, with the same kind of surroundings as the parent church.

Sometimes the chapel is surprising. Last year in Norwich Cathedral, for example, I discovered St. Catherine's Chapel, a new space recently carved out of the dean's vestry. Its thick glass door, looking like a block of heavy crystal, was inscribed with verses from T. S. Eliot's *Four Quartets*. Inside, a gleaming white plaster ceiling shimmered between weathered gray stone arches, and a soft green carpet covered the floor. A few chairs stood before a table with a simple contemporary glass crucifix. With its color, light, and warmth, the chapel instantly created a welcoming mood.

I loved Norwich Cathedral partly because it reminded me of Salisbury Cathedral, the first great cathedral I ever saw, whose spectacular spire, large secluded green close, and grand cloister have drawn me back to its precincts many times. (I later learned that Norwich was built first, and its plans were used to help in the design of Salisbury.) Norwich is much less crowded than Salisbury, simpler and more approachable. A short, elderly, sweet-faced priest in a black gown, a figure right out of Trollope, wandered around the church, smiling, commenting to visitors, and eventually taking the pulpit microphone to ask for a few minutes of silence and then the Lord's Prayer. The pipe organ played softly much of the time we were there. Just outside, the cloister held even a greater stillness, with only two or three people sunning themselves on the green lawn beyond the carved arches.

Though smaller English churches cannot offer the breathtaking light effects of the grand cathedrals, or the reverberation of choral voices in seemingly infinite space, or towers that reach into the sky, they do have something else that appeals to someone with a tendency to thoughtfulness. They have burial grounds. Smaller churches even have an advantage here, for it is possible to encompass a country churchyard in a fairly short period of time. Studying gravestones, making simple deductions to learn who married whom, what children they had, and how long they all lived, I am often able to follow generations of interrelated families in a small community. For someone who yearns for a sense of continuity, a country churchyard is reassuring.

Old churchyards are also, of course, remarkably quiet places. Most are well kept, with the grass clipped and the yews neatly trimmed. Seldom defaced by garish monuments or bouquets of bright plastic flowers, these green spaces hold just gray stones and slabs, perhaps askew or tumbled, but often delicately covered with lichens or tendrils of ivy. Photographer and naturalist Heather Angell, known for her television features on the English countryside, describes many churchyards as "undiscovered wildlife havens." Some look out on expansive views, while those in the center of busy country towns still preserve a walled silence.

Churchyards in America seldom offer such possibilities for contemplation. Separated from churches, our cemeteries are often unsightly stacking grounds barely fenced off from urban highways. Or they serve as pretentious parks that do not welcome casual visitors. In Ames, although I knew well the small college cemetery where my father was buried, I do not believe I was ever inside the gates of the town's main burial ground. It was at the other edge of town, behind a high wrought-iron fence, in a large green lawn dotted with trees. Once, when I was in high school, another student reported to me in horrified tones that our new French teacher, Mr. Dutoit, who was known to be war-damaged, had been seen with his wife one Sunday afternoon, holding a picnic basket and walking toward the cemetery. "He must have thought it was a park," the boy said. I was shocked. I knew that nobody who was right in his mind ever went to a cemetery except for a funeral or on Memorial Day.

Death somehow seems less terrifying in England, more an accepted part of life, and so, usually, do ghosts. When I am touring English country houses, I often think of Old Gregory. He is a character in Dorothy Sayers's *Busman's Honeymoon*, a detective romance that in one scene illustrates the English urbane acceptance of ghosts.

Sayers's heroine, Harriet Vane, visiting Duke's Denver, the ancestral home of her new husband, encounters a white-haired old gentleman in the library. He doesn't speak, but smiles cordially, waves his hand, and continues his reading. Moments later, when the door opens again, he whisks himself, and the flowered skirts of his dressing gown, out of sight. Harriet is dismayed to learn shortly afterward that she has made the acquaintance of Old Gregory, one of the many family ghosts.

Peter Wimsey, Harriet's husband, and his mother the Duchess, then lightly touch on the house's various hauntings:

> "You must waste quite a lot of time bowing and apologizing to the family spooks," said Peter. "You should just walk slap through them as Gerald does. It's much simpler, and doesn't seem to do either party any harm."
>
> "*You* needn't talk, Peter," said the Duchess. "I distinctly saw you raise your hat to Lady Susan one day on the terrace."
>
> "Oh, come, Mother! That's pure invention. Why on earth should I be wearing a hat on the terrace?"

Had it been possible to imagine either Peter or his mother capable of discourtesy, Harriet would have suspected an elaborate leg-pull. She said tentatively:

"This sounds almost too storybook."

"Not really," said Peter, "because it's all so pointless. They never foretell deaths or find hidden treasures or reveal anything or alarm anybody. Why, even the servants don't mind them. Some people can't see them at all—Helen, for example."

Sayers, whose Peter Wimsey detective stories are among the most eloquent apologias for the English upper classes, manages to make even their ghosts sound charming. I would not mind, I think, walking into the library at Athelhampton and seeing Old Gregory smiling at me. In the libraries of sunny, welcoming houses, sometimes I half expect to find him.

But I never do. Most of the haunted rooms I have visited in England have been uninspiring, with no obvious vibrations or uncomfortable feelings. (I may have been in more haunted rooms than I know, for only an occasional guidebook will mention ghosts. The National Trust, for example, is far too sedate.) Perhaps, like Helen, Peter Wimsey's insensitive sister-in-law, I am impervious to them. I have often thought, however, that I would not like to sleep in a dark-paneled Tudor bedroom, or in any antique four-poster bed hung with heavy curtains, nor would I like to walk alone at night through the great halls of most stately houses.

Occasionally a place in England seems so likely to be unpleasantly haunted that I do not want to linger there. In the chapel at St. Michael's Mount near Penzance, a short twisting stairway leads down to a roped-off dungeon. In recent times, excavators discovered there the skeleton of a nine-foot-tall man. No one knows who he was or why he died there. Even in a consecrated church, I would not relish encountering a spirit emanating from that cramped, dark cell.

Ghost-hunting can, in fact, be downright depressing. A few years ago, James and I stopped at the Old Jail in Bodmin. Having once loved Daphne du Maurier's *Jamaica Inn*, I thought the Old Jail, a dark hulk looming portentously behind Bodmin's main street, might be interesting. When we arrived, no other cars were parked in the dirty courtyard, and the building itself, imposing as it was, was clearly run-down and disintegrating.

Although our tickets cost several pounds, James and I stayed only a few minutes inside the jail. It had been converted into a chamber of horrors, with instruments of torture hung on the walls. A few sample cells had been reconstructed. Inside them, barely visible in a damp darkness that could not be dispelled by a few weak light bulbs, costumed dummies were hunched in chairs or posed on the dirty straw-strewn floor. One hung from the ceiling in a crude noose. Placards, in typically thorough English style, explained who each dummy represented and what he or she had done. One had stolen a loaf of bread, another was accused of infanticide, one old spinster had been convicted of witchcraft. Most of their stories were pathetic, their crimes questionable, and their ends appalling.

Shaken, we hurried back to the daylight of the courtyard. Ignoring the quizzical look of the ticket taker who had just admitted us, we quickly climbed into our car and escaped. As a student in London thirty years ago, I had lightheartedly toured Madame Tussaud's, though even then I did not much like the torture section. Now, much more aware of the history of human evil and suffering, I could no longer enjoy such a place. I wondered why I had even thought of exploring Bodmin Jail.

The ghosts who have most affected me in England have always been ones I have raised myself. Many times, when I've thought I'd permanently glazed over from too much exposure to historic settings, I have been suddenly galvanized by some artifact, some ordinary detail, that has made someone from the past almost shiver into life before my eyes. At Hever Castle, where the Astors' 1920s renovations seemed to have firmly muffled Elizabethan echoes with lavish fittings and comfy cushions, I stopped before a glass case containing Anne Boleyn's Book of Hours. She had taken it to the scaffold. Staring at it, I could suddenly see her small, graceful hands grasping the book, perhaps shaking in terror, perhaps gripping it like iron. For a moment I heard the murmur of the onlookers and saw the shining sword held high over her head. Who, I wondered, had turned aside in the bloody aftermath and picked up the fallen book?

In another virtually unnoticed glass case at Hever was a yellowed set of layette garments, sewn by young Elizabeth for her elder sister, Mary Tudor, who believed she was expecting a child. The child would have displaced Elizabeth from the next line of succession. The garments were beautifully made, with fine lawn and tiny stitches. I used to sew myself, years ago, and once I made a few little gowns for my own expected child. Looking at these unused swaddling clothes—for Mary, who was barren, had deluded herself—I found myself imagining what Elizabeth had thought, as she sat there, sewing. Did she know or suspect that Mary's pregnancy was only a fantasy? Did she fear it might *not* be? Did Mary walk by her and stop, perhaps approving, perhaps suspicious—she, too, may have wondered what Elizabeth was thinking—as she watched her younger sister industriously stitching at those royal baby clothes?

Such ghosts as I glimpsed at Hever appear on the spur of the moment and quickly disappear. They are flashes of history that momentarily brighten what little knowledge I already have. Some grand historic sites remain unenlivened, some less celebrated ones—like Bodmin Jail—are luridly illuminated.

My ghost-hunting in England continues. I am not always even sure what I am looking for. Sometimes, without realizing what is happening at the time, I find it. One sunny afternoon in Padstow, a Cornish fishing village, James and I took a tour of Prideaux Place, a handsome Elizabethan house, accompanied by Jocelyn, a young, friendly, and giggly guide. Despite touches of grandeur, the house had a happily worn and homey feeling. I could picture us living there quite comfortably—at least, I thought I could until Jocelyn told us about the ghost.

Jocelyn had heard this story from someone who knew someone who had recently been employed at Prideaux Place as a handyman. The handyman was working in the house late at night. The family was away, and he was alone, taking this opportunity to finish his tasks. "He was standing right here," said Jocelyn with relish as we paused at the foot of the main carpeted staircase in the hall. Turning to look behind him—he did not know quite why—the handyman realized that something was happening on the stairs. Slowly, step by step, a set of footprints was descending, visibly crushing the thick pile of the carpet. The handyman did not wait to see if anything would materialize above the footprints. He grabbed his toolkit and ran out of the house.

I looked at the staircase, its soft carpet now flooded with late-afternoon sun. The hall was still and peaceful. This, I thought, is my kind of ghost story. Footprints from the past, briefly glimpsed, perhaps only imagined. Gentle, teasing hints that did not have to endure the scrutiny of daylight.

"Has anyone else seen those footprints since?" I asked Jocelyn.

"No, I don't think so," she said cheerfully. "And now, if you look up on the wall over the landing, you'll see a seventeenth-century portrait of . . ."

We moved on. James and I were Jocelyn's last charges, and she was anxious to close the house and go home. We could not have been in the hall more than a few minutes. But those footprints still hover in Prideaux Place and in my memory, coming from somewhere I cannot see, going to someplace I do not know.

1960: Thumbs Up!

A man in a black bowler hat, with a folded *Times* under his arm, standing in a bus queue. A red double-decker, Number 77, pulling up to the stop, the conductor leaning out, clackety ticket machine hanging from his neck. Big Ben, behind a tidy bed of pansies, snapdragons, and petunias. Plump, rosy-cheeked children, scrambling over the statue of Peter Pan in Kensington Gardens. Sightseeing boats, their flags flying, moving up the gray-walled Thames toward the Tower of London and Greenwich. Square black taxis whirling around winged Eros in Piccadilly Circus. A bright red pillar-box, outpost of Her Majesty's Royal Mail, delivery four times a day. A blue-helmeted bobby, bending courteously to answer a question from a tourist in a helpless flutter among the pigeons of Trafalgar Square.

When I lift my small collection of slides to the lamp and squint, I become for a short while the eager and excited girl who took these pictures in 1960. The pictures are few—film was expensive—and painstakingly composed. I remember how fiercely I was determined to capture the essence of London, both to keep it safe in my heart and to show my family and friends back home. I had fallen in love with a city.

As I examine these pictures thirty years later, I can easily recall the greedy passion I felt when I took them. My city! I've caught it now! Here comes the bus! It will be a perfect shot! I'm so glad I can get the conductor in it, and the man with the bowler, too, if I'm lucky! Look at those kids, with their impeccably neat short pants and little jackets—oh, if only I had the nerve to ask one of the nannies just out of range to let me take her picture standing next to that dark blue hooded baby carriage! It's so—so *English*!

And yet most of my pictures are breathtakingly conventional. Westminster Abbey, the Houses of Parliament, Nelson's column, the London Zoo: they look to me now as if I might have purchased them in a packet at a store selling London souvenirs. But, I remind myself, this is what the city looked like in 1960—or perhaps more accurately, this is how I saw it. The London I had come to explore did not include factories, working-class neighborhoods, or most places outside the range of a standard guidebook. I did not go to Clapham, Wapping, or Wormwood Scrubs; I did not make pilgrimages to state schools, football grounds, or redbrick churches. I will never really know how much of what I absorbed that first summer in London was influenced by what I expected to see. From the beginning, my relationship with England was an inextricable tangle of imagination and reality.

Much of what I recall from the summer of 1960 are iconographic images that I did not record in pictures. They became so indelibly impressed on my mind that they still remind me of the England I knew then. Cornflakes, for example: English breakfasts began with cornflakes rather than with orange juice, and only with cornflakes—no Rice Krispies, Cheerios, Wheat Chex, or Sugar Frosted Flakes. I think of Cadbury's sixpence Bourneville candy bars, delicious semisweet chocolate, readily available through small vending machines in public places like railway stations. Although I had never been fond of Hershey bars, I adored Bournevilles. I still own a walking umbrella, reminiscent of one with which I tapped my way around London, affirming my safety and security with every metallic clang of its steel tip on the pavement. Transparent yellow parchment toilet paper, large copper pennies, handy public conveniences, jam tarts, women in stodgy tweed suits and brown oxfords, small dark Indian restaurants, silver-muzzled Labradors lying next to their masters' feet in train compartments, green city squares shut off by high wrought-iron fences, pubs with white frosted-glass windows, boxes of loose carrots, lettuce, Brussels sprouts, and potatoes outside tiny grocers' shops: I took my mental snapshots and never forgot them.

I also memorized maps. Two of my longest-lasting English souvenirs were a *Geographers' A-Z Folding Map* of London and a dishtowel printed with a full-color map of the London Underground. I used my old map on several return visits until it fell apart and I had to replace it. Once home, I refused to wipe dishes with my dishtowel; I just unwrapped it from time to time, gazed at the evocative diagram of the Underground, and wafted myself back to the top of a steeply descending escalator at Piccadilly, going down, down, down, or to the door at the Covent Garden station while the slow crowded lift creaked its way up, up, up.

Both maps symbolized the excitement of my first trip to London. I had visited several American cities, but I did not know any well, and I was uneasy about exploring them on my own. When I was growing up in Iowa, the only metropolis I knew was Des Moines, which I thought of as big rather than beautiful. Driven there for daylong shopping trips or high-school basketball tournaments or touring road shows, I did not know much more of Des Moines than its downtown, and I saw no reason to be curious about the rest of it. When I went east to Smith, my few excursions to New York were hasty overnights accompanied by more knowledgeable friends, whom I blindly followed through a labyrinth of hazardous streets and indecipherable subways.

Although I worked in Boston during the summer of 1959, sharing an apartment near Harvard Square with two other girls, I had neither free time, money, nor any compelling motives to take the MTA much farther than Park Square, from which I could reach the Public Gardens, Filene's Basement, and the shoe stores on Boylston Street. I had no sense of how Boston as a whole was put together. A small-town girl, I didn't know I could ever feel at *home* in a city. Yet almost immediately after arriving in London, I was astonished to find I could actually get around easily, cheaply, and with ever-increasing confidence.

My *Geographers' A-Z* was a marvel. Unfolding it to a particular square, I could concentrate on one small section of the city at a time. Since I did not have to stand on a street corner and spread out a large, unwieldy state highway map—the only kind I ever used before I came to London—I was not at all embarrassed about checking street signs, and then my *A-Z*, to see exactly where I was. Like most inexperienced tourists, I desperately didn't want to look like one, and my *A-Z* was a discreet companion, fitting into my purse, my pocket, or my hand with unobtrusive ease.

Consulting my *A-Z* at almost every turn, I soon began to see it as my personal guide to the city. I could wake up in the morning, study my map, and decide that in early afternoon, right after class, I would start off for Regents Park, or Oxford Street, or the British Museum, or the Cheshire Cheese in Fleet Street. I knew my *A-Z* would get me there.

Just casually browsing through my *A-Z* map made my heart beat a little faster. Sometimes I'd see the name of a street and gasp in recognition. I *knew* that street! So many places seemed hauntingly familiar—and yet intriguingly unknown. Berkeley Square—wasn't that where the nightingales sang? The Cadogan Hotel—something about Oscar Wilde, a terrible homosexual scandal. Scotland Yard and Baker Street: I had read every story Sir Arthur Conan Doyle wrote about Sherlock Holmes. Pimlico: what poem of T. S. Eliot's mentioned Pimlico? He had made it sound rather cheap and lower-class, I thought, but still, I ought to go there. And Holborn! At Smith I had just finished Dickens's *Bleak House*, and I remembered its mesmerizing opening page, an evocation of dark smog-shrouded London on a day when "it would not be wonderful to meet a Megalosaurus, forty feet long or so, waddling like an elephantine lizard up Holborn Hill." Well, swathed in my wool suit and raincoat, today *I* would waddle in the lizard's footsteps up Holborn!

I also liked the upbeat color printing of the *A-Z* map. Although later, because the *A-Z* ended abruptly at the edges of central London, I also acquired *London Street by Street*, a thick pocket-size book, I never became attached to it. It was a dull black-and-white set of grids printed in blurred ink on cheap newsprint. My *A-Z*, on the other hand, painted major roads in sunny yellow, parks a bright grass-green, the Thames and the Serpentine sky blue, and railway stations and Underground stations fire-engine red. In light italics it sketched the outlines of major landmarks like Westminster Abbey, the National Gallery, and Royal Festival Hall. My *A-Z* gave me a sense of London as a whole. I could see how green islands dotted the city, how the Thames cut through it, and how one section led into another. I could also see how close I always was to the Underground.

I loved the Underground—or as I quickly learned to refer to it, in a casual Londoner's tone, the Tube. After my few timorous forays into the New York subway system, where unruly crowds frightened me, routes and names of trains were mystifying, and I was always terrified of getting lost, I found it hard to believe that the Tube belonged to the same family. It was as if I had discovered that a hulking, greasy-haired, and rather threatening adolescent, who often pushed me rudely out of the way in his rush to get somewhere, had a staid, tidily dressed, and well-behaved aunt.

I never worried about getting lost in the London Underground. By studying large color-coded maps on each station wall, I could quickly see the exact route I needed to take. These primary colors were plain and friendly: all I had to do was follow the right one, brown for Bakerloo, dark blue for Piccadilly, blue for Victoria, red for Central, black for Northern, yellow for Circle, green for District. Zooming toward my destination, I could glance up at a colored map hung in every car and tick off my approaching stops: Victoria, Sloane Square, South Kensington. As each station flashed by, a sign outlined in colored tiles echoed the map above me. Gloucester Road is next. Time to get up and sway to the door.

The Underground was kindly disposed. It anticipated mistakes and forgave them easily. If I did take a wrong turning in a subway tunnel and found myself on a train going the wrong direction—Westminster, say, instead of South Ken—I simply got off at the next stop, followed color-coded signs to the other side of the track, and started again. Everything seemed so civilized. Whenever I saw the sign for the Underground, a red circle bisected by a blue bar with white lettering, I was reassured.

I felt safe on the Underground. Since it did not run after midnight, I never traveled at lonely or dangerous hours. In 1960, I had not heard of muggings on the Tube or on London streets, and for many years afterward, I do not remember more than pangs of mild unease about any other passenger in my car. Of course, I also eschewed adventure by not taking the Tube beyond the boundaries of central London. In fact, as I studied the names on incoming trains that indicated the end of their runs, I felt almost as tantalized as when, a child in Ames, I had stood by the tracks and watched the City of San Francisco or the City of Portland roar through the night. Cockfosters, High Barnet, Kennington Oval, Harrow-on-the-Hill, Uxbridge, Watford, Ealing Broadway: these names were equally mysterious.

Aside from the sudden dramatic eruption of a train from its black tunnel, the Underground held little other mystery, except why sometimes the next train did not appear for fifteen minutes, twenty, then half an hour. Once I had developed a dependence on London Transport, I became fussed by these delinquencies. I looked at my watch, clucked under my breath, and tapped my foot: it was as if an old friend were irritatingly and inexplicably late.

The only deviations I welcomed from my Underground routine were changes in the advertising posters hung on the walls next to the escalators. On my long descents, studying the wall, I became well acquainted with temporary employment agencies, Miss Selfridge, and the latest West End shows. Most ads were quintessentially British, concise, sometimes witty, and as polite as the passengers who quickly moved down to the right-hand side of the escalator so those in a rush could hurry down on the left. But a sprinkling of explicit lingerie ads leaped out from the row of neat glass frames. As my eyes focused only a few inches away from breasts and buttocks, I could never decide what these fleshy ads indicated about the British national character. I looked at the impassive, dark-suited, umbrella-carrying men standing stolidly on the escalator, and I wondered.

As I roamed throughout the city on the Tube, I eventually developed definite feelings about the different lines, as if they had personalities. Bakerloo (a homey brown) was dull and stodgy, stopping at only a few places I wanted to go and then vanishing into dreary outposts like Finchley Road or Elephant & Castle. Piccadilly was fast, bustling, and chic, whirling through Leicester Square, Green Park,

Knightsbridge, and South Kensington. The Northern, an uncompromisingly straight black line on the map, was stubborn, unpredictable, and almost always late. The Circle Line, cheerfully deceptive, tempted me to jump aboard its endless loop without always knowing which direction the train was going.

Most of the time I rode the Piccadilly Line, because it was the only one that stopped at my home station, Russell Square. After a few minutes' walk, I could be in my room at the University of London. I ranged around London bravely that summer because I knew I could quickly return to a secure, small space of my own. One college dormitory room is not so very different from another, and once inside my cubicle, I was in familiar territory.

My six-week summer course—English Art, Literature, and Music 1660–1780—was mainly a foreign experience because of the other American students. The only British student I remember was a talky Scotsman named Duncan, who wore thick glasses, had bad skin, and frowned a lot. Duncan had just graduated weeks before from the University of Edinburgh, with a degree he said was a *Third*, something he felt he had to explain and rationalize. I had not before understood about the classes of British degrees, or indeed about the ranking of British universities. From Duncan's defensive pride in Edinburgh and from his depression about a degree he now feared might be almost worthless, I caught a whiff of something unpleasant—a combination of narrowness, pressure, and exclusivity.

Almost all the other students in Art, Literature, and Music 1660–1780 were Southern girls. Having grown up in the heart of Iowa, I knew almost nothing about the

Deep South, except through history books, movies, and popular stereotypes. Although Smith had a few token representatives from states like Texas, Alabama, and Georgia, they simply seemed Smithies with soft accents. But the Southern girls in my London dorm were different.

As Melanie, my roommate from Atlanta, explained, she and her friends had come to London because their parents saw this noncredit program as a relatively inexpensive way for their daughters to gain some polish, not to mention a suitcase of souvenirs from foreign travel. Melanie's mother had particularly instructed her to travel to Brussels over a long weekend break so that she could buy some Brussels lace for her wedding gown. Melanie was not engaged—she had, in fact, recently broken up with her college steady— but Brussels lace was an essential part of her eventual trousseau. She was also bound to bring home a set of English bone china.

Most of the girls found the course both boring and arduous. London, despite Madame Tussaud's and a few imported American musicals, was chilly, damp, and unappealing. Huddling together, they sought refuge by shopping for cashmere sweaters and by going to the movies several nights a week. In the dormitory dining room, they sat at one long table and commiserated over cold toast about the lack of cute boys and how nice it would be to get home again. One of them even began going steady with Duncan.

Although I liked Melanie, who was bright and engaging, I found it hard to talk naturally with her friends. One night I noticed that an art cinema in London was showing the film *Black Orpheus*. When I had recently seen it at Smith,

I had wept because I had found it so beautiful and so sad. Joining Melanie and her table at dinner, I asked if anyone would like to go with me that night so I could see it again. There was a long, awkward silence.

One girl, an open and sunny friend of Melanie's who often stopped by our room, finally said with a certain strained frankness, "That's all with nigras, isn't it? I'm sorry. I don't know about you-all, but I just wouldn't feel comfortable."

Another chimed in: "It shows them kissing, doesn't it? No, I wouldn't want to see it, either."

Surprised and confused, I did not know exactly how to respond. A sheltered Northern liberal, I had lost my sense of a verbal common ground. It did not occur to me then, or any other time during the course, that perhaps I might learn something important by probing more deeply into what these girls thought and felt. Instead I went to the movies by myself.

Most of that summer in London I was alone. I didn't mind, and I established a pattern that made it easy for me to return alone in later years. I liked exploring the city, making unexpected stops and indulging momentary whims. London seemed to welcome and enfold me. Armed with my map and walking umbrella, I walked happily among the crowds on Regent Street or strolled along the almost deserted Embankment, wandered in and out of quiet squares and enchanting mewses, browsed in shops I couldn't afford, and usually stopped in midafternoon for a cup of tea at a convenient Lyon's Corner House.

Once, on a cold, rainy day, when my umbrella seemed ineffectual and my feet were wet and clammy, I dared to enter the glass-fronted shop of a dealer who sold prints and engravings in a scholarly street near the British Museum. I was encouraged by the emptiness of the shop, its warm interior light, and the piled folders of prints, some spread open, in the front window.

Craddock & Barnard was undoubtedly used to tourists. The gray-haired and gray-faced proprietor, not even blinking at the sudden appearance of a dripping-wet twenty-year-old American girl in a navy-blue raincoat who wanted to look at some prints, asked me what kind. I didn't know. What century? he inquired. I hesitated, mentally scouring my thin background in art history, wondering how to answer. "Ahhh . . . something not too expensive," I said. He brought me a large brown folder, courteously untied it, and left me to consider. A few minutes later I coughed politely, raised my eyebrows, and gave a tentative beckoning gesture. He approached. "Perhaps more, ah, in the neighborhood of a pound?" I inquired, with as much dignity as possible. He nodded gravely. He brought another folder.

For twenty years, until in a short-lived spasm of dispossession I sold them for a pittance, I kept the two small prints I bought that rainy day. One was a Dutch seventeenth-century vision of Judgment Day and hell, the other an English churchyard shadowed by a giant yew. I knew nothing about either artist or the provenance of either print. I bought them not because I was drawn to the subjects—though their gloominess seemed, on that gray-smeared day, somehow appropriately English—but because I wanted to buy *something* from the gentleman who had graciously offered me anything I wished to see in his venerable shop. After I moved into my first house, I framed and hung both prints in a prominent spot, reminders less of art and mortality than of a rainy afternoon in a side street near the British Museum.

Some afternoons, if I didn't have to attend a lecture, and many nights, I went by myself to the theatre. Although London theatre has now been celebrated for decades, I was not aware in 1960 how marvelous it was. But as soon as I glanced at the sedately alluring theatre section of the *Times*, rows of tiny boxes announcing play after play, I knew I had been invited to a feast. Already I loved the theatre. As a young girl in Ames, I sold tickets, worked on sets, did makeup, and acted in our intense high-school productions, directed by a dedicated and charismatic teacher who made us feel we were aiming for the professionalism of Broadway. I still remember the chill with which I heard an orchestrated unearthly moan from the dead residents of *Our Town*, and longing for a happy ending, I felt my heart wrench in the last scene of *The Heiress* when proud Catherine Sloper, now lonely forever, carried her candle up the dark staircase. I never thought of them as high-school plays.

Once or twice a year, touring road shows, drifting into town with a faint aging flavor of distant New York, played at a basketball auditorium in Des Moines. From somewhere in the bleachers, I gazed spellbound at *Teahouse of the August Moon*, *The Bad Seed*, and *Tea and Sympathy*. This, I was sure, was indeed Real Theatre. At Smith, I extended my range to uneven college productions of Shakespeare, Restoration comedy, and frequently forgettable modern drama.

Now that I often have to fight blinking and dozing

when lights dim in the evening, I remember with a certain sadness how ready I was at twenty to see anything, at any time, in London. No matter whether a play was magnificently or only adequately produced, Shakespeare sounded more convincing and more alive when I heard his verse spoken in a British accent. But I discovered more than vibrant Shakespeare. I could not quite believe that I could also watch Alec Guinness or Laurence Olivier for less than the price of a ticket to a new American Western in a Leicester Square cinema.

Olivier, I didn't need to be told, was a Great Actor—at Smith's Friday-night flicks, I had sighed over his Heathcliff in *Wuthering Heights* and admired his gallant *Henry V*—but I was equally elated by seeing Alec Guinness. In Ames, the run-down Varsity Theatre near the college campus showed occasional foreign films, like *The Man in the White Suit, Kind Hearts and Coronets,* and *The Lavender Hill Mob,* and I felt I somehow *knew* Alec Guinness. I had never dreamed, however, that one day I would see him alive, right in front of me. Alec Guinness! *My* Alec Guinness! Nor had I realized his dramatic range. When in that summer of 1960 I watched him flung to the floor, a shattered Lawrence of Arabia in Terence Rattigan's *Ross,* I was so impressed I unconsciously vowed that whenever I had a chance, I would always see any play that had Alec Guinness in it. On every trip to London afterward, I kept that promise. He became so much a part of my theatre-going life that I still find it hard to think of him as Sir.

Not just the theatre, but other arts, sparkled that summer in London, drawing me out of my dormitory room, away from my desk and down to the nearest Tube station.

At the ticket window, I proffered a precious pound note for the cheapest possible seat, and I almost always got change back—usually more than enough for a cup of tea and a cardboard carton of chocolate ice cream during the interval. I loved sitting in my plush-covered seat during intermission, daintily chipping away at my ice cream with a little wooden spoon and looking around at the swooping curves, velvet-draped boxes, and grandiloquent gilt of London's historic theatres. They bore absolutely no resemblance to the Des Moines KRNT Theatre.

From standing room at the top of Covent Garden, peering around a pillar and over elaborately curled heads, I could just glimpse far below the starry grace of Margot Fonteyn. I liked the feeling of being present at something that was happening right now, on the stage below me this very night—not, months later, in a diluted version passing briefly through the provinces. Experimenting with culture, I attended concerts at Royal Festival Hall, introduced myself to perplexing varieties of modern dance, and strained to hear the lyrics of Gilbert and Sullivan at the D'Oyly Carte. By the end of the summer, I became forever convinced that London, rather than Boston, New York, or indeed any other city on the face of the earth, was the undisputed center of artistic life.

Some of my enthusiasm sprang from my summer course at the University of London. Since I was not receiving academic credit, I did not expend much more energy on it than attending lectures and my discussion group. The lure of the city was far stronger. But despite my half-hearted participation, the course gently illuminated the borders of some of my dark patches of ignorance. I did not learn a great deal about Pope or Sir Joshua Reynolds, but

I began to listen with pleasure to choral and chamber music. Until that summer, I had never really liked much of the classics except what I could play on the piano. English Art, Literature, and Music 1660–1780 introduced me to Purcell and Handel, and I eventually realized I was no longer awash in waves of indistinguishable sound. I actually could hear lines and harmonies. That next Christmas, to my music-loving stepfather's delight, I asked him for an unabridged version of Purcell's *Dido and Aeneas.* I am sure he felt my request, which he honored, justified my whole trip to England.

Since I had recently switched majors from history, and knew more of American literature than English, I was scarcely aware how inconceivable it was to cover all of English literature from 1660 to 1780 in a noncredit, six-week survey—even without tossing in English art and music. So I did not fuss at our rather hurried, sometimes superficial pace, and indeed, sometimes our guest lecturers, who were often noted scholars, talked right over my head. I particularly remember the name of Milton being batted about, influencing this poet, echoing in that poetic form, intoning in yet another poet's cadence. Milton here, Milton there, Milton everywhere. Our English tutors assumed that every aspiring student of literature had read Milton, and I did not like to betray American philistinism by admitting I had not. I knew, I reassured myself, quite a bit about Thoreau and Faulkner, and fresh from a seminar in American literary realism, I could carry on quite an informed conversation about William Dean Howells. But these names were unlikely to cut much ice at the University of London.

One afternoon, in our tutorial session, when our rather

sullen group was attempting to discuss an assignment I hadn't completed by some minor poet I had never heard of, the tutor turned to me. "And what do you think, Miss Allen?" he asked unhopefully.

I tried to look both thoughtful and alert. "Um, I think I rather hear, um, some Miltonic echoes in this passage," I said as confidently as I could manage.

He looked disbelieving. "You *do*?" he asked. "And just *where*?"

I looked blankly at the dittoed poem in my hand. Scanning it quickly, I selected a few lines that seemed more ponderous than the rest. Milton, from what I'd gleaned, was no lightweight. "Um, lines twenty-five to thirty?" I volunteered, the rise in my voice betraying my uncertainty.

The tutor looked at his book, then at me. I could tell he had struggled hard to conquer his aversion to American students. "Well, perhaps," he finally acknowledged, "but I confess I don't hear it myself."

As my six weeks of glancing study drew to an end, I began to look forward to the rest of the summer. Before I left America, I had arranged to travel through England for a month with another Smith girl, Joyce Skaggs, after she had finished her similar six-week course at Stratford-on-Avon. Although, as English honors students, we knew each other slightly, we gambled on a mutual friend's recommendation that we would enjoy each other's company. The friend was right. Although I have never asked Joyce what she thought of me at Smith, I suspect I may well have appeared to be brash, nervous, and a little loud. On superficial acquaintance, Joyce was quiet and somewhat reserved. During our trip together, however, I soon discovered her warmth, wit, curiosity, and sensitivity. Our enduring friendship, which began that summer and has lasted to this day, was one of England's many unexpected gifts.

On warm, azalea-scented afternoons during the late Massachusetts spring before our trip, Joyce and I sat together on the lawn outside the library and discussed where we should go and what we should do. Neither of us had much money to spend. Both of us wanted to see as much of England as possible. After much brainstorming, calculation, and revision, we settled on a bicycle tour, renting bikes and the necessary gear in London, and staying in youth hostels. Consulting a map of hostel locations, we laid out a route that would cover between twenty-five and thirty-five miles a day, with a few long-distance hops on trains. We joined the International Youth Hostel Association, sent deposits to England, and received all our hostel reservations.

This plan was simple, thorough, and inexpensive. The only problem was that we had approached it with a theoretical air. Both of us, I suspect, believed a bicycle/hostel trip *sounded* suitable for two enterprising but impoverished college girls, but I don't think we ever considered whether we would actually *like* it. Neither of us was particularly athletic. Though I seem to remember Joyce, who was slight but strong, with a tennis racket or perhaps even a cricket bat in her hand, I had barely passed required gym by taking duckpin bowling. We knew nothing of long-distance biking. Although, like most Smith girls, we owned bicycles, I do not recall that we rode together that spring much farther than across campus to Davis Center for a cup of coffee. My own ancient Raleigh, purchased for five dollars from Smith's annual used-bike sale, barely had one gear. When I came to a hill, I got off and walked.

A daily thirty-mile ride through the English countryside sounded both fun and easy when we talked about it under sunny skies at home. But after several weeks in cold, rainy London, I began to realize that those thirty miles might not be so easy after all. They might, in fact, be soggy, slogging, and exhausting. Having taken a few day trips outside London, I could see that many roads were surprisingly busy—and lots of them were hilly. Would we struggle all day to get somewhere we might not then have time to explore? Would we get there at all? Halfway through my course, Joyce came to London, and we conferred. A visit to the London Youth Hostel Association, with its dauntingly professional assortment of packs, bags, bikes, and other equipment, convinced us. We had gotten in over our heads and needed to bail out.

Given our stringent budgets and our nonrefundable deposits on a chain of youth hostels, we could not start all over again with a radically new plan. We had to maintain our itinerary, but how were we to follow it? We could not afford many train trips, we did not know anything about the bus system, and we weren't sure we could get to our remote hostels except by automobile. Only one option remained. We would have to hitchhike.

Perhaps I remember that summer of 1960 with such affection partly because it was the first time I deliberately set out to do something I knew my mother would not approve. In 1960, according to what Joyce and I had heard from other students, hitchhiking through Europe was a quite acceptable mode of transport for girls traveling together—even, in those days, for girls traveling alone. But I knew my mother would never believe my assurances. I wasn't entirely convinced myself. Girls from Iowa didn't stick their thumbs out. They only did that in places like California, where the Beats, Kerouac, and other vaguely unsavory people hung out in smoke-filled coffeehouses and inveighed against society. I knew about *On the Road*. So I was unnerved as well as exhilarated by the idea of casually standing by the side of a highway, waiting for an unknown car to stop and pick me up.

But if I didn't dare to try something like this now, when I was abroad for the first time, when would I? I wanted to think of myself as someone who knew how to take chances. Next year I would be twenty-one. My life so far, I knew, had been mostly uneventful. In my freshman creative-writing class, I had realized that I had absolutely nothing to write about. Compared with the other writers, I was as empty as a blank notebook. I didn't drink much, I knew almost nothing about sex, and I had never shoplifted or crawled out of a dormitory window or even driven without a license. At home I had always been the kind of utterly dependable girl any parent would want for a baby-sitter. At Smith I was on Dean's List and a member of the Student Executive Board. Wasn't it time to stop being so responsible? To plunge into the unknown? In short, to hitchhike?

Joyce agreed. Perhaps because we both were rather conservative, we trusted each other's impulses. If Joyce could do it, so could I. If I could do it, so could Joyce. We

egged each other on, pointing out advantages and adjust-
ments. With such short distances to travel between hostels, we'd have plenty of time to explore Kenilworth, Loch
Lomond, Tintagel, and all the other literary shrines we'd
selected so carefully.

Since the Youth Hostel Association frowned on hitchhiking and, we feared, might refuse to honor our reservations if anyone at a hostel saw us get out of a car, we'd have
to be sure our rides dropped us off some distance from
each night's lodging. Then we could nonchalantly stroll
through the door, dump our packs on the floor, and sign
in like veterans. All we would need to carry were changes
of clothing, toiletries, towels, a metal plate, mug, set of
cutlery, and a sheet sleeping sack.

When I remember those four weeks on the road, I
always think first of my sleeping sack. I came to dislike that
sack, but I think I was also rather proud of it. It was a
visible sign that I was a student traveling abroad, making
do, and getting along. Since I did not keep a travel journal,
I have lost the details of the individual English hostels
where we ate and slept. A girls' dormitory lined with cots;
a long wooden dining table set with dented tin plates and
mugs; a cement-floored toilet; an unheated shower
room—they all merge together. But my sleeping sack—ah,
that had an individual imprint.

Rented from the London hostel center, a sheet sleeping
sack was required at every hostel of any student traveler
who didn't have a sleeping bag. When you produced your
sack, the hostel gave you rough brown wool blankets to
put on top of it. The sack was simply two old grayish
cotton sheets, sewed together in a narrow tube, with a slot

for something like a folded towel that might serve as a pillow. After only a few nights, bits of sand and grit from our bare feet began to cling to the pilled surface of the worn sheets. After a week, I slipped into the sack without looking at it very closely. Washing it was out of the question; we never stayed long enough at any one hostel to do laundry that couldn't dry in a day. The sack gradually turned grayer.

Hitchhiking through England and staying in youth hostels was not quite the adventure I had imagined. Perhaps that is why I think first of my sheet sleeping sack; it recalls a certain gritty reality. My fantasies of hosteling, inspired by vague recollections of other students' stories, involved staying up late, talking to other students, exchanging violent political opinions—though Joyce and I barely had any—and somehow, in the process, making lifelong friends. In fact, the hostels were places of convenience rather than camaraderie. Most foreign students traveled in small groups and stayed close to each other. Few from countries besides Britain spoke fluent English, and Joyce and I could manage only some halting French. Almost everyone arrived at different times, washed up, ate dinner, and soon went to bed.

Hostels reminded me a little of my early experience at Camp Fire Girls' Camp, where I lived with other campers from either outlying farms or distant towns that seemed unbelievably remote from Ames. Late at night, huddled into my blankets, I could listen to strange conversation from girls in nearby cots. Their lives seemed so different from mine, even their accents a kind of reproach to my carefully articulated, grammatically perfect, but somehow inappropriate English. The bookish daughter of an English teacher, I said things like "I am she." At camp, I am sure I often sounded stuck-up. Here in England, an off-key American, I felt I sounded just as foreign.

In the morning, after a breakfast of cornflakes, cold fried eggs, and toast, washed down with vats of strong black tea, we lined up at the director's desk for work assignments. Part of the hostel ethic was a commitment to daily chores before travelers went on their way. But only a few students could crowd into the kitchen, boys always drew heavy hauling jobs, and girls who weren't washing or drying dishes needed other tasks. Since the director did not want to encourage shirking, jobs had to be found. Although I remember a vista of the blue waters of Loch Lomond, I focus much more clearly on the oak staircase that led up to the second floor of the Loch Lomond youth hostel. I spent a long morning hour there flicking nonexistent dust from banisters and newel posts.

When Joyce and I turned each morning onto the nearest highway out of sight of the hostel, our hearts were light, even if our stomachs were sloshing with too much strong tea. One of my favorite snapshots from that trip shows me posing by the side of an English lane, banked by high hedges, my thumb stuck out, a grin on my face. Although I felt as adventurous as Kerouac, I look as respectable as my mother would have wished. I am wearing a brown plaid drip-dry skirt, beige blouse, and Shetland sweater, with my waterproof poncho slung over my shoulder. Both Joyce and I marvel to remember that we hitchhiked in skirts.

My mother, of course, did not know I was hitchhiking.

When I wrote her my carefully composed air letters, I merely said, "We arrived last night at Loch Lomond. . . ." or "It was a long day today, with rain until afternoon," or "We are tired but fine." I did not lie. I just did not tell the truth. That made me feel sneaky, even more like a renegade. Kerouac and me, on the road together.

Now that I have a twenty-year-old daughter of my own, I do not like her to take too many chances. "Don't jog around the lake in the dark," I warn her. "Watch out for drunk drivers. Leave any party where people are using drugs. Look in the backseat before you get in your car."

She listens, but she rolls her eyes. "Mom," she sometimes says, with the security of the young, "don't worry. Nothing will happen to me. Look, I took a jog after nine last night, with plenty of people around, and it was just fine!"

So, to bolster the authority of mothers, I wish I could here point out that Joyce and I ran into serious trouble as hitchhikers. At the least, we should have had some narrow and sobering escapes. But in fact, we, too, were just fine. The first morning when we stepped to the edge of the road, I admit I was frightened. Joyce and I tossed a coin to see who would go first. I lost. As I stuck my arm forward, turned my wrist, and extended my thumb, I felt as if my thumb had suddenly begun to grow, long, longer, longer even than Pinocchio's nose. Although the road was empty, I was sure people were staring at me, perhaps from behind the hedge.

But my thumb didn't stay out very long. In a few minutes, the first car that passed us stopped. We gave our destination, hopped in the backseat with our packs, answered a few friendly questions from the English couple in front, and off we went. Naturally, it wasn't always quite that easy. Sometimes the road was empty, sometimes too busy. On a few rainy days, we had to walk farther and wait longer than was comfortable. We walked, in fact, quite far enough on most days to justify signing in at the hostel with clear consciences. Just once, when a man driving a van picked us up and roughly urged us to come to his house for dinner, we looked at each other in alarm, made up a sudden excuse about why we wanted out at the next village, and afterward, relieved at our escape, decided perhaps we would not raise our thumbs for single men in vans.

Along the way, I learned a few unexpected and highly specific lessons. (None of them has been very useful in later life.) One, when you are only five feet five inches tall, it is hard to see anything over the top of a seven-foot hedgerow. Footpaths are scenic, roads on foot usually are not. Two, walking many miles in a pair of two-dollar black Woolworth sneakers will cause a significant tendon in the right foot to lose its lubrication. It will creak and hurt as your foot moves up and down. You will end up in the local surgery under the disapproving eye of an overworked doctor in the National Health Service. Buying a new pair of shoes, you will have new respect for socialized medicine. Nonetheless, if you continue to walk, your foot will continue to hurt. Three, when you are on the road, you will be eternally hungry. Whatever the hour, it will always be time for tea or a Bourneville bar or both.

Although I cannot now retrace the exact route Joyce and I took, I am amazed when I look back at how much of England we covered in those four weeks. We passed through the Midlands, paused at the Lake District, spent a few days in Scotland, skirted Yorkshire, swung down to the southwest, touched on the Devon and Dorset coast, stopped in Cornwall, and breezed through the Cotswolds. Because we absorbed so much each day, we did not feel we were traveling fast. Dedicated English majors, we chose many places for their literary associations. Scott's Border Country, Burns's Edinburgh, Wordsworth's Tintern Abbey and the Lakes, Austen's Lyme Regis: we felt we should do it all cover to cover, even if we hadn't yet read Burns or Scott or Austen.

As first-time tourists, we also wanted to see places we knew were starred attractions, like Canterbury, Blenheim, and Bath. How could I go home and say I hadn't been to Anne Hathaway's cottage? Or the Brontës' moors? So we walked, hitched, snapped pictures, grabbed imitation hamburgers in Wimpy Bars and devoured ploughman's lunches in roadside pubs, checked in and out of hostels, occasionally splurged on a bed-and-breakfast with a bath-tub down the hall, and set out to walk some more. Al-though I know it must have rained that August—my pictures show me carrying my poncho, and the country-side was green and flowering—I seem to remember that the sun always shone.

Although I now look back on those hitchhiking weeks as if they were bathed in a deceptively golden light, I must confess that most of the romance I had imagined for my first trip abroad did not happen—at least, not in the way I expected. From my courses in American literature, par-ticularly my readings of Henry James, I pictured Europe (and England) as seductive, dangerous, and entangling places. Would I, like Daisy Miller, find myself tempted to risk my reputation alone in the moonlight with an adoring foreigner, experiencing the English equivalent of the Roman Colosseum—say, Stonehenge or Warwick Castle or the ruins at Kenilworth? Would I glimpse evil and corruption? Would I delve for the first time into the complexity of life? Would I return to America subtly but unalterably changed?

No, I would not. But something did happen that summer. Romance is not always immediately recognizable, and my steadfast and continuing affair with England and its countryside began during those rainy, happy, vagabond days. The freedom with which Joyce and I traveled was energizing. We hitchhiked, ate in bars, and shared sleeping rooms with strangers. When we wanted to change our plans, we consulted only each other and our own whims. Armed with merely a basic map, our packs, some traveler's checks, and determination, we managed to roam throughout a foreign country, wherever and whenever we wished, with confidence and zest. England seemed to liberate us from the strictures of home.

As a result, when I left to return to college at the end of the summer, I knew that England was a place where I could successfully travel alone, where I could explore a newfound independence, and where I could somehow be myself in a way I did not yet fully understand.

Trifle with Me:
Spotted Dick and
Other Delights

B ut what about the *food?*" gourmet friends ask me,
trying to understand why I return so often to England. "Yes, we know, it's supposed to be better
than it was," they say. "But still, compared to Italy, say, or
France . . ." I understand why these friends are so skeptical.
In our other travels, James and I have savored bouil-
labaisse, pastas, tapanades, moussaka, and sauces that demand to be scooped up with a last surreptitious swipe of
crusty bread. When we talk about making another trip to
France, for example, we reminisce not about castles, gardens, or mountains, but about a tiny round of goat's cheese
wrapped in grape leaves at a village market stall or an
ambrosial soufflé aux fraises served in a sunny courtyard
surrounded by flowering roses.

And yet we do go back to England. In England, as my
censorious friends point out, a typical dinner in a provincial
hotel may still begin with watery tomato soup, continue
with a thin grayish slice of roast beef awash in overcooked
peas, slog along with a side dish of soggy roast potatoes, and
thud to an end with a slab of canned-apple pie smothered
in thick corn-starch custard. That, in fact, is exactly the

meal James and I were recently served in a moderately expensive establishment in Sidmouth.

It is not that my husband and I do not care about food. We do care, passionately, more than I think we ought to care. Nor does my affection for English countryside and culture extend indiscriminately to tinned peas or Bird's yellow custard. But just as I seem to thrive in cool rainy English weather more than under the white-hot Mediterranean sun, so, too, English meals seem to suit me. I like their timing, their temperament, their reassuring predictability.

Take a full English breakfast—which I always do. For most of my life, I have been a morning person, brightly awake when the world is barely astir. I have never voluntarily missed a breakfast. Blessed with a mother who believed in nutritional excess for growing children, I remember sitting down not only to juice, cereal, and eggs, but also, on varying mornings, to omelets, French toast, waffles, pancakes, crepes with hot applesauce, muffins, fried cornmeal mush, homemade bread, doughnuts, Norwegian kringla, crispy bacon or sausage links, washed down with lots of milk or cocoa. From time to time as a teenager, I went on diets that limited me to a single soft-boiled egg, but I knew what I was missing.

When, in midlife, the gloomy portents of modern medicine forced me to cut back on cholesterol, I certainly did not give up on breakfasts. Now when I awake, I merely ponder pleasantly whether to have Oatios with green grapes and banana, oat-bran muffins and yogurt sprinkled with slivered almonds, or possibly hot oat-bran cereal stirred with a dash of cinnamon and vanilla and drizzled with a thin ribbon of pure maple syrup.

I do not regard a so-called continental breakfast, with juice, hard roll, and coffee, as worth getting out of bed for. On my trips to England, I temporarily ignore cholesterol (travel, I tell myself, is *supposed* to be broadening). When James and I arrive at our favorite country-house hotel, Philip Chapman, the proprietor of Chedington Court, always inquires politely before we retire, "And what kind of breakfast will you have in the morning?" And James always enthusiastically answers for both of us: "The works!"

The works, of course, varies both in quantity and quality at each hotel, bed-and-breakfast, or farmhouse accommodation. At Chedington Court, breakfast is an art form. We begin with juice or stewed prunes, then muesli topped with sliced banana, and perhaps a croissant touched lightly with strawberry jam. Soon Philip sets in front of each of us a steaming-hot plate with fried eggs, bangers (sausage), bacon, grilled tomatoes and mushrooms, and a rack of toast. (If I wished, I could add kippers or kidneys.) The eggs taste fresher and more flavorful than those I have at home, perhaps because Hilary Chapman, Philip's wife and head chef, scours the countryside for the best produce. Or perhaps I am so pleased to be sitting at a breakfast table laid with white linen and polished silver in a spacious, high-ceilinged dining room looking out on a glorious garden that I am prepared to believe everything, including jam in little pots, will taste better than at home.

As I shamelessly chow down, I tell myself that this gargantuan breakfast will carry me through until evening. I can't imagine I will want any lunch. Besides, who knows where I'll be? On a distant footpath, in a museum, at the beach? No, I'll skip lunch, I assure my conscience, who is just now a stern figure clad in hospital whites watching in disapproval as I slice open the last juicy sausage. "Philip? Could we have some more toast?" carols James, whose mental minder tactfully disappears at the door of the dining room. James knows, but kindly does not remind me, that we both will in fact undoubtedly have lunch.

I did not immediately take to English breakfasts. My first ones, served in the basement cafeteria of my University of London summer dorm in 1960, seemed barely palatable. I didn't mind the watery juice or repetitious cornflakes, but I did not see how anyone could refer to a white, fattish slab of undercooked meat encircled by a tough brown rind as bacon. But I wanted to be tolerant, accepting, and adventurous—the right kind of American tourist. Even while I groused about English food with my American classmates, I tried to remember that World War II was really not so far in the distant past. I didn't know much about food rationing, but I decided maybe it lingered in spots, like some of the bomb craters that still punctuated parts of London.

So I concentrated on enjoying my tea and toast, which, over the years, I came to realize were the essential underpinnings of a classic English breakfast. To an American trained to the taste of melted butter soaking into just-popped hot bread, cold toast—even stacked in a silver rack—is at first a disappointment. But soon I began to like its crunchy taste, especially when heavily layered with butter and marmalade. English butter is remarkably sweet and creamy. Who could drive past the rain-soaked green pastures of the West Country and doubt that cows munching on that emerald grass and drinking from those tree-dappled streams would turn out superior butter?

I never eat marmalade except in England. After my first summer there, I brought a jar home, but it did not taste right. Although I then tried transporting different brands, I finally realized that once I'd recrossed the Atlantic, I no longer liked marmalade. It did not smear easily on hot toast; its slivers of rind competed with the grainy texture of my favorite whole-wheat bread; its slightly sour flavor overpowered my bland side dish of Oatios. But in England, that tangy flavor puts just the right edge on a slathery, swimming-in-fat breakfast of bacon, sausage, and fried eggs.

As I munch on my buttered and marmaladed toast, I sip my tea. England turned me into a dedicated tea drinker, although, as my life grew jumpier, I eventually abandoned Earl Grey in favor of herbal concoctions. When I first came to England, I had only just learned to drink coffee. Growing up, I could not imagine why adults swilled down such a strong, bitter, murky drink. But as soon as I arrived at college, I realized that I needed to add coffee and cigarettes to my core curriculum. So I experimented, dousing my coffee with ever more cream. Diluted and whitened, it didn't taste too bad. Then it began to taste almost good. Before long, I began chugging several cups at breakfast, then perhaps snatching an additional swallow or two just before class, stopping for midmorning and midafternoon breaks at Gino's Coffee Shop on nearby Green Street, and finally sipping a dark demitasse in the living room after dinner. By my first Christmas vacation, I had proudly become a committed coffee drinker.

Before I came to England, I felt tea lacked coffee's kick and cachet. Our housemother presided not only over nightly demitasse but also at weekly tea. Each Friday after-noon at four o'clock, Smith girls celebrated the oncoming weekend or entertained friends from other houses with big cups of nondescript Lipton's tea augmented by a plate of sugar, peanut-butter, or chocolate-chip cookies. The tea was incidental. It was merely an excuse to talk, relax, gossip, and eat lots of cookies.

But tea in England, I quickly discovered, was a very different thing. When I passed through the breakfast line my first morning at the University of London, I paused briefly in front of a heavyset, perspiring woman in a green apron who wielded enormous jugs of tea, boiling water, and milk. "White?" she snapped, without looking up at me. "Yes, please," I said quickly. I had never poured milk into my Lipton's at home, but the girl ahead of me had ordered white. In what seemed one swift gesture, the woman lifted, poured, and swirled a foaming whitish-gray liquid into a thick china cup. As I set it on my tray, its strong aroma made my nose wrinkle. Tea that morning *tasted* like something, though I wasn't quite sure what.

On subsequent mornings, as I rather glumly contem-plated my bowl of cornflakes and cold toast, I grew to depend on my cup of tea. Although I did not know for many years that tea held any caffeine, I knew that when I had a cup of tea, I perked up. As I wandered around London during the day, stopping for a snack in a cheap café or improvising a makeshift picnic, I observed how other Londoners around me ate and drank. I could not help but notice that not only ladylike shoppers but rough-looking workmen took their cuppa, too.

Everywhere I traveled in England that summer of 1960,

I was never far from a cup of tea. Coffee was scarce then and usually terrible, a muddy emulsion of Nescafé and tepid water that didn't even taste like the familiar instant I made at home. Tea, however, was dependable, even though it was often so strong that I just kept adding more hot water to my starter cup. As a bonus, the thick creamy milk I poured into my tea was almost a meal in itself. Like English butter, I was sure it came from cows whose green pastures were sprinkled with Shakespearean flowers— primrose, gilliflowers, buttercups, daffa-down-dillies—not mere alfalfa.

And of course I could always stop for afternoon tea. When my friend Joyce and I hitchhiked around England that first summer, we did not search out fancy tea shops or the public rooms of elegant hotels. Traveling on the cheap, we studied the menus in windows of small, dark, homey-looking cafés, willing to forgo cucumber-and-shrimp sandwiches for student-level prices. Often we were satisfied with lumpy buns and butter, a slice of heavy cake or apple pie, washed down with lots of tea. But here and there, we were regaled with spreads from a child's paradise: little iced cakes, bread-and-butter sandwiches, jam tarts, a plate of ginger biscuits and shortbread—and always hot, milk-laced, reviving tea.

When we toured the West Country, we discovered Devon, Dorset, and Cornish cream teas, calorie-laden extravaganzas consisting of tea and fresh hot scones, served with pots of strawberry jam and a small bowl of clotted cream. Devon/Dorset/Cornish clotted cream—it varied only by the name of the county in which it was made— reminded me of Mother's whipped cream when the Mixmaster whirred just a little too long, thickening the cream until it was almost butter. After a discreet inquiry in our first West Country tearoom, Joyce and I learned how to split the scone, top each little sandwich with a shaky mound of clotted cream, ladle jam on each side, and pop the scones into our mouths. Young and hungry, we could devour an entire basket of hot scones, ask for additional cream and jam, empty a whole teapot—and leave, at perhaps three or four o'clock, to work up an appetite for supper.

Sometimes, instead of supper, Joyce and I decided on high tea, a meal that even in 1960 was beginning to disappear. In out-of-the-way villages, however, we often found high tea advertised in the kind of dingy, cluttered windows that we knew promised a meal suited to our budgets. High tea was served after about four o'clock and ran very conveniently into our usual supper hour of five-thirty or six. I approached each high tea with the eager anticipation I had always felt at a Presbyterian church potluck in Ames: lots of everything would be on the table, most of it good, some absolutely delicious. Joyce and I ate cold meat pies, slices of cold ham or pork, Welsh rarebit on toast, sausage rolls, stuffed eggs, wedges of cheese with biscuits, bowls of stewed or canned fruit, assorted peculiar relishes of tomato or beets or cucumber, and of course scones, cookies, cake, and pie. We drank pots and pots of strong tea. When we had devoured the last crumbs of the last scone, we did not think of eating again for days—at least, until next morning at breakfast.

Although I remember English breakfasts and afternoon teas as highlights of our traveling day, I have blanked out most of our other meals on the road. In 1960, Joyce and I did not ever spend much money on lunch or dinner. The kind of meal we could afford was almost generic, whether in Bath or Salisbury or York or Canterbury, and nearly identical to the meal James and I had not so long ago in Sidmouth: grilled or roasted meat, or a fried fillet of fish, served with roasted potatoes or deep-fried chips (French fries) and an overcooked green vegetable, peas, sprouts, or cabbage. Sometimes we treated ourselves to a Wimpy at a Wimpy Bar, but an imitation American hamburger, a gristly paper-thin patty that did not taste at all like ground beef, only made us homesick, even when accompanied by a watery vanilla shake.

When Joyce and I yearned for a good meal, we looked for a menu with omelets. As I learned to venerate English cows, I knew I could never go wrong with a cheese omelet. After a long, cold, and often wet day of tramping along country roads, I still remember how, out of the same kitchen that would have produced, if asked, a tired arrangement of tepid meat, peas, and chips, emerged instead a hot golden omelet, made with at least three or four eggs, sautéed in butter, and oozing a mellow stream of melted cheese. The sharp local cheese was only the most distant relation, at least twice removed, to my old favorite, American Velveeta. With the omelet came a small salad, whose buttery green leaves, the color of English fields, also seemed quite unlike the pale iceberg lettuce from the Safeway cases at home.

When I left England that August, I had formed an assessment of English food that served me well for many return trips. I had devised certain strategies. Eat a big breakfast; do not stint on toast and marmalade. Drink lots of tea. Around lunchtime, drop into a food shop for slabs of cheese or pâté or quiche, or cartons of yogurt, and perhaps some takeaway coleslaw. Down the street, let a bakery provide brown rolls and a bit of dessert—jam tart, mince pie, macaroon, éclair, jelly doughnut, or a square of sugary apple pie.

Or stop in a pleasant-looking pub, especially in rural areas or towns not overrun by tourists. March up to the bar, study the chalkboard of bar snacks, and then order either a ploughman's lunch (a hunk of cheese or pâté, roll or bread, and a decorative swirl of lettuce on the plate) or the day's specialty, usually stew, cottage pie, steak-and-kidney pie, or quiche. Wash it down with a glass of sweet cider, as easy to drink as fruit juice—though an hour or so later, you may suddenly begin to nod off in front of even the most spectacular scenic wonder.

After a mandatory break for afternoon tea, the gustatory delights of the day have usually ended. Unless armed with a good-food guide, or staying among London's many ethnic restaurants or in a noted country-house hotel, I just find some place handy for my evening meal and get it over with quickly. Breakfast, after all, isn't far away.

It took me many years to discover that English food takes on new life if it can be prepared at home. When I spent seven months in England in 1978, accompanied by my six-year-old daughter Jenny and Laura, a baby-sitter/companion who was an ardent vegetarian, I knew that we would not be eating many meals in restaurants. Fortified by an American-sized refrigerator and stove in our flat, Laura and I took turns doing the cooking. From my first visit to the tiny grocery store on our South Kensington block, I began to expand my limited expectations. There, artfully arranged in small boxes under the awning, were fresh fruits and vegetables that merely asked for a little steaming, sautéing, or simply peeling and eating raw. Courgettes (zucchini), long French beans, aubergine (eggplant), small melons, and large rough oranges from Spain all reminded me of England's continental links and influences, as did the heap of croissants by the cash register.

England's produce held its own, too: tiny Brussels sprouts so fresh and green I almost wanted to pop them in my mouth, firm crisp cabbages, short stubby carrots with a surprising sweetness, dirt-encrusted new potatoes that tasted almost lemony, small yellow-red tomatoes that were unexpectedly ripe, and, in season, strawberries that, like the tomatoes, did not appear to have ever been treated with American growth hormones. When I sniffed, the tender strawberries had such a rosy seductive perfume that it was impossible not to snatch a punnet (box) and hand it to the smiling young Pakistani who hovered nearby.

A few doors down, I soon became decorously friendly with the local butcher, whose assistant, a shy boy in his teens with a white apron he must have changed several times a day, always referred my surprising questions to his employer. I often sent him scurrying to the back of the shop, for when I stared at the assortment of cuts in the butcher's case, I never knew quite what they were or what to do with them. Pork chops, lamp chops, and mince (hamburger) all were recognizable, but other roasts, chops, and unfamiliar lumps of flesh didn't even sound feasible when the butcher used explanatory words like haunch.

Laura excelled with English vegetables, and she introduced me to the delicacy—if treated with care and respect—of Brussels sprouts. I had always thought of them as a bitter and mushy mess, best pushed to the side of one's plate. Laura's recipe was simple. She carefully selected the smallest, youngest sprouts, cut their stems, and peeled the outer leaves, sliced them in half, and sautéed the halves in a generous swirl of English butter with an even more lavish helping of chopped garlic. After a few minutes, she added some lemon juice with salt and pepper, tossed, and served. They were crisp yet tender, juicy and sweet. Even Jenny, who looked askance at most vegetables, asked for seconds of Laura's sprouts.

Some years later, when I began to travel with James, I received another revelation about English cooking as startling as my discovery that, cooked at home, English food could throw off its dowdiness and dance in the kitchen. Early in the 1980s, James and I based our first trips together to England in country-house hotels. Since 1960, one of the most noticeable changes in England was a slow revolution in what was regarded as gourmet cooking. Certain hotels now prided themselves on their chefs, who imported and adapted French nouvelle cuisine and other continental favorites to English tastes. Using simple ingredients, based on fresh local produce—meats, poultry, and fish, such as English lamb, salmon, duck, and veal; asparagus, Cornish potatoes, watercress, young carrots, and spring peas; strawberries, blackberries, and apples—these cooks created menus for an increasingly sophisticated clientele.

James and I wafted from one English dining room to another in a blissfully satiated state. In my abbreviated travel journal I always managed to note our meals, something I would have previously done in England only in a spirit of resigned irony. One Sunday noon at Teignworthy, a small, luxurious country-house hotel near Dartmoor, Mrs. Newell, our hostess, announced that she would take advantage of the first sunny day in more than a week by organizing an outdoor buffet. The handful of guests, including James and me, sat at little tables under shady umbrellas while Mrs. Newell passed a carafe of wine and urged us all to return to the buffet for additional helpings. My journal rhapsodizes about a pureed spinach-and-cauliflower soup; homemade whole-grain crunchy bread; curried duck eggs with herbed-mayonnaise sauce; grilled quail, fresh trout, hamburger, sausage, pork slices; mixed salad; marinated tomatoes; hot potato salad; and for dessert, a fresh rhubarb flan "with huge dollops of Devon cream, thick as butter." Understandably, my next entry reads: "A brief nap after lunch."

With each trip to England, I have become more addicted to English food. I am now hopelessly enamored of English desserts—gooey puddings, moist cakes, flans, tarts, crunchy meringues—mostly childlike food innocently laden with uncountable calories. I relish currant-laden rice pudding, sherry trifle, caramel custard, floating island, meringues filled with ice cream, strawberries and cream, raspberries and cream, *anything* and cream. Only in England does the waitress routinely ask, as she dishes up anything on the sweet trolley, from chocolate gateau (pronounced deliberately flat, no French fanciness) to apple pie, "And will you have cream?" From her silver pitcher on the trolley, she is ready to pour heavy cream on any and every cake, pudding, pie, and tart. (Ice-cream stands in the West Country even offer a dollop of clotted cream as a topping to an ice-cream cone. If asked, the vendor would probably happily pour cream on top of *that*.)

And who could resist the disarming names of these desserts? Apricot fool? Summer pudding? Treacle tart? Once, studying the dessert menu at Winyard's Gap, a thriving pub on the road outside Chedington in west Dorset, I noticed an entry I had never seen before. Its name alone piqued my interest. "Go ahead," said James. I think he just wanted to hear me order it. When I said gravely to the man behind the bar, "And I'll finish up with some Spotted Dick," he didn't crack a smile, and James only grinned into his half-pint of bitter. What the barman soon placed in front of me was a heavy, custardy bowlful of raisin-and-fruit-studded suety pudding, topped with a thick hard sauce. Though it sank into my stomach like a stone, I ate every bite.

I realize the depth of my attachment to English food when I pack my suitcase of souvenirs at the end of a trip. In corners, wrapped in socks and sweaters, I tuck a bottle of sweet cider; boxes of cheese, cream, and water crackers; jars of gooseberry, damson-plum and bramble jam; Dorset honey; Coleman's mustard; herbal teas; Bourneville bars; ginger biscuits; and chocolate-covered sweetmeal digestives. (Chocolate digestives, despite their deceptively healthful name, are large, rich, crumbly, and rather plain-tasting cookies, gussied up with a thick coating of chocolate.) In my carry-on bag, well wrapped so nothing will reek before it gets to Minneapolis, I often stash chunks of one or two English cheeses, perhaps Wensleydale, Caerphilly, Double Gloucester, and of course, Stilton. For a snack on the plane, I treat myself to a small carton of Loseley's hazelnut yogurt.

So I listen politely when a friend, newly returned from Italy, regales me with tales of spinach fettuccine tossed with fresh clam sauce, or another recalls longingly a skewer of marinated lamb from a Greek taverna, or Francophiles take me, spoonful by spoonful, through a five-course, three-star dinner. When they're gone, I can go to my cupboard, spread a little Marmite on a Carr's water biscuit, and pretend I am looking ahead to afternoon tea.

My Voyage on the *Queen Mary*

*F*or years I dreamed about sailing to England on an ocean liner. Although my early airplane travel was exciting, it soon dwindled into the reality of cramped seating, tasteless meals, and lingering jet lag. So as scenes from old movies and sepia-toned snapshots began to flicker through my mind, I saw myself standing at the rail and waving goodbye to envious friends as the ship slipped away from the dock.

Tucked into a cozy rug by a solicitous steward, I was soon reading in a deck chair. Later I sipped cocktails in a glittering salon, watching discreetly for Cary Grant to smile and gesture me over to his table. Early next morning, we marked the sunrise from a lonely post at the prow. Mostly I imagined myself, profoundly meditative, watching the restless ocean rise and swell into the horizon. From New York harbor to the bustling docks of Southampton: this was the only way to go.

But until I saw the *Queen Mary* looming across the harbor of Long Beach, I had never booked passage. With limited vacation time, I couldn't lop off five days in order to spend that time afloat. Once, when I tried to tempt

James with a Technicolor multipage brochure, he reminded me, gently, about seasickness. A World War II tugboat captain and veteran of several transatlantic crossings, *he* of course was immune, James said rather smugly, but did I remember how I'd felt on our calm, sunny four-hour voyage to a Sicilian island? The constant hum of the engines, the slight motion of the ship? Could I recall lying prone on a bench, my face covered by a scarf?

So I had given up my fantasy until that winter Saturday in Long Beach. Late in the afternoon, after my literary conference had ended, James and I had walked in a gray, gusting rain along the sands of Long Beach. Looking up, and blinking away the rain, we could see the great ship in the distance while wind-whipped waves broke at our feet. Even though we knew the *Queen* was now permanently moored, a tourist attraction and partly a hotel, her glamour shone through the gray mist. Just then, a deep mournful whistle cut the air. It was as seductive and haunting as I'd heard it in my dreams. "Last call," my husband said without a trace of a smile. "Everyone going ashore had better get off. She's about to sail."

I was hooked. On Sunday, though I was coddling a lingering migraine, we had a few tempting free hours before our plane left. Outside our hotel window, beyond a freeway and a neighboring marina, the *Queen Mary* rode at anchor. Her three smokestacks, jauntily tilted, rose like red beacons of adventure. The sun had come out; the day promised fair weather and calm seas. I told James we had just enough time to tour the *Queen*.

The *Queen Mary* is not alone in the harbor. Tethered next door is an enormous geodesic dome, almost as large as the *Queen*, protecting the *Spruce Goose*, Howard Hughes's giant wooden plane. It flew only once in 1947, briefly rising seventy feet over Long Beach harbor, before retiring, like Hughes, to a reclusive life in the shadows. To view the *Queen Mary*, a passenger buys a ticket for both attractions. A Los Angeles billboard advertises both with a simple, singularly Californian slogan: SEE MAMMOTH! And indeed, "mammoth" may be just right, evoking gigantic extinct animals who could not successfully compete in the race for survival. Yoked together by two museum pieces, England and America become equally faded powers on this pier that celebrates unrecoverable glories.

Though the *Queen Mary*'s gangplank resembles a convoluted entrance to a Disneyland attraction, I pretended as I strode up it that I was boarding for a long voyage. At my side, James whispered to me that our trunks would have been labeled and whisked away at the dock, to appear magically later in our cabin. Our map directed us first to the lower decks and engine rooms, but with my head beginning to pound harder, I knew where to place our priorities. Sun, water, fresh air.

Before long we were at the stern, gazing out at the bay. It was an early Sunday morning in off-season, so only a few tourists drifted past us. I tried to feel like a passenger. But facing the crowded shores of Long Beach, I couldn't quite pretend we were two days from land. Ahead of us in the harbor squatted several oil islands, with incongruously planted palm trees and ugly cement towers. I squinted and turned to shut out as much reality as possible. I wanted to savor the feeling of relaxing in the sun on deck, pretending I had endless hours to do nothing but read, stretch, and nap. A few empty deck chairs were scattered here and there. But the wind was brisk, and despite the sun, I felt a little chilly. No steward appeared with a steamer rug. "They always sell deck chairs before the ship pulls out," James said offhandedly. "Then, when you're really out on the Atlantic, it's usually too cold to sit outside."

The promenade deck was satisfyingly long, stretching along the side of the ship farther than my nearsighted eyes could properly focus. Its scuffed and weathered floorboards showed the age the *Queen* hid so well from a distance, but the promenade revived my romantic pictures of shipboard life. I imagined myself as a passenger on a walk, getting her regular exercise. From a placard I learned that four times around it equaled a mile. At home I circled our three-mile city lake daily, watching the seasons change, noting different birds, greeting other regular walkers. That walk always went quickly. How would I feel about twelve laps around the promenade deck? I looked over the railing at the barely ruffled water and tried to picture wild waves, pounding at the sides of the ship. "If it were really rough," said James, "you wouldn't be out here."

Halfway down the promenade deck a stairway led into the ship, where a bakery/café had just opened its doors. The bakery walls were decorated with over-life-size photographs of some of the *Queen Mary*'s famous passengers. Hovering over the pastry cases was Greta Garbo, shielding her face from the camera. The Duke and Duchess of Windsor, arm in arm on the deck, were smiling brightly, next to Anthony Eden, Winston Churchill, and Clark Gable. Taking our plastic tray outside, we looked for a table in the sun, but the starboard side was now completely shaded. We drank our tea quickly.

Further along the deck, we wandered in and out of other exhibits. More photographs of more celebrities. I thought of them on board this ship, walking up and down this promenade deck, hidden behind sunglasses. When I was a young girl, I thought of movie stars as leading golden lives. Now, with so many public reputations awash in a littered tide of telltale biographies, I know better. Looking at the blowup of Gary Cooper accompanied by his wife, Rocky, I thought of his notorious love affair with Patricia Neal. I wondered about Greta Garbo, always frowning. I shuddered a little at the Windsors, whose sad and wasted lives now read like a modern morality tale.

After following our map to Piccadilly Circus, a radiating center of shops selling *Queen Mary* teacups and sweatshirts, we walked past a series of reconstructed rooms. One exhibit, a cutaway section of the *Queen*'s nightclub, showed two mannequins seated at a minuscule table while a waiter hovered over them and a pianist sat at a grand piano inches away. The black carpet, a sign said, had been a decorating sensation in its day. Passengers could dance and dine here till seven A.M.

I thought about spending a whole night at that cramped table, surrounded by black carpet, in a darkened room deep inside the ship. I imagined trying to keep conversation going till seven A.M. with even the most intriguing escort. I saw myself rising blearily, to circle once more around the dance floor. "Listen," I said to James emphatically, "let's just take a look at a first-class stateroom and then get out of here."

The stateroom was actually a suite: salon, bedroom, bathroom, and maid's room. I liked the gadgety bathroom, with its capacious claw-foot tub and double set of fresh- and saltwater taps, but I now felt quite foggy, and the narrow hall seemed stuffy. I looked anxiously toward the small portholes that served as windows. Of course they weren't open. "Even in here I hear a slight hum," I said to James.

He nodded. "The engines are going all the time," he told me. "And the fans have to keep recirculating the air."

I looked speculatively at the bedroom adjoining the living quarters. I love art deco furniture, and the bed frame was bird's-eye maple. A vanity and mirror were equally fancy, with enticing curves. But the ceiling was low, the light dim—and the porthole seemed to shrink as I looked at it. Even without a migraine, how could I sleep here? I wondered what it would be like to have a migraine and seasickness at the same time.

We walked briskly toward the exit, pausing briefly at photographs and life-size reconstructions showing how the *Queen* had been turned during the war into a carrier for fifteen thousand soldiers. (Her ordinary capacity, said our brochure, was 1,957 passengers, with officers and crew of 1,174.) James read aloud the placard about "hot bunks"; space was so scarce that each soldier took an eight-hour turn in bed and then had to give it up to the next sleeper. I imagined myself a soldier with a migraine.

The wartime exhibits were sobering. The *Gray Ghost*, as she was affectionately known, courted danger on every crossing from German U-boats that had been offered a high bounty by Hitler for sinking her. Once, nearing the

Irish coast, she'd accidentally sliced through the hull of a smaller cruiser that had suddenly crossed her bow. Obeying firm orders never to stop and risk becoming a target, the *Queen* had to sail on and leave hundreds of sailors to drown in her wake.

Taking a last turn on deck, we stopped at the *Queen*'s salon. It was a large magnificent ballroom, whose drapery and furnishings, though slightly shabby, recalled nights of lavish entertainment and high revelry. I could envision an orchestra, dozens of tables with white linen and sparkling crystal, music, laughter, and swishing long skirts along the polished floor. Here, as James and I stood alone in the empty room, I could at last see Gable and Garbo, Crosby and Astaire, even the Gary Coopers, all of them released from their human frailties. They danced the night away, stopping only for bits of lobster and glasses of champagne, tossing ermine and dinner jackets over the backs of chairs, turning their best profiles toward the ship's photographer. They had been turned again into stars. The *Queen Mary*, once more the ship of my dreams, was also a star.

But I am not, I thought. No matter how or where I travel, I'll always be a bit claustrophobic, prone to migraines, not liking parties, drinking very little, wanting to go to bed early. Not the ideal profile of a *Queen Mary* passenger. Not, probably, a contented passenger on any long voyage. As we emerged onto the deck again, the sun was almost unbearably bright on my headache-glazed eyes. "You know," I said thoughtfully to James, "I have a feeling that these past two hours on ship have saved us a lot of money."

We slowly descended the gangway into a world of

parking lots, freeways, and airports. I looked backward toward the *Queen*, whose tilted red smokestacks looked as gallant and racy as ever. A few visitors leaned over the stern deck, lazily gazing at the water. That was how I always thought I'd look on board a ship, comfortable and tranquil.

Just then, perhaps because it was noon, the *Queen*'s whistle blew, a loud, commanding note quite different from the mist-softened reverie we had heard on the beach the night before. What was the *Queen* telling me? To stay away? To come back? Or was she congratulating me? Had I now jettisoned all my excess baggage? Would I be able to plan, finally, an ocean voyage free of false illusions?

"On the other hand," I said to James as we drove away, "this may not have been a fair test." He raised his eyebrows slightly but said nothing. We turned into the endless current of California traffic, cars flanking us like moving walls. I thought of the *Queen* far out at sea, slicing through the water. I mentally lay back in my deck chair, watching the waves toss and waiting for the steward to bring my martini and another lap robe.

A View From
Waterloo Bridge:

Married and Alone in London, 1963–1975

S haken and tearful, I stood on Waterloo Bridge facing Lawrence, my husband of four weeks. His jaw was set, lips tight. Below us, the brown Thames swirled and moved sluggishly toward the sea. It was an early August evening in 1963, and the lights of London were brightening in the rain-streaked mist. Behind us, we could see people streaming across the vast concrete plaza of the Royal Festival Hall. We had eaten supper in its ground-floor cafeteria. The supper hadn't been very good.

The day had not been very good, either. Lawrence had been cross, and I had withdrawn into hurt feelings. Although I do not remember what words passed between us on Waterloo Bridge, I was distraught. My marriage was only a month old, and already I wondered if I had made a terrible mistake. On an impulse I wrenched my diamond engagement ring from my finger and held it out by my fingertips over the dark muddy water. "I feel like dropping this right now," I sobbed, but quietly, so no one except Lawrence would hear me.

"So why don't you?" Lawrence snapped. I looked at the brown water far below. I wished I had the courage to fling the ring into the water, but I didn't. During the months we had been engaged, I would sometimes look at the small but almost flawless diamond on my hand and think, "One thousand dollars!" Now, as Lawrence glared, I quavered. After what were probably only a few moments, I drew my arm back and slowly replaced the ring on my finger. Lawrence shrugged and turned away.

I had thought London would be the perfect way to end our honeymoon. It had been three years since I had spent a summer studying in London and hitchhiking with Joyce around the English countryside. When I flew back to my senior year at Smith, I was soon to confront major changes in my life: graduation, a fellowship to Berkeley, two hectic but exciting years studying and exploring San Francisco and the Bay area, romance, marriage.

Now, at twenty-three, I was ready to settle down. I was taking a year off from my Ph.D. studies in English, and I had lined up a temporary teaching job at San Francisco State. To begin our married life, I had found a spacious and inexpensive apartment with a view of the Bay, and I was eagerly planning to furnish it with thrift-shop finds. I had already bought *The Joy of Cooking*, *The New York Times Cookbook*, a stockpot, and a Mouli mincer. I had even acquired a wooden darning egg so I could mend Lawrence's socks.

But first I wanted to see London again. Looking back on that carefree summer, I thought that I would never again hitchhike or sleep in youth hostels or plan to bike with a girlfriend around Europe. Of course, Lawrence and I would travel, but it would be different. I felt I needed to say goodbye to the girl I had been—only three years ago?—in

London. I also had another reason for wanting to return, for I was hoping to share my passion for London with my husband. Lawrence was a theoretical scientist, I was an English major, and although we were very attracted to each other, we had some difficulty in finding areas of common interest.

When Lawrence and I began planning our four-week European honeymoon, I suggested we might spend some time in England. To my surprise, he was unenthusiastic. "When England invaded Suez," he said bitterly, "they betrayed the Hungarian Revolution. The English made it possible for the Communists to crush the Freedom Fighters." Lawrence's parents had both emigrated from Hungary. Lawrence went on: the English were also untrustworthy, snobbish, imperialistic, and, in addition, poor scientists.

I mentioned Shakespeare. Lawrence and I had been to the theatre together several times, and I knew he had read *Hamlet* in his western-civ course at Cal Tech. Well, yes, he admitted, there was Shakespeare. We talked some more. Finally Lawrence agreed that we could stop a few days in London on the way home. That would be enough, I thought. Surely he would be able to see London in a new way through my eyes. I would show him around, take him on the Underground, and get us tickets to Shakespeare.

On our European honeymoon, as we drove from Germany through Austria, Switzerland, and Holland, I increasingly looked forward to those days in London. Although I dutifully marveled at mountain villages, Baroque castles, tulip fields, and museums filled with Old Masters, I was often preoccupied and, to my surprise, often unhappy. No one had warned us that a European honeymoon might be stressful. We were both gradually worn out by constant traveling, sightseeing, and coping with foreign languages and customs. We fretted about money; in charge of budgeting the trip, I had seriously underestimated what everything would cost.

We also had a new and unexpectedly heavy responsibility. For a wedding present, Lawrence's parents had offered to buy us a car to be purchased in Europe and then shipped home. We had decided on a Porsche, a bright red convertible with a black top. A plump little sports car with a low throbbing voice, it was so diffidently seductive that I still remember the model number—a 356B Cabriolet—as if it were a muttered endearment.

When Lawrence saw our new red Porsche, gleaming like a polished apple, in the yard of the Stuttgart factory, he instantly fell in love with it. Fluent in German, he listened intently as the factory representative explained just how the car had to be driven for its first thousand miles. As we carefully turned out of the lot, Lawrence in turn explained to me. The tachometer, a clocklike dial on the dashboard, was marked in zones. If the car was in the correct gear, the little black arrow would stay in the dark green zone. If the gear was too low or too high, the arrow would move out of the dark green into the light green or, worse, into the red. Terrible things would then happen to the engine. "If the car doesn't get broken in properly," Lawrence said ominously, "it could be ruined."

We spent many anxious miles breaking in the Porsche. When we crossed the Alps, we had to crawl along in a line of traffic that would neither move fast enough nor slow down enough to keep the little arrow in the dark green zone. The road was narrow as well as crowded, so we could not pass. Lawrence fussed, I tensed, the arrow wobbled. Although we drove past flower-strewn meadows, below snow-covered peaks, and across vertiginous passes, I remember the wobbling arrow much more vividly than the Alps.

So I disloyally anticipated our time in London, when we would have no car. We intended to ship the Porsche home from Amsterdam and fly the Channel. I also fantasized about our desirable hotel room in London, which, like all our accommodations, I had arranged long distance, guided primarily by an outdated edition of Frommer's *Europe on Five Dollars a Day*. In London, our last stop, I had decided to splurge on a private bathroom. This, as things had turned out, would be wildly welcome.

For as we were breaking in the Porsche, I was having a difficult breaking-in period myself. A month before the wedding, I had consulted our family doctor for a premarital exam and acquired a prescription for birth-control pills. Almost as an afterthought, I asked the doctor if I should possibly also own a diaphragm, just in case. He agreed, gave me cursory instructions, and sent me on my way with a casual but alarming send-off: "You're awfully tight. Don't expect it to be easy."

Nothing was easy. The night before our wedding, nervous and keyed up, I forgot to take my pill. During the ceremony, I began to bleed. We flew from Iowa to Chicago, Chicago to Germany, and still I bled. Frightened, I took at first double pills and then none at all. I decided to use my diaphragm instead. I soon found myself having to struggle with this strange and slippery device under decidedly unromantic conditions in cramped rooms often equipped only with cold-water sinks.

So London began to look almost idyllic. We would be in a city I loved, where I knew the streets and spoke the language. We would finally have a comfortable and well-equipped hotel. Although we might be having a hard time on our honeymoon now, everything would be all right in London. Only, of course, it wasn't. By the time we dragged our suitcases up four flights of the dingy third-class hotel in Earl's Court, we were exhausted. After a month together, we were also tired of each other's constant company. We needed to go home and resume the relative separateness of our everyday lives. But first we were committed to three days in London.

The Earl's Court room was small, noisy, and dark. Its private bath turned out to be a primitive shower rigged on a cement platform in one corner of the crowded room. The toilet was down the hall. "This dump is costing how much?" asked Lawrence incredulously. When I told him, he snorted.

I wanted to show off my beloved city, but cold and rainy, London refused to cooperate. Nothing went right. After weeks of tender veal schnitzel, aromatic sauerbraten, and crunchy hard rolls, the peas in London's cheap restaurants were mushier than I'd remembered, the potatoes soggier. Even Wimpy Bars no longer seemed amusing. We couldn't get tickets to the Shakespeare play I wanted. Lawrence did not find the Tube particularly fun, and he was unimpressed by my insider's knowledge of its vagaries and routes.

Worse, I realized as I led him through my favorite streets, Lawrence did not walk down the Strand and think of Dickens or Thackeray. He did not particularly want to eat lunch with Samuel Johnson's ghost at the Cheshire Cheese. He did not thrill to the names I mentioned that were laden with English history or literature, just as I would probably have been equally unenthralled if he had taken me on a tour of a radiation laboratory or introduced me to a cyclotron. But I was still crushed.

When we left Heathrow a few days later, I did not know if I would ever return to England. There are other places I want to see, I consoled myself, places like Norway, Denmark, France, Greece. Lawrence and I could travel there. But somewhere in the back of my mind, tucked away like an overlarge suitcase I wasn't sure I'd be able to use again, I carefully stowed my old image of London. My London wasn't a cold room in Earl's Court or greasy sausage rolls in the Festival Hall cafeteria or the polluted water under the Waterloo Bridge. It was an enthralling city where I had once been independent and adventurous.

When Lawrence and I moved in 1964 from Berkeley to Minneapolis, London seemed more remote than ever. Although I eventually settled with contented permanence in the Twin Cities, at first they only painfully reminded me of my recent loss of San Francisco, just across the water from Berkeley. San Francisco, with its golden bridge over a sparkling blue bay, was the second city I'd loved. Different as it was, San Francisco still reminded me of London. It too had a certain foreign air, with its winding streets, flower carts, and gingerbread houses. As in London, I learned to find my way around the city, made it my own, and then had to leave.

As the Christmas of 1969 approached, Lawrence and I had been separated, off and on, for almost a year. We had parted the previous Christmas, eventually entered counseling, tried a reconciliation, and separated again. I became so embarrassed about telling people, "Yes, we're back together," or "Actually, we've separated again," that I often wished I could fly a coded flag in front of our house. One flag would signal, *He's living here*, another would signal, *He's not living here*.

The more I thought about Christmas, the more depressed I got. Perhaps Lawrence would move back for the holiday, but then again, perhaps not. In either case, the season didn't promise to be very festive. Sitting in my Macalester office one mid-December day, I took a break from grading end-of-semester English papers and leafed idly through a recent issue of *Publications of the Modern Language Association*, something I only did when desperate for distraction. Suddenly a small notice leaped out at me: *Christmas in London*.

I read the notice several times. Ten days in London, including Christmas. Then I looked out my office window at the bleak empty courtyard edged with dirty snow, and I thought of London at Christmas. Theatre, pantomime, Christmas pudding, Dickens, holly, carolers. "God Rest You Merry Gentlemen," shoppers scurrying along Regent Street, rosy-cheeked English children in Hyde Park. After-Christmas sales at Harrod's and Selfridge's. On an impulse, I called the listed number, a travel agency in New Jersey.

The lady there was eager to help me. Was I a member of the MLA? In that case, even though the tour had officially closed, I could still join. No more seats on the plane were available, but I could pay a little extra, take a flight an hour earlier, and wait for the group at Heathrow. The group numbered eleven. No, we would have no planned activities. Just a group rate on the airfare and at a nice hotel. Of course, I would have a private bath.

The more I thought about the trip, the better it sounded. I'd have company, but I wouldn't be constrained to any itinerary. I could avoid deciding how to spend my Christmas and with whom. Although I didn't want to be alone in Minnesota at Christmas, being alone in London would be just fine.

Although I am usually a meticulous planner, for once I acted on the spur of the moment. I called the lady in New Jersey again and told her I was putting a deposit in the mail. When Lawrence heard of my plan, he did not like it at all. He expressed himself vigorously at our next counseling session. He was close to coming back again, he said, but now I was leaving—and at Christmas! I wavered, but our counselor uncharacteristically called me at home that night. Go, he said, it's a good idea.

So I did. On the plane from New York to London, excited and exuberant, I was anxious to talk. I discovered that the man sitting next to me was single and taught at a college not far from mine. Another man across the aisle heard us talking and joined in; he, too, was traveling alone to London. He was just going through a divorce. Both men gave me the phone numbers of their London hotels. The man next to me said he would love to see a new musical version of *The Canterbury Tales*, and perhaps I would see it with him. I said that sounded great. The other man and I made tentative plans to meet for dinner.

Years afterward, when I was single, I remembered that

plane trip with some astonishment. At the time, I was happily surprised to discover that I could still attract male attention. But I didn't realize then how rare it was to meet single men so easily. After my divorce, they seemed to be almost extinct. But on the plane, I flirted gaily and thought that perhaps being divorced, starting all over, might not be so bad. Or perhaps, I concluded as I ordered another drink, this simply might be part of London's long-distance magic.

At Heathrow, I glanced at the familiar tabloid signboards near the airport newsstands. Today's headlines were all about flu. FLU KILLS DOZENS! FLU EPIDEMIC RAGES! NO RELIEF FROM FLU! AVOID CROWDS, DOC SAYS! For one uneasy moment, I looked around at the crowds pressing through the terminal. Then I picked up my suitcase and determinedly plunged ahead.

For three or four days, I was swept up in a joyful reunion. Although I quickly made friends with several people in our group, it was London I had really come to see. Hello, London! Hello, Liberty's! Hello, Piccadilly Line, pound notes, Hungerford footbridge, public conveniences, country rectors' indignant letters to the *Times*, rainy afternoons at the V&A, foggy mornings in the park! Hello and Merry Christmas!

Then, overnight, I got the flu. My nose clogged, my chest filled up, and I ran a high fever. Weak and dizzy, I fell into bed. For almost all the rest of our stay, I huddled under the covers of my narrow bed. I tried not to think too often about how I had depleted my little bank account for this trip.

And yet I was not unhappy. My new friends from the group usually brought me breakfast in my room, sometimes tea and snacks in the afternoon. Lying snugly in bed, I watched the BBC. I had never before had access to English television, and now I became hooked. Historical dramas, offbeat and slapstick comedies whose humor I didn't always understand, news programs, weather, garden bulletins, even old American movies and sitcoms: I watched it all. Without any commercials, the BBC seemed so dignified, so understated, so—as I remembered my British slang—*tony*. If my eyes got tired, I turned off the TV and tuned in the radio. As I drifted in and out of fitful sleep, I listened blissfully to the elegant Oxbridge accents of the BBC announcers.

Even being sick in London was something like a holiday. I was only sick enough to be in bed, uncomfortable but not in pain. Removed from all responsibilities, I had no house to care for, no pets to feed, no telephone to answer. Sleeping or dozing or leafing through magazines, I let the strain of the past year relax and slip away.

Christmas Day came and went. I was well enough to make a visit to a nearby restaurant for a meal that ended deliciously with a little Christmas pud (rhymes with *good*), dark, heavy, and raisin-studded, with a sugary hard sauce. Three of us from the MLA group went to dinner together and then walked slowly to the hotel in a drizzling cold rain. I went back to bed. I did not get to a Christmas panto, or smell any roast goose, or hear any carolers, except on the BBC. But I didn't mind.

After I was divorced, I did not forget how satisfying it was to lose myself in London. Teaching, caring for my young daughter, and trying to squeeze in time for friends and relaxation, I could seldom indulge in out-of-town trips. But a few times during my eleven divorced years, I did manage ten-day or two-week vacations.

When I knew I could go somewhere, only one place really tempted me. As a single woman, I did not know an American city where I could go out at night alone without fear. Much as I loved San Francisco, what would I do there after dark? Suppose I didn't feel like a symphony, opera, or a touring road show? I briefly considered New York, but I did not want to picture myself alone in the theatre district late at night, unsuccessfully trying to hail a cab. Boston? I wasn't even sure it *had* theatre. So when I could, I went to London. "Won't you be lonely? Won't you get depressed?" Several of my friends asked anxiously before I left. I shook my head. I couldn't imagine being either lonely or depressed in London.

But I did plan carefully. After many air letters flew like wafer-thin birds between Minnesota and England, I found just the right base of operations. The Knights Hotel was a narrow, crumbling building, once a substantial town house, in a still-genteel cul-de-sac a few short blocks from Harrod's and Hyde Park. It had only nine or ten rooms, it lacked both lobby and restaurant, and its breakfast room was a windowless subterranean space, but it was clean and moderately cheap.

And it was in Knightsbridge. To my snobbish ears, *Knightsbridge* had a distinctly different ring from *Bayswater* or *Paddington*. Although my guidebooks cited inexpensive hotels in many locations, I shuddered when I remembered my honeymoon in Earl's Court. Nor did I want a tatty hotel in the endless row of dispirited bed-and-breakfast signs that lined the street in Sussex Gardens.

No, I wanted Knightsbridge. I thought of its fancy shops, staid museums, and discreet Regency and Victorian houses with curlicued wrought-iron gates. I pictured myself window-shopping among the cashmere sweaters of the Scotch House and the lacy lingerie boutiques in Beauchamp Place. I imagined quick visits to the Victoria and Albert Museum, which was close enough so I could nip in and out with the practiced ease of someone who lived in the neighborhood. If I decided to take an early-morning ramble in Hyde Park, I could watch horses with undoubtedly titled riders cantering along Rotten Row. As I repeated my address to myself, I loved its sound: "Knights Hotel, Beaufort Gardens, Knightsbridge, London, SW1."

Furnished only with a twin bed and a two-drawer dresser, my hotel room was small and plain, but I was determined to make it home. As soon as the manager closed the door behind me, I quickly assessed my few square feet of space, dragged my bed across the floor, and shoved it directly under the one window. When I went to sleep, I could keep my face turned to the sky. Then I surveyed my tiny bathroom: its sink, toilet, and shower were all sized to fit into a second-class train compartment, but they were mine. I happily stuck my toothbrush into the one glass.

As soon as I had unpacked, I left the hotel. Although I had been in a plane all night, I had no intention of wasting time on an afternoon nap. I was about to meet London as a recently divorced woman, now on her own and definitely in charge. The moment I was swept into the hurrying stream of pedestrians along the Cromwell Road, London's familiar cool damp air brushed away drowsiness. Briskly I strode through Harrod's, not stopping to shop, but peeking into the baronial Food Hall, with its high ceilings and long aisles stacked with cheeses, meats, game, jams, relishes, breads, crackers, and caviar. There in the next two weeks I could join the jeweled and furred matrons, whose chauffeurs were waiting outside, to pick up a spot of something for lunch.

Down Knightsbridge, past Hyde Park and Marble Arch, across Green Park and St. James's all the way to Piccadilly I walked and looked, checking for double-decker red buses, square black taxis, Underground stations, W. H. Smith & Sons, bobbies in chin-strap helmets, and men carrying wood-handled umbrellas. I wanted to make sure everything was still there. I walked until I was so groggy I knew I'd have to find someplace for a cheese omelet and then go immediately to bed.

Next morning at breakfast, as soon as I started on my second steaming pot of tea, I took out a little spiral notebook I'd bought at W. H. Smith the day before. Marking off days to make a calendar, I began to schedule my next two weeks. I knew that if I had something definite each day, I could not possibly end up sitting in my hotel room, wondering what to do, and perhaps feeling sorry for myself.

As soon as I turned to the theatre and entertainment ads in the *Times*, I got so excited I swallowed a cup of fresh tea without blowing on it and burned my mouth. What riches lay in front of me! Alec Guinness! John Gielgud! Deborah Kerr in something I'd never heard of, but still, Deborah Kerr, in a limited run at the Haymarket! Jean Simmons and Hermione Gingold in *A Little Night Music*!

Two, no, three Shakespeares at the National and at the Aldwych! The Royal Ballet, the London Festival Ballet, Ashkenazy at Festival Hall—how could I ever do it all? I began circling ads with my pen, making notes about matinees and closing dates, estimating ticket prices.

That second day in London I hurried from one box office to another and bought tickets for everything I intended to see. By suppertime, I was irrevocably committed, except for a few days designated for possible train trips, cheap-day-returns, to Cambridge or Canterbury or Broadstairs. When I leafed through my notebook, I felt as pleased as if I were looking at a full dance card, with every scribbled name a high-stepping partner in top hat and tails. Back in my hotel room by six o'clock, I spread out all my new theatre, ballet, and concert tickets on one end of the bed and admired them. Then I sat cross-legged on the other end and ate a picnic supper of yogurt, raw carrots, and apple, finished off with two jam tarts. Not quite as good as a cheese omelet, but cheaper and faster. Before long, I'd have to hurry back to the Knightsbridge Tube station in order to catch a seven-thirty curtain on Shaftesbury Avenue.

No day in London was ever long enough. Every morning I went out in search of adventure. Sometimes I clambered to the top of a double-decker bus and rode across the city, perched in the front seat for a panoramic view. Although I wrinkled my nose at smokers' fumes—smoking was only permitted upstairs—I liked looking down on Marble Arch, over park walls, and into the streets. As the bus rolled and rumbled through the streets, I felt as if I were sitting atop a swaying elephant, high above the crowds, moving very slowly to a distant tent for afternoon tea.

Filled with high-toned intentions, I tried to visit one museum every day. My favorite was the V&A, whose endless succession of jumbled rooms reminded me of a grandmother's attic filled with cobwebby treasures—old porcelain vases, scroll-backed chairs, and faded needlework—all awaiting fresh discovery. I also liked visiting the Blakes at the Tate. Some people, I knew, thought of the English as irretrievably dull and conservative. They obviously hadn't looked very closely at William Blake. On one trip to the Tate, I followed a shop assistant into the basement archives so I could locate and buy a black-and-white photograph of a Blake drawing called *The River of Life.* It showed mysterious angelic figures surrounding a woman who was swimming upstream, head held high, with a baby holding on to each arm. Though I only had one child, that was how I sometimes felt.

Some days I did not get to a museum. On my way to the National Gallery, I might pause at the stores on Regent Street, or I'd suddenly get off the bus at the Burlington Arcade on Piccadilly. I never admitted to anyone, including myself, how much time I spent shopping in London. During the 1960s and through most of the 1970s, prices in England seemed low, or at least reasonable. Although I had little money to spend, that only made me sharper-eyed.

From my first visit to London, I became enamored of the *English look.* Although I knew that many English homes were filled with clashing patterns, not to mention brown-and-gold floral upholstery in shades no flower ever bore, rackety metal lamps with bulbous shades, and painted china dogs, I nonetheless took my English style from other sources: National Trust shops, *Country Life*, Wedgwood plates, Jaeger jackets, Crabtree & Evelyn boxed soaps.

Hard to define, I knew the English look when I saw it: sprigged flowers on a china teacup, paisley prints on a Liberty scarf, a heathery blue tweed skirt, delicate violets and lily of the valley on an oval white canister of perfumed talc from a Boots pharmacy. Sometimes it had the woodsy charm of an English cottage garden, with warm soft colors artfully but informally arranged against the blue of sky, the white of clouds, or the green of flowing green grass. Or it might be the art deco sleekness of the London Transport sign or the clean bright graphics of the Underground map. I even was fond of quaintness, in selected instances: teapots in the shape of Tudor cottages whose roofs lifted off, umbrellas with parrots' heads, and jam jars covered with flowing script that identified the manufacturer as Purveyor of Jam by Appointment to Her Royal Majesty.

My favorite store for the English look was Liberty's. There I could indulge colonial fantasies, fingering Oriental silks in the yard-goods department, wistfully flipping through a row of tropical-weight Liberty-print lawn blouses, and pausing at a three-foot-high brown leather elephant to wonder in what unimaginably cushioned parlor it might feel at home.

I always looked for something I could buy in London to wear. In the London I had known in the early 1960s, style merely signified a nicely cut tweed skirt or a triple-ply cashmere sweater with brass buttons. By the 1970s, English fashion designers had emerged from the turbulent later 1960s with new confidence. The King's Road, starting at Sloane Square, had become a mecca of trendy shops, specializing in costume melodrama. Tweed gave way to floppy rayon, rosy red to shocking pink, classic to razzmatazz.

Exploring beyond Regent Street, I found that London's fashion world was careening along a different road. At a time when women's clothes at home seemed predictable and dull, London skirts sank and swooshed, dramatic hoods fell over shoulders, poetic blouses ballooned, and boots shot sky-high. I still have a flounced mauve raincoat from a fanciful South Kensington shop. When I wear that raincoat, I think of the eccentric side of England, with its occasional outbursts of defiant individuality—though William Blake would not like to be coupled in anyone's mind with a flounced mauve raincoat.

Of course, I brought home some clinkers. Once, in the Burlington Arcade, trying to escape a cool glance from the beadle, who stalked in his gaudy antique uniform up and down the vaulted passage, I slipped into Wetherall's. There I unaccountably purchased a dark-green-and-rust reversible wool cape, in a light double-faced wool, for a sum of money I have conveniently forgotten. At home in Minnesota, it was never warm enough for winter and its colors were far too autumnal for spring.

On another London visit, I spied a massive tweed kilt, much reduced, at the impeccable Scotch House. I think I was won over by the kilt's authentic pleating, leather straps, and pewter buckle. The saleslady assured me it would last forever. It probably has. I found it so heavy I drooped from its weight, as if I had two sagging blankets draped uncomfortably around my hips. After it hung reproachfully in my closet for a year or two, I managed to give it away, but to whom I have also conveniently forgotten. I do not like to remember failed bargains.

I did not shop every day in London. On Wednesdays and Saturdays I almost always had a scheduled double-header, a matinee in the afternoon, followed by an evening performance an hour or two later. Between shows I raced to a grocery store for a portable snack or tried to find a restaurant that could produce a cheese omelet in a hurry. Wednesdays and Saturdays were long, entrancing, and somewhat dazing. After three hours of luridly lit Jacobean tragedy, I would emerge into daylight for a freshly cut sandwich and an orange squash, sometimes devoured as I raced from one theatre to another. Then I would dive again into the darkness for, say, three and a half hours of *Giselle*.

When I hurried out of the Knightsbridge Tube station late that night, my mind was humming with music and whirring with images. I walked quickly to the Knights Hotel, tapping my umbrella so that it rang sharply on the almost-deserted street. I wished I could talk with someone about everything I had seen that day. But I was too sleepy to feel lonely very long.

Back in my closet-sized room, I curled up on the bed underneath the window. For a while I listened to the muffled sounds of taxis rumbling down Brompton Road. Sometimes I'd hear heels tapping on the pavement below and snatches of murmured talk from guests returning to the hotel. Perhaps I might see them at breakfast. Listening to those low voices, I felt comforted. They reminded me of a familiar world, one of friendship and conversation, shared secrets and laughter. In less than two weeks, I'd be back in that world. Meanwhile, I was keeping company just with myself—and with London. I was pleased with both, and for now that was enough.

Sheepdog Trials:
A Field Trip

SHEEPDOG TRIALS—LEWES—SAT, JULY 21. Although it was only a crudely painted sign stuck on a roadside fence, it caught my attention. As James and I had tramped around the English and Welsh countryside over the years, we'd sometimes watched in admiration as a small black-and-white dog in a nearby pasture moved a flock of sheep across a field and through a gate. I had only a vague image of sheepdog trials, but a few days before, I'd tuned into the last minutes of a BBC television program called *One Man and His Dog*. Its chatty host was interviewing a taciturn man in mud-spattered clothes standing next to an intelligent-looking, bright-eyed sheepdog. They were talking about a trial the dog had just won. I wished I'd been able to see the man and his dog in action.

At the time, I assumed that the program featured different dog stories each week—perhaps a champion Jack Russell, a corgi related to Queen Elizabeth's, or a Labrador who'd recently saved a baby from a burning house. I did not know that sheepdog trials were a popular competitive sport with regular regional meets, national champions, and international contests, nor could I have guessed that such trials provided weekly tension-filled moments for a popular TV show.

I was about to learn. It was not easy to find the Lewes Sheepdog Trials, even though an accommodating hotel clerk had telephoned the Lewes Tourist Information Agency and learned that the trials began at nine A.M. Sunday at Deans Farm on the Puddingham Road. She wasn't quite sure about Puddingham. Neither were we. But if the trials were a major event, we'd be sure to find it, perhaps on a public parade ground or soccer field outside Lewes, a thriving market town not far from Brighton.

Early Sunday morning we packed a picnic lunch and set out for what we thought would be an easy half-hour drive. We allowed for plenty of time. "This is probably going to be crowded," I warned James, "and we'd better be early to get good seats. We don't want to be so high in the bleachers that we can't see anything." Sheepdog trials somehow brought to mind other contests and races I knew about, greyhounds, horses, stock cars, the Minnesota State Fair. Lots of fans, crammed together in a stadium, noisily stamping their feet or clambering over each other to reach the beer or popcorn vendor.

So we left our holiday flat near East Grinstead soon after eight A.M., zooming along the multilane, high-speed A26 toward Lewes and Brighton. But I had forgotten how hidden many of the back roads of England can be. The A roads sometimes seem edged and banked with a clear invisible shield that insulates the countryside from intrusion. Unless you intuitively sense an opening, it is hard to break through the shield.

Once near Lewes, I couldn't spy any signs for Puddingham Road. We didn't see any outdoor bleachers or soccer field or fairground. The highway swept us into the center of the town, where we circled fruitlessly on confusing one-way streets—fortunately, on Sunday morning Lewes was almost empty—until finally we stopped a passing pedestrian.

"Puddingham?" he asked, puzzled. Then light dawned. "Oh, you must mean the road to Piddinghoe!"

I looked on my map and saw an almost unnoticeable marking for a tiny village called Piddinghoe. The clerk at East Grinstead, half an hour away, had evidently not traveled much in her neighborhood. Yes, I said, I guessed that was what we meant.

Now I was sure we'd be late. We'd never get a seat, and we'd miss at least the first hour. Did the trials last all morning? Or would everything be over quickly? Leaving Lewes, we determinedly set our course for Piddinghoe. Eventually we turned off the main road down a narrow one, passed through the village, and at last, about to give up, caught sight of another hand-lettered sign, with a reassuring arrow: LEWES SHEEPDOG SOCIETY CHARITY TRIALS.

The arrow led us into an even narrower track, barely wide enough for our Ford Escort, that ran up and along a steep ridge. Although only an hour by train from London, we were now deep into the Sussex Downs, high grass-covered hills that roll south to the sea. The hills seemed empty. Hedgerows blocked our view, but when we occasionally glimpsed the fields below, we could not see any farms. No one passed us on the road. It was a quiet sunny morning, with barely a breeze.

After a mile or two, we rounded a curve and emerged

onto the top of the ridge. There, just in front of us, clustered in front of a gate, were several young girls in what
looked like scouts' uniforms and an older man sitting on a
portable chair. One of the girls held a large roll of tickets.
They were the first people we'd seen since we left the
main road from Lewes. I looked beyond the gate. Far
below, in the bottom of a broad shallow basin of green
grass that swooped up to the sky, I could see what must
be the sheepdog trials.

No bleachers. No crowds. Only vast green fields, a
square of golden wheat on one far horizon, three or four
windblown trees on another, lots of blue sky. Strung in an
odd-looking straight line across the valley floor were perhaps two dozen cars, mostly station wagons, vans, and
hatchbacks with their trunk lids flung up. Behind the cars
stood a large tent and a white semitrailer truck with a sign
on it. I kept my eyes on this rigid line of bright cars, an
incongruous slash in the green flowing landscape, as we
bumped slowly down a precipitous path to the valley
floor. There, at a gap in the fence, standing guard near a
pair of portable toilet cubicles, another uniformed girl
took our ticket and waved toward the grass.

As we slowly rolled across the field to the cars, I could
now read the semi's cheerful logo: DI'S FARMHOUSE
KITCHEN. A flap in its side had been opened to form a shelf.
Tea, I thought comfortably. Scones, freshly cut sandwiches, cake. Ah, the English. As we passed the tent I
noticed many empty tables set up beneath it. If a crowd
ever arrived, the organizers of the Lewes Charity Sheepdog Trials were certainly prepared.

A few people were standing by their cars or sitting on

folding chairs, two or three walking from one car to another. Most were looking at the field where, just barely visible in the distance, a small black-and-white shape was moving down the valley, not far from a cluster of other, slightly larger, white shapes. We pulled up in an empty space in the line, slowly and quietly, careful not to slam the car door as we got out. Next to us two border collies were tethered to a temporary fence between the cars and the field. They, too, were watching the valley intently.

Directly ahead of us in the field was a gatelike structure, two sections of wooden fence forming a wide opening, and on either side were two identical structures. These gates were clearly the obstacles, but what was the dog supposed to do? Where were the sheep supposed to go? To our right was a wooden circular pen, just large enough to hold a half-dozen sheep. Now I noticed a man standing in the field not far from the pen, whistling loudly through cupped hands. Then he shouted a series of commands I couldn't follow. The dog dashed to and fro, the sheep hurried this way and that. They seemed as confused as I was.

"The program explains it," James said helpfully, handing me the printed handout he'd gotten at the hilltop gate. I tried to read it quickly, following a sketch of a typical course and matching what I read to what was going on here—or *not* going on, since the man and his dog had just abruptly left the field, disappearing behind the line of cars. The sheep milled aimlessly.

"Too bad," said another man, leaning on the hood of the van next to us, to a woman behind the wheel. "Sam just wouldn't stop for him." I decided to ask for help. Though the English have a reputation for reticence, I have seldom failed to have my inquiries answered with full and polite instruction. They usually like to educate ignorant but well-meaning Americans.

"Excuse me," I said. "Would you be kind enough to tell me why that man took his dog off the field so suddenly? Did something go wrong?"

"Lost too many points. He knew he didn't stand a chance," the man answered. He pointed to the program in my hand. "It explains it all in there."

"I know, but I don't seem to quite follow everything," I admitted. "This is the first time I've been to a sheepdog trial."

He stood up and walked over to us. "Now, see," he said, waving toward the field, "there's a maximum of twenty points on the fetch." He began to describe each section of the trial, growing more enthusiastic and voluble as he went on. In a few minutes, another man joined him, adding his own comments and explanations. James and I listened carefully. Gradually I began to understand what they were telling us.

At the beginning of each trial, the competitor stands with his or her dog at a post just beyond the temporary fence. Over a loudspeaker, an announcer calls both names, equal billing for dog and handler: "Next, Robert Stephenson with Moss," or "Douglas Parkins with Jet." All the dogs at Lewes had one-syllable names, sturdy and straightforward: Dan, Sweep, Ben, Roy.

One of the judges waves a flag—here at Lewes, it was a makeshift cloth tied to a long-handled black umbrella—toward the far end of the field. There, so far away I could only make out their white shapes by squinting, another official releases five sheep from a holding pen. At a hand signal from his owner, the dog sets out to retrieve the sheep.

When a sheepdog leaves the post, he begins his *outrun*, the first phase of the trial. (Each phase has an optimum number of possible points that can be awarded.) To avoid coming at the sheep head-on, and alarming or scattering them, the dog circles widely to the right or left, an approach that is ideally pear-shaped. When the dog contacts the sheep, he has completed his second phase, the *lift*. Now he must drive the little flock back toward his handler.

Watching the eager border collies streak up the field, James and I could scarcely believe their speed. Crouching low, a black-and-white blur in the tall grass, a dog usually reached the end of the field in moments. "Oh yes," our neighbor assured us, "he can get up to forty miles an hour, can a good dog." Speed is not the only consideration, however. In the third phase, the *fetch*, as the dog brings the sheep down the field, he is supposed to herd them in a straight line. But sheep do not like straight lines. They have their own ideas.

Nor do they have any desire to cooperate in the *drive*, the next phase, a triangular course that passes through two gate obstacles. The dog is supposed to move, turn, and keep the sheep in line without upsetting them. As with people, I gathered, it was better to nudge, suggest, and persuade rather than to intimidate. Yet sheep have the irritating habit of bolting this way or that, separating from the flock without warning, or turning at the last possible moment to skirt a gate. And some sheep, our neighbor told us, are simply a bad lot. "Occasionally you get a rogue. Real trouble. Not much you can do about it."

In the final two phases of the trial, the *shed* and *pen*, the dog has to perform even more intricate maneuvers. First, at a signal, the dog must identify two sheep specially marked by large collars and then cut them off from the flock. Finally, after again collecting the sheep, the dog is supposed to herd them into the pen. The sheep do not tend to file into the pen without a fuss. The handler, standing at the gate of the pen and holding it open, can wave his shepherd's staff and try to block the meandering sheep with his body, but he or she cannot let go of the gate. Too many shouts, gestures, and stick brandishings cost points.

During the trial, the handler uses several kinds of signals. To James and me, novices in the art of sheep herding, the most intriguing was the whistle. Holding his hand cupped before his mouth, sometimes the handler almost seemed to be playing a virtuoso instrument, varying in pitch and tone. Some handlers used a mechanical whistle, others depended only on their own innate skill. As the piercing, rolling trill rang out over the field, the dog seemed to hear its notes like a private musical language. All James and I caught was its urgency.

The more we saw of the trials, the more we were awed by the skill and temperament of these fast, smart border collies. A prizewinning dog needed patience, tact, flexibility, ingenuity, and firmness—many of the qualities, it occurred to me, of a successful parent. Once, when a particularly recalcitrant sheep had broken from its fellows and bolted for the third time, a frustrated dog lost its control, snapped at the sheep, and seized it by the wool at its neck. My own daughter having just grown up, I was very sympathetic; I knew how that dog felt. But, like parents, a sheepdog pays for loss of control. Grabbing a sheep was a severe fault, costing the dog's handler many points.

After giving us basic instructions, our neighbor returned to his absorbed perch on his van. Before long, it would be his turn. Almost all the spectators were also competitors.

"How long will the trials go on?" I'd asked him, still worrying we might have missed too much.

"Oh, all day," he'd said casually. "Sometimes the judges don't post any ratings until the very end, so we all have to hang around till six or seven."

Now I understood why Di's Farmhouse Kitchen had settled for the day behind the parked cars. James and I wandered over to its window to buy ourselves some tea and cake.

As the morning deepened, so did our interest. Although we could not judge the finer points, we could follow the basic maneuvers. For me, it was rather like watching baseball: I can cheer strikeouts and home runs, but I don't notice a batter's stance at the plate or the spin on a pitcher's fastball. Watching sheepdogs, I did not know why one managed to pen its flock on the first try—and why others never managed it at all.

James and I realized that most successful handlers used the fewest signals. If properly trained, a dog understood immediately what he was supposed to do and required little further guidance. Sometimes, however, a dog in a difficult situation had to check with its handler constantly. Then, while continuing to stare down the restless sheep, the dog had to follow a series of rapid-fire signals— "Move!" "Stop!" "Stand!" "Keep quiet!" "Hunker down!" *"Move!"*—and react with precision timing.

As we understood more, our tension mounted. I found myself straining to see the faraway lift and assess the fetch. Soon we knew when a dog had a bad start, running too directly (not in the recommended pear shape) toward the waiting sheep. When the sheep swept too fast down the field, rushing past the first gate obstacle before the dog could turn them, we realized his handler was in trouble. We waited with bated breath as a dog almost drove the sheep into the pen—and then missed, as one sheep bolted and dashed away, distracting the dog's attention from the rest of the flock, who then hurried off to the edge of the field.

Our hearts went out to both dog and owner. Each time a dog took its place at the post, we wanted him and his owner to do well. Once an attractive young woman with fiery red hair, announced as Rosie Adams, walked confidently onto the field with a handsome, restless dog. (Although the title of *One Man and His Dog* correctly telegraphs that most dog handlers are male, some sixteen of the fifty dogs at the Lewes trial were run by women.) We gave enthusiastic though silent support to Rosie, whose Jock looked particularly lively.

But when Rosie gave the signal, Jock dashed off to the right a short distance—and then stopped. He dropped down into the high grass and looked back expectantly at Rosie. She blew her whistle impatiently and waved him on. He started off again, at a fast clip, but in moments he had stopped once more. He circled, ran in another direction, and then sank again in the grass. A third time, Rosie, now shouting as well as whistling, tried to urge Jock to the end of the field, where his five sheep were waiting. But Jock started, stopped, and looked back at Rosie, cocking his head. Finally, in obvious disgust, Rosie turned on her heel, whistling the dog to her side. Grabbing his collar, she leaned and spoke sharply to him and stamped off the field.

Although our informative neighbor had returned to the privacy of his own van, I walked over and interrupted him one more time. "Pardon me," I said apologetically. "But what just happened?"

"Dog probably couldn't see the sheep," our neighbor said laconically. "The grass is too high. They should have cut it."

I looked. Yes, the uncut pasture was indeed high, thick and high enough so that a small crouching dog might well be looking through an impenetrable jungle. Jock couldn't figure out why Rosie was signaling him to herd phantom sheep.

When I reported my findings to James, he sighed. "Too bad," he said. "You know, it reminds me of the time I took Frank to his piano recital, and halfway through he forgot his piece, and so he started over, but when he got to the same place, he stopped again. So he started over once more, and he still couldn't remember. And he tried again. Finally he had to just give up and leave the piano. It was obvious to everyone he just wasn't going to be able to get through it. We both felt terrible."

Soon after Jock's fiasco, the other man who'd earlier

helped us understand what was happening walked by. "Enjoying it, are you?" he inquired pleasantly.

"Oh yes," I said, adding, to prolong the conversation, "and now when I watch *One Man and His Dog*, I'll know what's happening."

I couldn't have made a less propitious remark. His face darkened, and for a moment I thought he was going to spit, if not at me, at least in the general direction of my unwitting idiocy. *"Television,"* he said with great emphasis. "You can't think that *television* show has anything to do with a real sheepdog trial. Bloody deceptive, that's what that is. And I say that even though I'm going to be on it in a few weeks myself. Oh yes. Why, they spend ten, twelve hours just getting the camera angle set up, in the hills, or on the fence, or maybe even in the trees. Sometimes they build a tower just to put a camera in so they can look down the field for the proper close-up or stare into a dog's eyes. Close-ups, that's all they care about. And then all that folderol about the dog and its owner. Pat your dog on the head for the camera." He looked again as if he would like to spit. "No, don't tell me about *television."* He waved at the field. "Now this," he said with emphasis, *"this* is the real thing."

I followed his wave. It took in the deep valley, its green billowing grass spotted with red poppies; the silence, broken only by the low murmur of the onlookers, the handler's whistle and shouted commands that were almost lost on the wind; the blue sky with huge white clouds, the sea just over the downs, the clear clean air, the sense of remoteness, the absolute sweep of it all.

Toward noon, James and I consulted. We had only

watched about a third of the trials, but we had promised ourselves a walk along the sea. This was the only day we'd be able to get to the coast. So regretfully, we climbed back into our car, as quietly as possible, not wanting our neighbor to notice our early departure, and timing it so that the current sheepdog would be at the far end of the field. I was sorry we couldn't stay to see his fetch.

Ronald Reagan and
My Night at the Savoy

*A*ctually, it was two nights. That was two more than I thought I'd ever spend at the Savoy—or at Claridge's, the Dorchester, the Connaught, or Grosvenor House. Of course I knew all about these great London hotels. Characters in novels sometimes stayed in them. Movie stars, rock singers, and politicians often held press conferences there. (" 'No, we have no wedding plans,' said the actress, interviewed in her suite at the Savoy.")

When I browsed through travel guides to London, I occasionally paused at the Deluxe Hotels section on my way to Budget or Moneysavers. I enjoyed reading about the gold-leafed Palm Court at the Ritz ("still the most fashionable place in London to meet for afternoon tea, including cucumber and smoked salmon sandwiches and specially made French pastries, scones, and cake"). Turning with a certain moral superiority to a list of bed-and-breakfast hotels in Paddington, I'd mutter to myself ominously, as if I could hear tumbrils rattling along the Strand: "Yes, yes. Let them eat cake."

My righteousness evaporated, however, during an unex-

pectedly hot spell in June several years ago. After two
weeks in the English countryside, James and I had returned
to London for five nights before flying home. We had
booked a small, spiffy hotel, but our room, fronting on the
Brompton Road, was surprisingly noisy. After two sleep-
less nights, I decided we ought to move. Consulting our
backup list, we quickly walked to an old-fashioned but
rather expensive hotel near Harrod's, one recommended
enthusiastically by an upscale guide. Just as we arrived, we
saw Douglas Fairbanks, Jr., instantly recognizable, standing
in white-haired elegance on the steps of the hotel. In a
moment, he hailed a cab and was gone. We looked at each
other. If this hotel was good enough for Douglas Fairbanks,
it was surely good enough for us.

"Do you think he's a shill?" James mused aloud several
hours later. "Or maybe he was visiting some old friend
here? Someone down on his luck?" We were sitting on
lumpy beds in a hot dark room, haphazardly furnished.
Dusty light filtered through one narrow window.

At the reception desk, we'd been taken aback to learn
that only this room was available. "It's Wimbledon week,
you know," said the clerk impatiently, waiting to turn to
a new customer. "This is all we've got. It doesn't have a
private bath, but there's one just across the hall."

James and I consulted wordlessly. Only three nights left;
my self-assured guide in my pocket; Douglas Fairbanks in
the background. "Okay," James said, with a nod from me.
"We'll take it." We did not ask to see it first. Now the
room seemed to get gloomier—and stuffier—by the minute.

The next morning, after tossing restlessly all night, I

thought longingly of our first hotel, its large windows, its Laura Ashley prints. In retrospect, its raucous street sounds seemed almost welcoming. But the manager had been miffed when we'd canceled our stay; we couldn't retreat.

"We'll just have to make the best of it," James told me admonishingly as he headed down the hall to the w.c. "If we can't adjust to a place like this, even if it is a little dingy, well, something's wrong with us."

Fifteen minutes later, James returned, looking grim. "I've changed my mind," he said. "Let's get out of here." Briefly but succinctly, he described the distant toilet cubicle: tiny, windowless, its walls painted black. "Black!" he repeated, with the full force of an architect's distaste. The night before, he confessed, it hadn't seemed so bad. But in the morning light, it was an affront.

"But where can we go?" I asked. "You heard the desk clerk. It's Wimbledon week. And the height of the tourist season. We can't just traipse around London with our suitcases."

"Call up the Ritz," James said, trying to open the single window another inch. "Call up Claridge's. Isn't that the name? I mean, let's splurge for these last two nights. I don't care what it costs."

I had never heard James say that before. Unlike me, he did not pinch pennies, and he was not much of a bargain hunter. But he was not extravagant, either. I somehow had also lost my own usual caution. Perhaps it's the heat, I thought. London isn't supposed to be this hot. It addles the brain. "Right," I said crisply, grabbing the phone book. "Claridge's is full," I reported a few minutes later, holding the receiver aloft. "What about the Savoy?"

"Go for it," James said. Now we were both a little giddy.

The voice at the reservation desk at the Savoy was cool, polite, and precise. Yes, madam, we do have a room available. But only one. It would be a River Terrace room. I thought a few seconds, realizing that of course, the Savoy must overlook the Thames. I had only noticed its majestic front on the Strand. "Yes, indeed, a River Terrace room," I assured the cool voice. "And how much will that be?" When he told me, I felt an even cooler sensation in my stomach. But I did not give in. "Fine," I said, "we will be there within an hour." Once I'd given my word to the Savoy, I knew I could not retract it.

"Actually, James," I said reassuringly as we trundled across London in a taxi, "we should think of this as a minivacation. Not really just a hotel. Sort of like a short cruise." James, who was beginning to return to his sensible self, looked at me and rolled his eyes.

Handsome as it was, the lobby of the Savoy still looked like a hotel, a grand hotel, true, but nothing that resembled my romantic fantasies. But when the bellboy wafted us up eight floors, down a thickly carpeted hall, and then through a heavy painted and gilded door, I tried to restrain a small gasp.

The room was enormous, not only in floor space, but in height. The pale painted walls rose past ornamented moldings to a ceiling that soared airily overhead. On the river side, the wall was given over to double-glazed windows. Looking out on the full sweep of the Thames, I could see barges and pleasure boats moving slowly downstream. From this distance, the imposing bridges I'd crossed so many times—Waterloo, Hungerford Foot Bridge, Westminster—looked almost like delicate bracelets clasped across the water. On the opposite shore were the monumental arts centers of the South Bank; I could spell out the current plays from a giant neon sign, as if the National Theatre were beaming personally to me, Susan Toth, presently at home on the eighth floor of the Savoy, in a River Terrace room.

As soon as the bellhop left I gave a subdued whoop and jumped up on one of the stately twin beds. Ensconced among downy pillows, I lay back and surveyed our domain. The standard hotel variety of French Provincial furniture is often tacky and overdone, but here everything had a discreetly antique and expensive air. I wondered if I should get up just to try out the satin-covered chaise longue.

Under the river-facing windows, a solid-looking round table was flanked by comfortable armchairs. "James," I said suddenly, "let's not go out. Let's order dinner from room service and eat at that table. We'll never find a view of London that can compare to this."

"Good idea," he agreed. "I don't much like leaving this cool room, anyway."

Yes, I realized, it was marvelously cool here. In my awed inventory, I hadn't quite noticed that. Or the quiet, either. I had never been in a London hotel in which I could not hear some sounds of the city—the rumble of buses, the whir of traffic, the bleep-bleep-bleep of ambulances. But here, sealed on the eighth floor, we were almost unaware of the rush along the Embankment below.

While I shamelessly scoured the gilded desk for any bit of stationery engraved with *The Savoy*, James went to draw a bath. He called for me to come and see the bathroom. It was as large as some hotel rooms I'd known, with a deep tub like a porcelain-lined swimming hole, surrounded by blindingly white towels the size of lap rugs. Two white bathrobes dangled invitingly from gold hooks. A heavy white cord hung over the tub.

About twenty minutes later, as James lounged in the tub and I returned to blissful incumbency on the bed, I heard a tap on the door and then a respectful voice.

"You rang?" a young man in uniform inquired.

I was too startled to say anything, and he disappeared quickly into the bathroom. He emerged almost as quickly and vanished into the hall.

I heard James laughing. When he came out moments later, wrapped in his fluffy robe, he explained: "I yanked the cord. I thought it was something to hold on to when you got out of the tub. But it was really a call button. That guy got here so quickly he must be lurking outside the door, just in case."

As twilight settled over the Thames a deferential waiter wheeled a large linen-covered cart into our room. He whisked out a creamy tablecloth, heavy silver, and fine white china. Fortunately, we had bathed and dressed properly, just as if we were going out for dinner. James had even put on a tie. We sat solemnly, a little self-conscious, as the waiter deftly served us veal marsala, green beans, and roast potatoes from silver salvers and poured us each a glass of white wine.

When the waiter left, we leaned back in the velvet armchairs and toasted each other. Then we toasted London. Then the Savoy. The meal was delicious. We ate slowly, looking through the windows past the treetops in the park below to the lazily moving river. Lights began to twinkle here and there. Here on the eighth floor, behind our double-glazed windows, it was hard to imagine how hot it was on the pavement below. I tried to think of jostling playgoers hurrying down the Strand, late business-men racing into the Tube, sweltering tourists sitting uncomfortably in cheap restaurants. I couldn't quite picture them.

"You know," I said to James, "I suddenly think I understand about Ronald Reagan."

"Oh?" James asked.

"Yes," I continued. "He's probably a nice man. The problem is, he lives like this all the time." I waved my hand dramatically about the room. My glass of wine was having an effect. "Absolutely insulated from any noise, or dirt, or bother. Someone is always waiting on him. He gets dinner served like this, whatever he wants. No worry about what it costs. No dishes to do. He doesn't get hot and sticky from standing in the sun in a long line at the bus stop. It's so easy to *forget* even how it feels to be hot and sticky. To be one of those people, down there on the pavement." I waved again, this time at the Embankment, far below.

"I could get used to this," said James, sighing, as he slowly finished his wine.

"Me too," I agreed. "I'd probably get used to it even faster than Reagan did."

Two days later, we regretfully left the Savoy. I took a stroll while James paid the bill, because I didn't want to know, and he had promised not to tell. As soon as we settled into our cramped coach seats on the crowded airplane, our sojourn seemed like an impossibly distant dream.

Not long ago, I read a travel article that mentioned how

the Savoy keeps files for important guests: preferred rooms, meals, drinks, and miscellaneous desires. I idly wondered if perhaps we had an entry: River Terrace room, veal and green beans, the house white. But in the past few years, as the dollar has fallen against the pound, I have realized that it is very unlikely we will ever return. Our file has probably long since been closed.

Yet I often think of those two days and nights. Among other enlarged travel photos, I keep a bit of the Savoy on our bedroom wall. Just after dessert that first night, I stepped back into the middle of the room and snapped a picture: James, in neatly knotted tie, sitting at the linen-draped table. Silver bowls, crystal glasses, heavy crumpled napkins. My empty green velvet chair. Behind our thick windows, the wide gray river. The thin red-and-black ribbon of the Hungerford Foot Bridge, where hot and dusty pedestrians—the others, the ones below—are tramping across the Thames.

The Royal Family and Me

*A*s I reached for the tabloid with Princess Diana on the cover, I looked around surreptitiously. Although this grocery store was more than a mile from my house, would anyone I know see me? Could I skim the story quickly before the woman ahead of me unloaded her last six-pack of diet cola?

Of course I know I'm not the only one who is curious about the royal family. I even know why. In today's media-hungry world, the royals provide a real-life running soap opera—love, separation, marriage, divorce, family squabbles, a search for meaningful work. Will Princess Anne marry again? Is Margaret an alcoholic, and can she ever find happiness? Is anything wrong with Edward? Will Charles and Diana separate? What is Charles going to do with the rest of his life?

Our hunger for royal news may go deeper. Several cultural historians, beginning with de Toqueville, have speculated about our democracy's secret longing for an aristocracy. If we can't find it ensconced in pink stucco mansions in the Hollywood Hills, we look for it hidden behind the medieval walls of Windsor Castle. I've even

uncovered a theory that our royalist fervor is somehow
Oedipal, a trauma roiling ever since we overthrew George
III in the American Revolution. According to this theory,
when Charles and Di arrive on our shores, we throng to
see them out of guilt.

But none of this analysis completely explains my own
long, if one-sided, relationship with the royal family. Ad-
mittedly, most of the time I neglect it. Weeks, even
months, can pass before I find myself, seized with an
embarrassing sudden flare-up of the old fever, devouring
some tasteless tidbit. But when I do, I have to acknowledge
that my involvement with England over the past thirty
years has been extended to an involvement with its royal
family.

Simply by being a reader, I was predisposed to royalty.
Kings and queens ruled over my nursery rhymes, from Old
King Cole to the London-going pussycat. I remember
being particularly moved by A. A. Milne's King John. In
Now We Are Six, Milne tells the melancholy story of King
John, a lonely man so unpleasant that he had no hopes for
any Christmas presents. Milne's poem made me think for
the first time that a king might be human. After all, I
always had a satisfying stack of presents under *my* Christmas tree. Although I had no idea what an India rubber ball
was, I badly wanted King John to have one: "And oh
Father Christmas, if you love me at all, send me a great big
India rubber ball!"

Any reader who grows up with fairy tales lives for a
time in an imaginative world dominated by kings (either
good, tyrannical, or on their deathbeds, issuing complicated instructions), queens (unhappy, because they don't

have children, or evil, because they have stepchildren), young and handsome princes (never old), and princesses (beautiful, but usually not very bright).

Like most children, I did eventually learn to distinguish between that enchanted world and the one I was going to have to live in. I stopped hoping that a talking bluebird would drop to my shoulder, a pumpkin would turn into a coach, or a prince would arrive on my doorstep with a glass slipper to replace my Buster Browns, extra wide. Despite my sister's teasing, I realized that a troll did not live under the ancient wooden bridge our car thundered across on the way to Lake Carlos—though being wary of trolls, anyway, I decided privately, was not such a bad idea.

Fortunately, I didn't have to give up believing in everything. One element in fairy tales turned out to be surprisingly real. Though I saw that kings and queens were both distant and rare—they all lived in Europe, and as I grew up they were disappearing with rather alarming rapidity—they did evidently sit quite firmly on the British throne.

It was a real throne. I knew, because in 1953, I actually saw it. When Queen Elizabeth II was officially crowned, the ceremony was filmed and rushed to the States for a widely publicized television broadcast. Our family did not yet have TV, but my best friend, Kathie Howell, invited me to her house so I could watch. Sprawling on the floor of the den, a little room off the kitchen, we arranged ourselves in front of the set. Kathie's mother made us popcorn and cocoa to sustain us through the long slow spectacle.

Mesmerized by what was unfolding on the small black-and-white screen—this had all happened only a few hours ago!—I got the magic of television all mixed up with the magic of the coronation. Here in Ames, through the inexplicable wizardry of some tubes behind this screen, I was present at an ancient rite in a country thousands of miles across the seas. I gave myself up to the spell of it all: the measured, dignified procession of lords and ladies; the dazzling display of velvet robes trimmed with ermine, diamond tiaras, and long white gloves; the elaborate ritual intonations of Anglican priests.

I had never seen anything like it. Even though I knew St. Cecilia's, the Catholic church downtown, had some fairly ritzy goings-on—incense, silver chalices, Latin chants—I was a good Presbyterian, so I naturally had never attended a service there. Ames did not offer much else in the way of enchantment. Here at last was pomp and circumstance, and I loved it.

As I grew up, the royal family continued to float into my dream life. I didn't know much about the Duke of Edinburgh, but when I saw him at the coronation, I thought he looked splendid. Tall, handsome, and dignified, Prince Philip had sex appeal. News stories gave hints of his independent spirit, his sharp remarks, and even his occasional grumpiness. Yet in public, Philip walked several paces behind his wife, shoulders thrown back, his hands firmly clasped. I liked that.

Knowing little about Prince Philip only made him more attractive. As their public-relations experts had long ago realized, the British royals had to remain somewhat mysterious. Only then could they properly embody the myths and fantasies of their subjects. For me, a dreamer already making up stories for myself, the royals provided a ready cast of characters.

The most poignant story I had to puzzle out was Princess Margaret's, when (as breathlessly reported in *Life*) she was forced to give up her one true love, Peter Townsend, because he had been divorced. Since at the time I could identify only two people in Ames who had been divorced (and one of the divorces, involving an old family friend, I was not supposed to know about), I rather understood Queen Elizabeth's dilemma. Yet, deeply and intensely believing in the triumph of true love, I wanted to rewrite Princess Margaret's ending.

I never did find a satisfactory moral for the story of the Duke and Duchess of Windsor. Although I'd read about his abdication—oh, the romance of it! he couldn't go on without the woman he loved!—I couldn't quite attach that passionate abnegation to the couple I saw in magazines and newspapers. His wife, the duchess, had a hard face. He looked small and rather faded.

By the time I entered college, and embarked on an English major (kings and queens everywhere), I was probably as passionate a monarchist as was possible for an Iowa girl brought up by a liberal-Democrat mother. What brought my royalist sympathies out into the open was my first trip to England. There I thrilled to the slightest whiff of the royal family. At Windsor Castle, I wondered if the queen were upstairs, right now, even though a guard had told our group that she was not in residence. I looked at the high windows of Buckingham Palace as I passed by, and I suspected she was in one of those rooms, signing papers or reading bulletins or conferring with heads of state. At Kensington Palace, treading in Princess Margaret's imagined footsteps, I kept hoping she might decide, at just this moment, to take a sudden quick stroll in the gardens.

What I remember best about the royal family in 1960 is not a sighting, however, but a batch of postcards. Leafing through a rack of souvenirs at Windsor, I found photographs of Queen Elizabeth, Prince Philip, young Anne, Charles, little Andrew, and assorted corgis. (Edward, born that year, did not appear on these cards.) One was a startlingly informal group portrait, as far removed from my image of Elizabeth's regal coronation as a Brownie snapshot might have been. Though obviously posed, everyone managed to look quite relaxed. They were casually dressed, Philip in some kind of tweed jacket, Elizabeth in a skirt and cardigan set. I wasn't sure I'd ever seen a picture of the queen without some kind of hat. The prince had his hand on his wife's shoulder, and the queen was smiling.

I bought that postcard, as well as several others like it. I examined it again and again. Philip looked so handsome. They seemed so happy. Gazing at this picture made me realize that the royal family *lived* in Windsor Castle. Standing on its meticulously groomed lawn, they acted as if it were simply their own front yard, which of course it was. They almost looked like an ordinary family. I was fascinated by the incalculable distance between us, so effortlessly bridged in that postcard.

In recent years, critics of the monarchy have sometimes disparaged it by pointing out how hopelessly middle-class the Windsors are. In 1960, I was pleased to discover that perhaps they weren't as different from me as I'd thought. I wanted what Elizabeth had: not the castles, really, or the Leonardo sketches, or the gilt coach, but a handsome, affectionate husband; nice-looking children; scampering dogs. I wanted to stand on our own bit of green lawn and smile for a picture that could go into a family album. It seemed feasible, even possible. In a world where the Queen of England could sit on a throne, yet later play with her corgis in her yard, fairy tales could still come true.

When I got home, I stashed the postcard somewhere and forgot about it. I could not think of England again for a while. I did not know when I would travel abroad again. First I had to finish college, then graduate school. Three years later, in 1963, I married my own prince, and as part of growing up, I learned about romantic confusion, deceptive appearances, and unmanageable plots. I found I had not written myself a fairy tale with a happy ending.

During the years after my divorce, as I returned to England, I lost much of my enthusiasm for the royal family. I no longer looked for royal postcards. I was only mildly interested in news items about Charles's education or Anne's temper tantrums or their aunt Margaret's continuing disasters. What I read now about Elizabeth made her sound rather dull, her children rather spoiled and not especially interesting.

The years passed. I continued to visit England. Although I sometimes glanced with a twinge of nostalgia at the "Court Circular" in the *Times*, I never arranged my schedule so that I could stand with a small crowd outside the Marylebone Center Trust Charity Bazaar or St. Bartholomew's Hospital and glimpse the queen as she emerged. I began to pride myself a little on the fact that I had never bothered to see her, or indeed any of the other royals, in person.

But as I grew older, my interest in the Windsors slowly revived. In a perspective coinciding with a slow tilt in the way I looked at my own life, I began to view them with a curiosity mixed with pity. I had slowly realized that I had an increasing need for solitude and privacy. I drew back more and more from parties, public gatherings, and occasions where I had to perform. Having developed a bubbly, social personality in my early years, I was now struggling with the notion that I might not be the outgoing person everyone, including me, had always assumed I was.

In fact, nearing fifty, I began to suspect I wasn't entirely sure who I was, or exactly what I wanted to do next—the sort of identity crisis about which my college students had always prided themselves. Although I found this change unnerving, one of my friends, who had recently studied Jungian psychology, cheerily explained: "It's simple. Jung could tell you all about it. You're simply discarding your false self and embarking on an interior journey. It's that time of life."

So, as I thought about myself, I considered more carefully some of the lives I saw around me. What had other people done? How had they coped? I also became more curious about why some people made certain choices. What might it be like to live as he did, or she did?

As Charles and Diana brought the British royal family into the glaring public spotlight, they reminded me of my old belief that the Windsors represented a charmed life. Now, however, I knew better. *Nobody* leads a charmed life. I followed the marital fortunes of this young royal couple with sympathetic interest. How could any marriage, any man or woman, survive such constant and intense scrutiny?

I began to watch the royal family for clues of how they

all *did* survive. Did Philip and Elizabeth have anything to say to each other? What sort of a marriage was it? Where did Philip find most of his satisfaction? What did the various royals tell themselves to get through the day? What happened if one of them had a migraine, or didn't want to go out, or needed to stay home with a child who had the chicken pox?

The last time I glanced at the "Court Circular," I was stunned by the relentless schedules it laid out. "The Princess Royal will attend the naming ceremony of the British Rail locomotive 'The Guide Dog' at King's Cross station at 9:45. As patron, she will preside at the Youth Employment Concern's annual meeting at the Royal National Hotel, WC1, at 1 P.M. She will be attended by the Hon. Mary Montague, Lady in Waiting, and Sir Angus Montague. At 4 P.M. The Princess Royal will open the Herbert Spencer Department of Clinical Oncology at the Royal Free Hospital of Brighton." Later, I gathered, the indefatigable princess would join the Prince of Wales, the Duke of Edinburgh, and the queen at a state dinner for the visiting prime minister of Tojo Lago. It sounded dreadful. How did the princess do it?

Suddenly my own schedule didn't seem so bad. Whatever I had to do that week, I didn't have to smile constantly for ten or twelve hours. I didn't have to make polite conversation with people I didn't know at both lunch and dinner. No, I didn't have a waiting limo or a lady-in-waiting, but there were compensations. No one was watching me with a telephoto lens. I could discreetly scratch my nose, or anywhere else, and I wouldn't end up on the front page of the *Daily Mail*.

As I consider the Royal Family these days, I am glad I am not an icon. THE *SUN* CRITICISED OVER PHOTO, read a note in the *Daily Telegraph* last summer. The offending tabloid had published a picture of Prince Andrew naked (the righteous *Telegraph* did not give any details), and Lord McGregor of Durris, chairman of the new Press Complaints Commission, had noted that this "clear invasion of privacy" was "not justified in the public interest." After pondering for a few moments just when a photo of Prince Andrew naked *might* be in the public interest, I shuddered.

So I have come full circle. Happily married, busy with work I usually enjoy, avoiding most parties, escaping as soon as I can from the modest publicity surrounding a new book, and struggling with some success for time to myself, I no longer envy the royals. I have my problems, but I wouldn't want theirs.

Last summer, browsing through the National Portrait Gallery, I paused for some time on the landing that houses portraits of the current royal family. These portraits strikingly reflect changing attitudes toward the monarchy. Sir John Lavery's 1913 portrait of George V, Queen Mary, the Duke of Windsor, and the Princess Royal, for example, is formal, stately, and quite forbidding. Standing sternly erect, his hands clasped on a ceremonial sword, George VI is posed like Donatello's famous *St. George.* Queen Mary, seated below a crystal chandelier in a grand stateroom, is wearing a diamond tiara, long strands of pearls, and a filmy formal gown. By 1950, James Gunn could paint a "conversation piece" of George VI sitting at a family dining table while Queen Elizabeth (now the Queen Mother) cozily pours tea for him and the two young princesses.

But I stood longest in front of a haunting image of Prince Charles in 1982, a man dressed in slightly rumpled polo clothes, seated in front of a plain board fence, and looking uneasily at the viewer. The artist, Bryan Organ, manages to suggest that the prince is not particularly happy. Uncertain, perhaps even anxious, yet touchingly determined, Charles seems to demand in this picture to be accepted as an ordinary human being. Yet, in the act of having a royal portrait painted, he must have known that was not really possible.

Twenty years ago, or thirty, I would have thought of none of this. This time, too, I bought postcards: Pietro Annigoni's dramatic, robed, and solemn Queen Elizabeth of 1969. Michael Leonard's 1986 painting of Elizabeth as a smiling, gray-haired matron, holding a bright-eyed corgi against her lap. Diana after her engagement in 1981, Diana in 1988, and I noted that unlike Charles, she appears increasingly confident. The queen mother as an enchanting seven-year-old with long curls and a ribbon in her hair. She was now, I knew, in her nineties.

As they all continued to age, so would I. What would happen to them next? What would happen to me? As I tried to decide about the shape of my own evolving narrative, I could observe and ponder theirs. A cat merely looks at a king. A writer, notebook in hand, lurks around the throne and wonders. The royal family and I went back a long time together, and until England no longer excited my imagination, they would probably be part of it.

1971: Who Is That Woman on the Platform?

Susan? Can I talk to you a minute?" Dwight looked even more timid than usual, shifting uncomfortably as he stood in the door of my hotel room. Short and unprepossessing, with large black-rimmed glasses, Dwight was not my favorite student in the traveling seminar. Most of the others laughed at my jokes, but Dwight, cool and impenetrable, just stared at me. He was not staring now, however; he was keeping his eyes on his feet.

I knew Dwight was very bright. The year before, when he was a sophomore in one of my classes, I'd given him an A, with justice but a little reluctance, because he wore his learning so heavily. His essays were clogged with multisyllabic words and obscure references. I often wrote in the margin: Can you say this more simply? Once, after I lost patience with an especially pedantic essay, I lowered his grade to a B-plus. He came to my office, stiffly, to complain.

Dwight didn't say much in class, but his timidity was something of a cover. Of the ten students with me this January in England, he was capable of the most sharply critical remarks, usually delivered in a low voice only audible to one or two others next to him. They liked to repeat his sallies, however, so when Dwight found fault with some part of the seminar, I soon heard about it.

Although the other students treated him with a casual friendliness, Dwight usually kept to himself. I was surprised to see him now at my door, but I wasn't concerned. Whatever it was couldn't be very important. The month was over. In an hour, we'd leave for the airport. Tomorrow we'd be home.

"Oh, hello, Dwight," I said, "please come in." I suppressed a sigh; I still had some last-minute packing to do.

"I just thought I ought to tell you," Dwight said, and stopped.

"Yes?" I asked politely. Had his suitcase broken? Was his toilet stopped up? Had someone else in the group done something he wanted to report? Maybe spilled a pint on the rug in his room? One more day, and I'd no longer have to worry about any of it.

"Well," Dwight went on, at first hesitantly, and then with a kind of desperate rush, "this morning I went for a walk in Hyde Park. And I bought a sugar cube from a guy. He said it was LSD. It only cost a pound. I've never tried anything like that, and I don't know, I guess I was curious. So I bought it, and I took it an hour ago, and now I feel kind of funny."

I looked blankly at Dwight. My mind raced. Yes, I knew LSD often came in sugar cubes. Although I was wary of drugs, and had never even tried pot, I knew something about them. This was 1971, and I had left Berkeley only a few years before. Pot was one thing, LSD another. LSD spelled freak-out. Dwight had chosen his last possible moment to have An Experience Abroad, and one of the worst possible ways to do it. Would he start to hallucinate on the way to Heathrow? On the plane? What would I do? Should I rush him to a hospital? Would we have to miss the plane?

"Oh, my God," I said, still blankly. Dwight now looked at me, no longer impenetrable, with fear in his eyes. "So how do you feel, exactly?" I managed.

"Kind of nauseated," he said.

That didn't sound too bad. Maybe, just maybe, the entrepreneur in Hyde Park had spotted Dwight for a patsy. Maybe he was selling sugar cubes soaked in orange juice or soy sauce. "Okay," I said with a confidence I didn't feel, "let me know if you have any other symptoms. Are you dizzy?" He shook his head. "See spots or anything?" He shook his head again. I didn't know what else to ask. Did he think he could walk through walls? Commune with colors? Enter paradise? "Then get your suitcase downstairs and let's try to get on that plane." If he goes to pieces in the air, I thought, at least the stewardess can help.

On the plane, I kept glancing surreptitiously back at Dwight. He met my eye with a weak smile. It was the first time all month he had smiled at me. Thank God, I thought, it must have been orange juice. I wished Dwight had paid more than a pound for it.

Nothing, I told myself as the plane blithely sailed onward, nothing at all ever turned out quite like I thought it would. This January in England, for example. What a cushy deal it had seemed last spring. Easy, fun, almost a scam. Well, it hadn't been a disaster, but it certainly hadn't been easy.

Watching a student who might suddenly burst into mania at thirty thousand feet was not what I'd envisioned last March. When I found the printed notice among the detritus in my faculty mailbox, I knew immediately it was meant for me: "Plan your UMAIE interim course abroad now! Deadline approaching for submission of course description!" I glanced over the list of previous off-campus courses taught by faculty who belonged to the Upper Midwest Association of small colleges offering International Education. Many of my colleagues packed up for balmy places during a Midwest January: "Biology in the Hawaiian Islands," "Archaeological Studies in Crete," "Flora and Fauna of the Florida Everglades." Others soberly promised "Studies in European Political Systems" or "Nineteenth-Century Art in France" or "Mozart in Austria." Yes, here was England: a course in theatre (London), Shakespeare (Stratford), English educational systems (Oxford, Cambridge, Reading).

Why couldn't I do this? Think of some literary topic? Go to England, all expenses paid? Escape my interim course here, where I'd have to layer on clothes each morning and then warm up the car for fifteen minutes before driving on icy streets to meet a sleepy class with runny noses and bronchitis? It couldn't be that cold in England in January, could it?

The more I studied the brochure, the more excited I became. My marriage, scarred by several separations, had sundered once more. My husband and I were in counseling again but still living apart. Who knew where I'd be next January? Maybe I could be in England.

But leading fifteen or twenty students? Planning, directing, and teaching a whole month's course? This was only my second year of full-time teaching, and I still felt very new at it. I had also painfully learned that I wasn't as independent as I had always thought. I was hanging on to my failing marriage partly because of what I thought of as love, partly because I wanted a child, and partly because I was terrified of contemplating a life alone. I wasn't sure I wanted to do this alone, either.

Quickly running down the list of our fourteen English faculty, I realized I had only one real possibility for co-leader. I couldn't ask any of the single or divorced men who were close to my age. Even if they liked the idea, even if the college approved, even if everyone understood how irreproachable it was, my husband would not. He always told me he could not help being jealous; he was, after all, Hungarian.

But I might, just possibly, be able to ask Herbert Morton. Almost twenty years older than I, a bachelor who lived with his mother and sister, Herbert would not be, in Lawrence's eyes, any threat. Gentle, funny, and phenomenally well read, he would also be a good traveling companion. In any case, if Lawrence disapproved, next January was a long way from this March, and I might not be living with Lawrence, anyway.

Herbert rather liked the idea. He had not been in Europe since his service in World War II, and he often talked wistfully about returning. Without totally committing himself, he promised to help devise a tempting proposal. Since the number of interim-abroad courses was limited, and many professors from the UMAIE group wanted to spend January in England, we didn't think we had much of a chance. That made it all seem more of a lark. Over several bag lunches, we talked about possibilities, jotted notes, looked at a map, and decided without too much thought on an impressive prospectus.

"Backgrounds of the English Novel" had everything. It was vague, so we could plan later exactly how to approach the subject. In our proposal we mentioned Hardy and Lawrence, who were Herbert's specialties; Austen and Woolf, who were favorites of mine; and Dickens, whom we both loved. Our itinerary would focus on London, but we'd also travel. "Yorkshire," said Herbert, who often taught the Brontës. "Salisbury," I said, because I wanted to see the cathedral again. Ah yes, said Herbert, that would fit in with Hardy. And what about the Midlands? Lawrence country? So we figured lots of time in London, then Nottingham and the coalfields, a whiz through Yorkshire, Salisbury, Lyme Regis for Jane Austen, and maybe Edinburgh so we could say we'd been to Scotland. A few other stops here and there. Very comprehensive, considering we had only a month.

Academically, we agreed, this would be a solid course. We'd give our seminar a reading list before departure; we'd make Xerox copies of some critical passages; the students could buy paperback texts in London. We'd have evening seminars to discuss the novels, and then in the daytime we'd visit relevant sites.

Herbert and I enjoyed talking about our plan, making changes, and adding refinements. I'd pop into his office with an idea, he'd put a clipping on my desk. We'd never actually get the assignment, would we? Certainly not! But wasn't it fun to think about? Neither of us was prepared six weeks later for the official notification that our course proposal had been accepted, and our final itinerary had to be filed with the Collegiate Travel Agency in Appleton, Wisconsin, by August 1.

Herbert turned pale. He reminded me he had not absolutely promised he would go. He was going to have to think of whether he was needed at home. He might have some health problems. He was not sure next January would be the best time for him to travel. While Herbert dithered, I wondered whether I should give up this free trip to England. But Lawrence and I were still in counseling. I didn't have much else to look forward to.

The letter of acceptance specified that unless our course enrolled a minimum of twenty-four students for two instructors, it would be canceled. I called the UMAIE office. What if there were just one instructor? Then I only needed twelve students, the director assured me. But all twelve would have to pay their deposits by October 1.

I decided to drift. Maybe I wouldn't get twelve students. Meanwhile, I'd let the Collegiate Travel Agency go ahead with the itinerary Herbert and I had outlined. Maybe they'd come up with an outrageous fee no one could afford, and that would settle the whole thing.

The fee was indeed hefty, and on October 1, I had only enrolled ten students. Lawrence told me he thought he might come back home soon; it seemed to him our counseling was going well. He did not like the idea of my going to England in January. He said he thought I should try to get out of it. But somehow, with everything against my plan, I didn't want to give it up. Maybe, I told myself, I didn't really need Herbert. Maybe, I also thought, for a few brief moments I quickly blanked out, I didn't even need Lawrence.

I called the UMAIE office again. "Ah yes, Professor Toth," the secretary said. "I'd meant to get in touch with you. We've decided we don't want to disappoint those ten students who have already signed up for your course. The Collegiate Travel Agency says that if we cut a few extras from your proposal, it will be financially feasible." I saw no problem. "Well, that's fine, then," she chirped. "We'll just go ahead and notify the students."

Now I had given my word. In one of our counseling sessions, I told Lawrence and Dr. Gingrich of my decision. Lawrence said he thought I was running out on our marriage. Dr. Gingrich said we should talk about this. The fall passed quickly, between teaching three classes and meeting with Lawrence and Dr. Gingrich.

Suddenly it was January, and I was on a chartered plane, filled with students and faculty on their way to Europe. As soon as I'd sunk into my seat, I tried to stop thinking of the house I'd just left, where Lawrence was stewing, returned but still angry. Forget my marriage, what was I going to do with this course? I'd packed my copies of *Mrs. Dalloway*, *Women in Love*, *Bleak House*, *Jude the Obscure*, *Pride and Prejudice*, and *Jane Eyre*. Maybe we couldn't read them all, but I might select certain chapters in the longer ones. Once settled in our London hotel, where we'd stay for two weeks, I could work out specific assignments. I wished I hadn't gotten stuck with Lawrence and Hardy.

After London, we'd be on the road for ten days. I opened the folder covered in gaudy gold print: PERSONAL TRAVEL PLAN FOR PROFESSOR TOTH FROM COLLEGIATE

TRAVEL AGENCY. It was surprisingly thin. It held an itinerary, a few instructions about our coach tours, and vouchers for our hotels. As the leader, I'd been told, I would have a single room, with private bath, if possible. For most of the detailed tour arrangements, I'd be on my own. Besides some personal spending money, I was carrying some UMAIE traveler's checks for group expenses. My budget, I'd been warned, was very tight.

After a while, I got up and walked down the aisle, looking for my ten students. I wanted to hand out a one-page syllabus with the general order of readings. It would convince them I was organized. As I checked off my list, I tried to memorize faces. I was relieved to see everyone looked quite normal. They were chattering eagerly among themselves. Even Dwight, who took the syllabus without a word, had put down the book he was reading. As I sank back into my own seat a few minutes later, I shut my eyes and relaxed. Actually, maybe this *was* going to be fun.

Though I must have supervised our passage through customs and somehow guided us all into London, I only remember arriving at the Hotel Leinspat. The small, dirt-streaked Leinspat, its front awning torn and its sign askew, stood in a cul-de-sac in Bayswater, surrounded by many equally dreary small hotels. It was late in the day, and the city was already dark.

In the Leinspat's cramped lobby, as I waited for a clerk to find our assorted keys, I looked around to assess our home for the next two weeks. The blackish-red carpet was worn to threads, an ugly brown wallpaper with faded yellow flowers was peeling from the sagging walls, and a strange odor, of something not quite fresh being fried rather too long in yesterday's grease, drifted in from a back corridor that led to the kitchen. Perhaps this was what the UMAIE coordinator had meant by "giving up a few extras."

"You, Professor, have a room to yourself," the clerk announced. The Leinspat did not have any private baths. I quickly assigned roommates among the eight girls, though later, I said, they could rotate. We only had two boys; I couldn't quite think of them as men. Ben, tall and self-consciously masculine, who wore a tweedy sports jacket and sported a small mustache, would have to room with Dwight. Ben looked at Dwight. It must have occurred to Ben whose roommate he would be for the entire month. But after a moment, he picked up his bag and simply said to Dwight, "Okay, let's go."

"Oh yes," the room clerk added as he took the keys from the mailboxes behind his counter. "I should just mention that you won't be getting any mail. The postal service went on strike two days ago. Several strikes going on, actually." At the time this hardly seemed important. I was thinking only about getting to my room. Maybe taking a nice, long, hot bath. Going to sleep.

When the room clerk opened my door, I stepped quickly in, thanked him, and shut the door behind me. I was suddenly very tired and depressed. Even after I had turned on every light I could find—a dim lamp with a cracked shade over the bed, a bare bulb over the rust-stained sink gerrymandered into the corner—the room seemed unaccountably dark. Then I realized its one narrow window was tightly shuttered. I saw some cigarette ashes scattered at the edge of the rug. Stepping over them,

I sat on the edge of the bed. In a minute I would turn back the stained cover and crawl in.

Just then I heard a knock at my door, followed by a quavery voice on the other side. "Mrs. Toth? It's me, Margit." I had sized her up quickly on the plane, taking in her 1960s look, long stringy hair, large dangly earrings, a defiant lack of lipstick on her wan face, a vague air of dissatisfaction. Now, when I opened my door, even in the Leinspat's yellow-spattered darkness, I could see that something was wrong with Margit.

"I'm sick. I'm really sick. It may be the flu, I'm not sure. I started feeling funny on the plane, and now I know I have a terrible fever. I've got a sore throat. I keep throwing up. I think maybe I'm going to faint." Her voice dissolved into sobs. "I want to go home," she said.

Trying not to think of my waiting bed, lumpy as it was, I grabbed my coat and purse and took Margit's arm. I didn't know a doctor, I figured the room clerk wouldn't either, and it was practically the middle of the night. We'd have to find a taxi and go to the nearest hospital that had an emergency room.

Several hours later, after having waited in a crowded drafty hall at the hospital, we found a harassed doctor who examined Margit quickly, told her she did indeed probably have flu, and advised her to stay in bed a few days. We returned in exhausted silence to the Leinspat. This time I didn't bother to turn on my lights. It was so cold in my room that I didn't even undress. I just took off my shoes and fell into bed.

The next morning, after a congealed breakfast cooked, I was sure, in the same fat I'd smelled the night before, I

assembled our little group in the front room that served as
the Leinspat's public space. Sleep-deprived, chilled, and
bleary, I didn't know how I looked, but I thought my ten
students looked terrible. Before I could begin trying to plan
our day, Dottie, a fragile-looking freshman from Macalester, who had a shy smile but a determined attitude,
spoke up. "I don't know about you, Mrs. Toth, but we
didn't have any heat at all in our rooms last night. We just
about froze to death." Several of the other students nodded
vigorously. "I had a kidney infection last month," Dottie
went on, "and I was on antibiotics for weeks. My parents
almost didn't let me come on this trip. Well, after last
night, I can feel it flaring up again. Do we really have to
stay here?"

I felt like a beleaguered public-health nurse. I had not
known I'd have to worry about flu and kidney infections.
But Dottie had a point. I, too, thought the Hotel Leinspat
was a health hazard. "We paid plenty to come on this trip,"
volunteered Ben. "If we're going to be staying in places like
this, where did all that money go?" He looked at me
suspiciously. Actually, that question had occurred to me,
too. I wondered if anyone from the Collegiate Travel
Agency in Appleton had ever stayed in the Leinspat. If
anyone there got a kickback from the Leinspat. Was *related* to someone at the Leinspat. *Owned* the Leinspat.

Claire, a thin, almost wispy-looking blonde with a face
that wasn't exactly beautiful, but made you want to look
at her again, put her arm supportively around Dottie.
Claire, I'd been told, was the darling of the art department
at Macalester. Already, at nineteen, she had shown such
talent as a painter that the chairman was talking of giving

her a one-woman show. Rumor whispered that a much older visiting professor, himself a noted painter, married with six children, had fallen in love with her. "I think Dottie's right," Claire said. "We were in the same room last night, and she was coughing really badly. I think we ought to move." Claire had a soft voice, but it commanded attention.

An hour later, we were on the street. It was a cold, windy January morning, with the sun buried behind a smear of gray. I shivered a little, despite my heavy wool coat. Swathed in bright purple, with a rather loud purple pom-pom hat, I felt like an aging Pied Piper as I led a bedraggled parade of ten students out of Leinspat Square. They were all pulling, dragging, or lugging overloaded suitcases. I had told them we could not afford taxis. Besides, I was not sure where we were going.

The manager of the Leinspat had been incredulous, then angry, when I announced our departure. Did we realize that our ten-day bill had been prepaid? That this was nonrefundable? That we could not under any circumstances break our booking? I was too demoralized to get up a full head of steam, but I mentioned the cold. The dirt. The illness of two of my students already. I could not afford *not* to move.

"Let's get this straight," I told my students. "I'll have to use up all my extra money just to pay for a new hotel. Some of my funds have to be reserved for expenses further down the line. So I think you'll all have to chip in a little extra. I'm hoping that UMAIE will get our money back from the Leinspat, but without any mail, I don't know when that will be. Is that okay?" Then I sent them upstairs to pack, hurriedly, before the Leinspat bolted its doors and locked us in forever.

Where should we go? I had only moments to decide, and my only guide was a handbook on traveling cheaply in England. Quickly thumbing through it, I found several listings for reasonable lodgings not far from Leinspat Square. Although I led my little band bravely down the street, I did not feel very confident. I was wondering if I could indeed pay for a new hotel and how long my supplemental funds would last. It was a worry that continued all month.

The first hotel we stopped at was too expensive. The second did not have enough available rooms. By the time we reached the Norfolk Arms, the third hotel on my list, my students were muttering and grumbling. I pretended not to hear. Heartened by a bright yellow door and freshly painted black knocker, I told everyone to wait while I went inside. My London luck came through. By noon, we were all happily settled in a clean, cheerful budget hotel, briskly run by a Dutch matron who had fled to England with her husband during the war. Though the rooms were small, and the girls had to share triples rather than doubles, no one complained.

After checking in and unpacking once more, we gathered in the parlor. I had planned to begin some formal studies on our first day, but we were clearly all too tired. Margit, still suffering from flu, had gone back to bed. "This afternoon I think we'll just have an orientation to London," I announced. "I want you to get to know the city a little, and most important, learn how to use the buses and Underground. Especially the Underground." So, bundling up again, we set off. Once more, I led the way, followed by nine muffled figures. Clustering in the middle of the sidewalk when I gave instruction, scurrying down the long Underground escalators, crowding into the train, comparing handfuls of change to identify the coins, scrambling for the doors at the right station, everyone clung together with a sense of camaraderie.

We had a good time that afternoon. We walked through Piccadilly Circus, Regent Street, and the Burlington Arcade. I pointed out Fortnum & Mason's and advised everyone to try an ice-cream soda there, just once. On the way home, we walked through Hyde Park. After we returned to the Norfolk Arms, several students explored our new neighborhood and reported on possible dinner stops: Indian, Chinese, Italian, and French restaurants. I bought a newspaper and pointed out the tempting list of theatres and movies. After dinner that night, everyone not too worn-out headed back to the West End. I went to bed.

The next day, I thought it was time to get down to serious business. Before I organized any seminar discussions, I decided on a quick background check. I asked the students which of the books on the suggested list they'd managed to finish. Nobody had read any of them. A few students assured me that although they hadn't read *Bleak House*, they felt they knew Dickens because they had done *A Tale of Two Cities* in high school. One or two had been exposed to Jane Austen; someone had read Hardy in Professor Morton's course; Dwight, from mine, was conversant with *Mrs. Dalloway*. They figured they'd sort of pick up what they needed to know this month. I decided I should continue my orientation to London for at least another day.

After a few more days, it became clear to me that my plans for the course would have to be jettisoned. I could certainly take my students to selected literary sites and explain why they were important. I could talk about novelists, and through descriptions of novels I knew and loved, I could try to tempt everyone into future reading. But if I asked my students to buy books and then take the necessary time to study them, nobody would be free to explore London. Did I want them to sit in the hotel reading *Sons and Lovers*, or did I want them to wander through Kensington Gardens, admire the wrought-iron fences in Mayfair, browse in Foyle's, have lunch in a pub and talk to the locals, stroll along the Embankment and count the bridges across the Thames, and at night, go to the theatre?

So I decided that Backgrounds of the English Novel would concentrate on backgrounds. As I improvised the rest of the course, I soon considered almost everything background: shopping on Bond Street *(Mrs. Dalloway)*; a walk down the bustling Strand (Dickens was a journalist); a trip to the zoo (was it Marianne Moore who had written about the zoo?); an early-morning visit to Covent Garden (Shaw's Eliza Doolittle); the changing of the guard around Buckingham Palace (I told my students to go and think of Christopher Robin). We went to museums and monuments, shops and parks, fancy pubs and cheap restaurants. If I couldn't think of any specific literary connection for a place we visited, I'd generalize: "Lots of people in eighteenth-century novels rode their horses on Rotten Row."

The official curriculum ended at suppertime. Often I'd announce that I was going to a play that night and would be glad of company. I seldom went alone. Some students wandered off to the pubs, others to movies in Leicester

Square, and a few just hung around the hotel. Sometimes we had evening seminars, but these were unlike any seminars I ever taught, before or since. At breakfast, or simply by passing the word later in the day, I'd call a meeting, about eight P.M., in Dottie, Claire, and Margit's triple, the only room big enough to hold us all.

Sitting cross-legged on the floor, I'd talk at first about what we'd seen that day, or I might outline tomorrow's plans. I might give an informal minilecture about the Bloomsbury Group or Dickens's philosophy. Soon we'd adjourn, and whoever wanted to leave could go downstairs to the bar or off to the corner pub. Those who stayed behind would start asking me questions. Who were the Stuarts and Cromwell? Why were Virginia Woolf's novels so hard to read? What did I know about *Who's Afraid of Virginia Woolf*? But after a little while, their questions would tack and veer, and soon we'd leave Backgrounds of the Novel far behind.

"When was the first time you were in England, Mrs. Toth?" "Can you tell us what it was like, being at a women's college?" "You were in London on your *honeymoon*? Was that neat, going to Europe on your honeymoon?" "Is your husband a professor, too?" "How did you meet him?" It was cold and dark outside, and we had the whole evening ahead of us. I wasn't always anxious to return to my room to read, and with a mail strike, I had no incentive to write letters. So I considered each question and answered it thoughtfully. Ben and Dwight had usually disappeared, in different directions, and I felt I could talk comfortably to the remaining girls. They listened intently.

As I talked I found that my answers gradually turned

into stories that I hadn't realized were waiting to be told. It was as if I'd opened an old trunk and found, neatly folded on top, memories as fresh and bright as if I'd tucked them away the day before. "I hitchhiked around England with a friend from Smith," I'd begin. "Before we left, I wasn't sure it would work out. I was a little frightened by Joyce because she was so smart. In fact, she graduated summa." I could see some blank looks. "Maybe I'd better explain about summas." And off I went, into the painful saga of my academic ambitions.

Although I did not recognize it at the time, those story-telling nights with my students were my real beginning as a writer. Until they gave me their eager attention, I had never realized that anyone might be interested in the anecdotes that seemed to form a narrative of my life. I was surprised that they could sympathize with stories that troubled or haunted me and that they would laugh at the odd or humiliating or ironic details I could now, at some distance, finally see as funny.

It was not that I was unused to personal conversations. Back home, my women friends and I talked freely about our lives. We reported on what was happening that day, or what might happen the next night or the following month. We discussed our husbands, our mothers, our cats, our diets, and our work, but we almost never talked at length about our pasts. Until Dottie, Claire, and the rest of my small audience in a crowded triple in the Norfolk Arms wanted to hear my stories, I don't think I even knew I really *had* stories.

Sometimes, as I finished, I'd find myself submerged in feelings that surprised me. I'd see something as if in a telescope that brought it startlingly close to my mind's eye. Or I would discover I'd turned the telescope around. From this distance, I looked back, through the small end of the lens, to my faraway house on Jefferson Avenue in St. Paul, where Lawrence was now perhaps feeding the cats or watching the evening news. In Ames, Iowa, if they were finished teaching, my mother was baking bread and my stepfather was running the snow blower. Since, with the mail strike, I hadn't heard from any of them, everything back home seemed eerily frozen in time.

As the month went on, I began to look forward to these storytelling evenings. Often we gave up any pretense of holding a seminar at all. Most of my students, except for Dwight, stopped calling me Mrs. Toth. "Susan," Claire would beg, "won't you come to our room tonight? Dottie bought a package of chocolate digestives, and I've got some sherry. We're going to have a little party." Most of the time I was happy to accept, although those gatherings in the triple were the only time I socialized easily with my students. They often invited me to join them for pub crawling, but I never did. I was still young enough to worry about how a professor maintained appropriate distance, and at thirty, I was also old enough to know I didn't want to pretend I was twenty anymore.

My students told stories, too. Their lives seemed much more complicated than those of myself and my friends when we'd been in college. Dottie, who was white, was in love with a black football player. Her parents hoped she wouldn't marry him, but she thought she might want to. Would they get used to the idea? One night Claire came to my room to talk. She had once been involved with one of her high-school teachers. Now she was in love with the older visiting professor of art, the man who had six children. What should she do?

Although I answered every personal question my students asked me, in one way or another, I did not tell them everything. I skimmed lightly over my troubled marriage; Lawrence had, after all, moved back in and presumably recommitted himself. We were supposed to be in the midst of a new beginning. Nor did I dwell on any of my secret fears or share some of my misgivings about myself and my abilities. I knew that these were my students, not my intimate friends.

Sometimes I felt precariously poised between their world and mine. At the end of our block was a small discount dress shop, where Dottie, Claire, a few other girls, and I all liked to browse. One late afternoon, Dottie and Claire walked into the dressing room while I was trying on long dresses. Stripped to my bra and panties, I felt quite awkward, but the girls merely grabbed some other clothes from the racks and began trying them on. Eyeing my selections carefully, they gave me their considered opinions: yes, absolutely, buy the blue wool floor-length shirtwaist. And of course, the form-fitting rayon jersey with the bright red flowers. It was incredibly slinky. It made me look *great!*

That night after dinner, no seminar was planned. I went to my room to read. I knew most of my students would be crowding into the tiny saloon bar of the Norfolk Arms, where Claire had entranced Stanley, the bartender, who, between fervent efforts at pinning her down to some kind of date, was happy to serve everyone whatever they

wanted. After a while I decided to try on my new dresses.
I looked critically in the mirror. Yes, the girls were right:
the jersey dress *was* slinky. I walked back and forth a few
times, relishing the slight swish around my ankles. Although the low scooped neckline of the dress was a bit
chilly, I sat down to do some reading. But I couldn't concentrate. I was restless. I wished I had somewhere to go. I
realized I wanted to show off my new dress.

Not quite sure I was doing the right thing, I walked
downstairs and into the bar. Dottie and Claire greeted me
delightedly, made room for me on one of the high stools,
and returned to an animated conversation with two young
men and a woman I didn't know. The bar was full, with
my students, other hotel guests, and their friends. Nobody
paid attention when I ordered a sherry and sat there quietly, sipping, feeling a little out of place. No one else in the
bar was wearing a long dress. "Hey, Stanley," Claire suddenly called over to him, "did you know that Susan is our
teacher?"

"Oh?" said Stanley, with an unbelieving stare I took as
a compliment. He walked over and began polishing some
glasses just in front of me. "What are you teaching them?"
I was unpracticed in flirtations with bartenders, but I
managed to keep Stanley in front of me, polishing, until I
finished my sherry. At some point, he asked how old I was.
"Thirty?" he said. "Oh, go on! Pull the other one! Well, for
thirty, you don't look half-bad. Not much like a professor,
I'd say."

Not long after that, I went back upstairs. Stanley had
returned to the pursuit of Claire, and I did not see anyone
else I could talk to. But I wasn't unhappy. In fact, I was

surprisingly cheerful. Until that night, I hadn't realized how old I'd been feeling.

Thinking about being old made me think of home. Although I was trying to pretend I didn't have any life except here in London, I couldn't help remembering that my fears about aging were closely tied to my marriage. After several years of trying, I'd been inexplicably unable to get pregnant. Lawrence and I had had all the tests, but they'd shown nothing wrong. For almost two years, Lawrence had been worrying intensely about this. You're getting old, he'd told me. He went to the library at the university medical school and read about infertility. He quoted statistics about how my chances of conceiving were dwindling astronomically with each year, practically with each month. Would we ever be able to have a family? Could we stay together without one? I had begun to feel more forty than thirty. Barren, and over the hill.

Before I slipped out of my slinky dress that night, I looked in the mirror once more. I could hear Stanley's admiring comment: "You don't look half-bad." For another half hour, I read *Jane Eyre*, and that night I dreamed that Mr. Rochester had swept me into his arms and carried me off on his horse to Thornfield Hall.

The days in London went by as quickly as the nights. I settled into a predictable routine: a morning excursion with my students, mostly free afternoons, a seven-thirty curtain, or an evening seminar. Then, just as everyone was zipping confidently around London, adopting favorite pubs and restaurants, and making a few friends, it was suddenly time to leave. Our two weeks in London were over, and the touring portion of our course was about to begin.

On the road, Backgrounds of the English Novel remains
something of a blur. I cannot even reconstruct its exact
itinerary. I recapture only brief pictures: the windswept
Cobb at Lyme Regis, a precipitously steep road down to
Robin Hood's Bay, a room under the eaves at an old coaching inn at Salisbury, students huddled in the biting cold
among the great monoliths at Stonehenge. "Think of Tess
stretched out on this horizontal slab," I urged them. By
now I could quickly deliver on-the-spot critical synopses
of novels, a sort of annotated Classics Comics with real-life
visuals.

I can also see us, quite clearly, jammed into two taxis,
whose drivers I instructed to drive us from our Nottingham hotel to Haggs Farm. I had no idea what we were
doing in Nottingham, a site chosen by Herbert Morton,
except it was D. H. Lawrence country. In a last-minute
rush before leaving Minnesota, I had photocopied a few
pages from an illustrated biography of Lawrence. It had
mentioned Haggs Farm, just outside Nottingham, as a
place where the novelist had spent time as a boy. "If Mr.
Morton were here, he'd be able to tell you exactly what
we ought to see around here," I said apologetically. "But I
know we're supposed to visit Haggs Farm."

I had no map. The taxi drivers had never heard of Haggs
Farm. I doubt that they had heard of D. H. Lawrence. But
my purloined pages gave a general sense of direction, a
nearby village, and the name of a road. Somehow we
managed to barrel along the main highway out of town,
then down several winding lanes, and finally along a dirt
track that led into a farmyard. The two taxis jerked to a
stop. I got out. Faded curtains hung limply at the windows

of the house. Under dark skies, about to pour rain, the farm looked both bleak and forbidding.

As I stood uncertainly in the farmyard, a man came from one of the sheds. He did not look particularly welcoming. By now the students had piled out of the cars and stood in the farmyard, looking about them. "Is this Haggs Farm?" I asked the man as soon as he was close enough to hear me. I had a sinking realization that we were trespassing.

"Aye," he said, and closed his mouth.

Of course I hadn't been expecting one of those blue-lettered circles that covered so many London landmarks: GEORGE ELIOT, THE NOVELIST, LIVED HERE FROM 1854–1880 or HOME OF SAMUEL JOHNSON, 1709–1784. Still, shouldn't this place have some reminder of Lawrence? "D. H. Lawrence, the novelist?" I went on. "Isn't one of his novels set here?"

"Can't say," returned the man. He glared at the students.

"Well," I said, turning to them with a certain desperation, "this is Haggs Farm. We'll talk more about it tonight. I'm sure you'll find this all very interesting. Now perhaps we should be on our way." We piled back in the taxis, whose meters had been relentlessly running, and sputtered up the drive toward the nearest public lane.

If we didn't learn much about D. H. Lawrence's background in and around Nottingham, we did have a fleeting brush with what I suppose was his passionate spirit. On the first night of our three days in Nottingham, Claire managed to meet a middle-aged businessman in the hotel bar. His name, I think, was Charlie. He was separated from his wife and traveled around England for his firm. He was lively and full of good stories, she said, and she learned a lot about England just from talking to him. I noticed Charlie in the bar the next night, deep in conversation with Claire, but I paid little attention to him. He was a bit paunchy, balding, a pleasant enough face, quite ordinary.

But the third morning, when we were scheduled to leave Nottingham at noon, I woke very early, long before breakfast, to a rapid knock on my door. It was still dark, so I switched on a light, grabbed my robe, and hurried to the door. Dottie stood there. She, too, was in her robe, and she looked very agitated. "Susan, I don't know what to do," she said very fast. "The others don't think I should tell you, but I'm really worried. Claire didn't come in last night. I saw her in the bar with Charlie about ten, but then I went upstairs. She didn't come back to the room at all. I don't know where she is."

It wasn't hard to figure out where, in a general way, Claire probably was, but that didn't help. What did anyone know about Charlie? Suppose he was some kind of creep? A pervert or worse? What would happen to *me* if something happened to Claire? I wasn't supposed to supervise my students' private lives, but I didn't think that disclaimer would cut much ice back home. In any emergency, I was the adult. The one in charge.

"Oh God," I said. I thought for a few moments. I had no idea what to do next. "Well," I finally said slowly, "I don't think there's anything anyone can do to find Claire right now. Later, I suppose, if she doesn't show up, we could contact the police. Do you know Charlie's last name?" Dottie shook her head. "Great," I said bitterly. "So go back to your room, but be sure to come and tell me the minute she comes in."

Not long after breakfast, and before our morning meeting, Dottie popped her head into my room to say, quickly but with obvious relief, that Claire had returned. At the meeting, tight-lipped and furious, I delivered a rare stern lecture to my students. I did not need to mention Claire by name. I talked about my sense of responsibility for them all, and what ought to be their concerns for themselves. I spoke about safety, common sense, and good judgment. In short, I sounded (as I realized years later) just like a mother. For the past few years, that is what I'd been desperately wanting, but this wasn't quite how I'd imagined it.

I do not remember where we went after Nottingham. After this sharp memory, our whirlwind trip around England dissolves in my mind as if washed away by the incessant rains that seemed to drip, drizzle, hover, and pour every day. Umbrella in hand, I bought train tickets, got my students to the station, directed them where to go and when to get on and off, flagged taxis, allocated passengers, figured tips and paid drivers, instructed coach drivers where to go and how long to stop. En route, I tried to deliver short lectures on what we were about to see.

At the hotels, I combined the job of tour arranger with den mother. On arrival, I assigned rooms, checked out nonfunctional faucets, and scrounged for additional blankets. I held more or less constant open hours for consultation. I talked to students who were tired of their roommates, didn't like the food, or thought they were coming down with colds. I brewed herbal teas, dispensed cough drops, and took temperatures. When I couldn't improve practical conditions, I commiserated and consoled.

If I had a previous incarnation, I often thought on that trip, it was surely as a bustling, many-skirted housekeeper on a grand English estate. I could so easily see myself with a billowing white apron and a huge ring of keys at my waist: keys to every door, every workroom, every storeroom, every trunk. Although I often felt tense and harassed, I was also rather smug about my efficiency. At the end of each day, my relief was mixed with self-congratulation.

But confidence in one's powers of organization is not necessarily an endearing trait. I knew my students probably chafed under my constant instructions, decisions, and caveats. So I was completely taken aback by a moment's incident at the Nottingham train station the day we left. I was rushing around the platform, directing people here and there, answering questions, and trying to shepherd everyone aboard before the train pulled out. Everything was so hectic that I was both half shouting and laughing. Claire suddenly appeared at my elbow. She smiled quietly at me, put her hand on my sleeve for a moment, and then said, before turning away, "Your husband must love you very much."

Later, as I watched the misty green countryside rush by in a blur of rain, I thought for a long time about her words. After my sharp scolding in the morning meeting, I was touched by the affection Claire had offered me with her gentle gesture. I was puzzled, too, because I was not used to seeing myself as lovable. I was also frightened. For although I had promised myself not to puzzle anymore about my marriage, at least until we were in the plane on the way home, I knew what I had almost blurted out to

Claire in response. It had risen to my lips instantly, and I had suppressed it because I did not want to shock her, or myself: "No," I had wanted to say, "actually, he doesn't."

The train rattled on toward Yorkshire. I walked down the aisle once, checking the compartments, to make sure everyone was there. My students settled back in their seats, talking to each other, playing cards, and sharing chocolate bars. Dwight read. One or two who'd been out late, including Claire, put their heads against the steamed-up windows and fell asleep.

I was in a compartment that was almost empty. I looked out my own fogged window, trying to plan a short talk on the Brontës, wondering what had made Claire spend the night with Charlie, thinking about the mail that was piled up in the London post office. I glanced at the folded *Times* in my lap, which I was saving for later. That wasn't the kind of news I wanted, anyway. What had been happening to Lawrence? Had he missed me? Had I missed him? Why did I seem to be so clear and definite here, and so uncertain and indecisive there? Who was the thirty-year-old woman Claire had seen, but I hadn't, on the Nottingham station platform?

The train clacked on, and my eyes began to flicker. It was going to rain all day. I might as well nap before we got to York. Then I'd have to organize some kind of afternoon walk around the city. Tomorrow, we'd go to the moors. Then back to London. The month was almost over. Some of it, probably all of it, was part of Backgrounds of the English Novel, but I would not know for a long time what our real syllabus had been and what I had actually learned.

Watching for Badgers

Badgers are not necessarily why one comes to Dartmoor. To my sixteen-year-old daughter, who had never been to England, I had explained that we would stop one night in that wild region. "It's a fascinating place, really spooky," I hinted seductively. "Have you heard of *The Hound of the Baskervilles?*" She hadn't. I tried again. "When the mist descends on the moor, you can hardly see a foot ahead of you." I warmed to my romance. "It's treacherous. All kinds of bogs, like quicksand. One step, and you're gone. And of course you find mysterious ancient monuments, standing stones and circles, sprinkled over desolate countryside. Not to mention the famous prison. You shudder just passing it." Driving over Dartmoor two years before, I assured her, I had been spooked by dark scudding clouds over the foreboding hills.

Now, on another summer day, James and I had returned, with Jenny and her friend Annelise, to experience Dartmoor a bit more closely. Since we were about to luxuriate for several days in a country-house hotel, I had decided our one night in Dartmoor should be different. From a guide I had selected Old Walls Farm, so remote it needed to be identified in terms of other places: Ponsworthy, near Widecombe, Newton Abbott, Devon. As a Midwesterner, I had vaguely pictured an English version of a farmhouse, perhaps a small stucco building, surrounded by a few sheds. Mr. and Mrs. Fursdon, the owners, I imagined, would be taciturn, plain, and unpretentious, if not actually chewing on straws of hay.

As we drove through Dartmoor that day, the sun shone brightly. Instead of mists, we looked into a cloudless blue sky. Sheep grazed peacefully on green splashes of grass. Weekend escapists, determined to enjoy the sunshine, crowded the highway, almost bumper to bumper. Along the roadside, elderly couples sat in folding chairs, drank tea, and read the newspaper. Families picnicked. Climbers set off to near and faraway tors, disappearing like ants in the distance. On top of one high hill, a club of kite fliers flew their huge colorful birds, abstract dots of red, green, and yellow against the blue.

"So what's scary about this?" asked Jenny, in the tone she uses to point out how, once again, I have exaggerated danger. Soon she and Annelise donned their Walkmans and dozed.

When we pulled up in front of Old Walls, I could see that I had again miscalculated. The large, pleasantly furnished house seemed more like a small manor. Mr. Fursdon, now retired from active farming, was a distinguished-looking man with silvery hair, perhaps in his seventies. His wife (I would not have dreamed of calling her Liz, as did the guidebook) was a dignified, gracious woman who welcomed us and then left us to our privacy.

When we asked about the many silver cups that dotted

the dining room, we were startled to learn that they were awards for high-speed auto races. In the 1930s, Bill Fursdon had driven racing cars, and pressed, he brought out pictures of a Monte Carlo rally in which the car he had piloted won the luxury-outfitting category. The stately black sedan, with its shaving mirror and sink, bar, and convertible bed, was part of an England now even more remote than Dartmoor.

Soon after we had settled into our rooms, we met Mr. Fursdon outdoors. Inquiring whether we enjoyed nature, he said he could promise us a treat after dinner that night. He had discovered a nearby family of badgers, and when it grew dark, we could catch a glimpse of those nocturnal animals. I was always delighted by a sighting of English wildlife, whether pheasant, rabbit, or fox, and I had never seen a badger in its natural setting. The girls were not quite as eager as I would have liked, but they decided to come, too.

When we returned from dinner in Widecombe, Mr. Fursdon was standing by his front door. We squeezed into the car and drove through the growing dusk. The road we took seemed deserted, winding across backstretches of the moor, which looked to my untrained eye exactly like the stretches we had just passed.

Suddenly Mr. Fursdon said, "Here!"

James obediently stopped the car.

"Just pull over on the edge," Mr. Fursdon directed. "When you unroll the windows, talk in whispers. We don't want to frighten them away." He pointed toward the moor.

We all strained our eyes. About four hundred feet from

the car, high on the hillside, was a group of rocks. Mr. Fursdon explained that we should regard them like a clock. We could whisper, "Six o'clock," if the badgers appeared on the lower rocks, "twelve o'clock," if on the upper. Even with the binoculars (Mr. Fursdon had brought three pairs), I could barely separate the rocks. I began to realize that if Mr. Fursdon had discovered these badgers, his sight and senses were remarkably keen, certainly sharper than mine. "They don't come out until dark," he said. "We'll just have to wait." His voice was full of joy.

So we waited. As the dusk darkened, we sat in the car and whispered. Was that a rock at three o'clock, or might it be a lurking badger? Had the bushes moved at ten o'clock? We handed our binoculars from one to another, hoping to confirm a sighting. Time passed. The car was stuffy. I tried not to think of the cool evening outside the car, a leisurely walk near the farm, a stretching of tired muscles. Jenny, who obviously now believed the badgers were no-shows, tried to be polite as she nudged us homeward. "Maybe the badgers aren't coming tonight." Ten minutes later: "Perhaps they've moved."

But Mr. Fursdon didn't give up. We continued to wait. About twenty minutes into our vigil, tension heightened when a car approached on the lonely road. "Quick!" he hissed. "Put your glasses down! If someone sees us, all of Widecombe will be out here!"

We put our glasses down as I inwardly marveled at a community whose life was so slowly paced, so peaceful, that an event like a badger sighting might cause a panic. James, however, had not acted fast enough. His binoculars remained in view for a few critical moments. The car drove slowly by, its occupants staring curiously at us, and five minutes later, it returned, pulling up discreetly behind us. For some time longer we all sat there, silently, in our cars, gazing at the hillside.

Then, just as Jenny kicked the same spot on my shin twice, James cried—in a whisper: "There! At two o'clock! I think I see one!" And soon we all were excitedly swapping binoculars, counting and describing. "There's another! And two babies! It must be a family, all right! How big they are!"

Six badgers of various sizes, emerging from their den, were now frolicking like boisterous children, tussling and rolling about, disappearing and reappearing at different places on the hill. Their sharp black-and-white faces swam into focus with startling clarity, then merged into a blur of brown bodies scampering up the hill.

Mr. Fursdon was completely caught up in their antics: "Oh golly," he said with pleasure, "what a party they're having!"

The badgers continued to float in and out of our field glasses, scrambling up the hill and then returning to the rocks to play. A few did not come back. After another half hour, the dark was so complete that we could barely make out the badgers' shapes. Jenny and Annelise, yawning, had given up their turns at the binoculars. I, too, felt I had now seen enough badgers.

Gently I tapped James on his shoulder. "Dear," I said, "I think . . ." James nodded, and Mr. Fursdon reluctantly put down his binoculars. We started the motor, still whispering, and slid slowly away.

On the drive home, we were all quiet, even though the

badgers could no longer hear us. I had no idea what James and the girls were dreaming about. But I was thinking of the Fursdons, their kindness and hospitality, and Mr. Fursdon's love of the moor and its wildlife. As I looked out the window at the rolling hills of Dartmoor, I could still not have told anyone exactly where we were, but I knew the moor no longer seemed barren and empty. It, and the night, were full of life.

Up the Primrose Path

*A*t the far end of the High Garden of Dalemain House in the Lake District, I could see a red-painted wooden door in the gray stone wall. Although the door was shaded by a spreading vine, it was impossible to miss. It was also impossible not to want to know what was on the other side. Walking up to it, I read a sign hung just above the heavy iron latch: TO LOB'S WOOD, and in smaller letters, PLEASE CLOSE THE DOOR.

Lifting the latch, I stepped out of the garden. In front of me, a path beckoned. It disappeared through trees that covered a sloping bank above a briskly flowing stream. As I walked along the hillside, I could hear below the faint sounds of water slapping against stones. The sun was rapidly fading that afternoon, and I did not have time to follow the path to its end. I could only imagine how it must continue, past the stream and beyond the woods, hurrying toward a mountain lake.

In my Dalemain guidebook, I found a short note about that enticing red door: "Lob's Wood above the Dacre Beck at the top of the High Garden was so called after Lob, the character in J.M. Barrie's play *Dear Brutus*, where one is to be given a second chance in life through the doorway." I wished I had a Lob's Door in my own garden, and then every day I could pass through it and follow the path to its very end.

Perhaps I love England most for its paths. They lead across pastures and cultivated fields, over stiles and through gates, into valleys and over hills, along the banks of rivers and canals, beside lakes and ponds, atop mountain ridges and seaside cliffs, past moors, meadows, bogs, and dunes, and through every English garden. Any Ordinance Survey map of England, especially the Pathfinder series, is covered with thin crooked broken lines whose tiny dashes indicate footpaths.

Some footpaths are thin overgrown tracks, almost impossible to trace among hip-high weeds. These paths tend to brush a careless walker with stinging nettles or slap a leg with prickly burrs. Other paths are as wide as a country lane, even sometimes metamorphosing into dirt roads. Most paths are flattened grass or dirt, but well-used ones, especially those on National Trust property, are often pebbled, paved, or covered with wood chips.

Paths come in all sizes. The park of any great country house has a catalog of paths, from swept avenues lined with trees to brick-edged garden walks. At Killerton House in Devon, one thyme-covered stone path winds in and out of a Victorian rock garden sheltered in a steep dell. It is so narrow that only one walker can thread its intricacies at a time. Not far from the rock garden, a broad Beech Walk, named for the stately handsome trees that shade it, offers a promenade where several houseguests could stroll abreast or even drive a small pony cart.

A path can easily change character. Across Brendon Common, my favorite patch of Exmoor, the path to the Doone Valley begins high on the moor. Here I can step firmly over a cobbling of small stones with an occasional crunch of wiry heather. But before long, the path dips into a boggy hollow. Now I have to watch carefully for insidiously bright green tufts of grass: they thrive on water, and a wrong step will sink into ankle-deep muck. Anyone who remembers malevolent Grimpen Mire in *The Hound of the Baskervilles* might understandably look at those boggy spots and think of more than mere wet feet.

Paths can also disconcertingly peter out, leaving a walker studying his or her map in perplexity. Others can fork in confusingly different directions, not marked on the map, although most alternatives still seem to end up more or less at the same place. Exploring a footpath for the first time is never boring.

For the English footpath at its quintessential best, I think of Aira Force, a popular waterfall in the Lake District. Its path begins rather unpromisingly as a wide walkway, level, tarred, and suitable for wheelchair access, with wooden railings for support.

Tapping his walking stick a little reprovingly on the tarred surface, James said, "Let's take a look at the falls and head on to Levens Hall." He had not particularly wanted to stop at Aira Force, since its large parking lot and information booth signaled it was the kind of frequented spot we usually avoid.

"Sure," I answered. "I don't think this will take long."

The waterfall was dazzling, a sheer seventy-foot drop of white water down a glistening rocky chasm. The path near the falls was still wide and easy, an unobtrusive graveling of pebbles in what seemed like a mixture of dirt and cement. Slate steps set in cement gave visitors a secure footing to an upper stone bridge from which they could watch the falls boil over the edge.

But the path did not end there. It led up the ravine, following the ghyll along its banks, passing another beautiful waterfall, and gradually turning rougher. No longer paved, it was packed dirt, then just a worn trail. We continued along the banks, up and up, past mosses and ferns, trees leaning precariously over the rushing water, and huge lichen-covered rocks.

Soon we had left the falls far behind, and we were keeping to the path with some difficulty. It was now wild and narrow, almost a mere scraping in the bank. Sometimes it seemed to disappear among exposed and tangled tree roots and then reappear several feet straight above us. More than once I grabbed at a tough root and scrambled hand over foot. Here the ghyll ran far below, in a cleft so precipitous that if we had slipped and fallen, we would undoubtedly never have set foot on another English path.

After climbing and clambering for perhaps half an hour, we found ourselves moving away from the ghyll, on level ground again, through woods, and toward a gate. Passing through, we emerged onto uneven grazing land, part of the lower fells, open, treeless, and untamed, with distant views of Ullswater far below. The path, increasingly damp and squishy, eventually turned into a muddy farm track that led to some outbuildings and a stone cottage. An arrow pointed in another direction to Gowbarrow Fell, but we reluctantly decided to turn back. Our path undoubtedly had more surprises in store, but we would have to save them for another day. Undeceived by its tame beginning, we would not take it for granted again.

"That was the most wonderful path we've been on yet," I said enthusiastically to James as we drove away from Aira Force.

He smiled. "Better than the Cliff Walk at Lynton?" he asked. "Or the path across Brendon Common? Or the one that leads from the door of Lastingham Grange out over the Yorkshire moors?"

"Well . . ." I admitted, finding it impossible to choose. On every trip to England, I find myself on a footpath that seems just then to be more enchanting, or exciting, or unexpected, than any other. Afterward, I add it to my mental collection of footpaths, something I can delve into during occasional early-morning hours when sleep eludes me.

On such an interminable night, I might picture myself walking along the path to Watersmeet, one of England's publicized "beauty spots," where Hoar Oak Water and the East Lyn River meet below Exmoor. Beginning in Lynmouth, the lightly graveled path curves along the side of a wooded gorge, above the shallow East Lyn, which softly sings its way over jumbled stones. Although trees edge the path and climb the hillside, they do not block the sun but fling out fans of leaves that filter light onto the path. Under the trees on the hillside, rhododendron, foxglove, and other flowering plants and shrubs rise from a carpet of ferns and grasses. From leaves to moss, I do not think I have ever seen so many luminous shades of green. It rained yesterday—it will probably rain again today—and as I walk along the path a moist, rich fragrance hangs in the air.

Or I might re-create the path around Stourhead, perhaps England's greatest landscape garden. When Henry Hoare created his park in the eighteenth century, he planned carefully composed tableaux from different viewpoints around the lake, centering on classical eye-catchers, including a Temple of Flora, Pantheon, Temple of Apollo, and Grotto. All are set among rare trees and shrubs. I have seen Stourhead blazing with azaleas and rhododendrons, in almost unbelievable variations of purple, pink, red, orange, yellow, and white, and I have walked around its glassy lake in fall, when the lime trees, maples, and copper beeches reflect russet and burnished gold into the water. But when I invoke Stourhead in the middle of the night, I see myself walking on the lakeside path and just looking up at the sky through intertwined webs of green leaves.

An English woodland path lies under a canopy of leaves that might have been cut by innumerable delicate-fingered artists out of impossibly thin paper. Their ever-changing patterns of light and shade are so absorbing that I sometimes think of lying down on the path, letting other visitors pass, as I look up through that green lace. But Stourhead, like most English landscaped gardens, is decorous and dignified, and at least in England, so am I.

I do not try to put myself back to sleep by reciting the names of the trees on my path. Even in elementary school, I was not a success at identifying leaves, and despite acquiring several informative books on English flora, I still usually find myself nonplussed in front of a specific tree. On a recent circuit of Stourhead, I dipped into the inviting shadowy cave beneath the lower branches of a giant red-wood. There I found another tourist, camera slung around his neck, with a pencil and pamphlet in his hands. He ignored me, looked up at the tree, consulted his pamphlet ("Guide to the Trees of Stourhead"), and made a check mark with his pencil. He smiled, rather smugly, I thought, and left. On to the next tree. I remained under the red-wood (*sequoia sempervirens?*) for a while longer, idly brushing my feet through a thick layer of needles, and watched the uneven flicker of sunlight through its high branches. Then I folded my own pamphlet in my pocket, decided not to bother with it anymore, and went on.

Once I think of Stourhead, if I still haven't fallen asleep, I might move on to other woodland paths. Nowhere but in England, with its damp moderate climate that encour-ages trees to grow for centuries, have I found such shaded and serene places to walk. I might put myself back at Pencarrow in Cornwall, where a path through fifty acres of wooded parkland took me past sheep browsing in a nearby field, through a grove of bamboo, under many specimen conifers (unusual and prized evergreens), and beside many monkey-puzzle trees. (Monkey puzzles were supposedly named at Pencarrow, when a nineteenth-century guest touched one of those prickly leaves and said wryly, "It would puzzle a monkey.")

Or I could remember Pretty Corner, an aptly named woodland not far from the Cromer beach in North Nor-folk. Easy to miss without a guidebook and a local map, lying unsuspected just off the well-traveled A148, it is not exactly what Americans would call a park, nor is it a noted landmark. It is just Pretty Corner, an uneven ridge covered with birch, beech, ash, rowan, pine and fir trees, a changeable terrain intersected everywhere by footpaths. Locals take their daily constitutionals or walk their dogs here, marching with assurance down ravines and through woods that seem likely to swallow me up at the next turning. Remembering Pretty Corner, I move mentally a few miles to Sheringham Park, landscaped by Humphrey Repton, whose path provides views of the gray sea just over the horizon . . . and by now, with any luck, I ought to be asleep.

When I am walking a new footpath, I do not of course feel sleepy at all. Each footpath is an adventure. But these are adventures of a properly English kind, civilized, documented, and signposted. Signs for footpaths appear all over England, sometimes at the very edge of busy towns. Driving along even a main road, an alert motorist can spot at surprisingly short intervals that thin familiar board, shaped like a blunt arrow, pointing the way. FOOTPATH TO CRANBROOK 3 MI., it may read tersely, or less helpfully, FOOTPATH TO PIXEY GREEN. Who knows how far it is to Pixey Green? Two miles? Five? What *is* Pixey Green?

If the sign announces only PUBLIC FOOTPATH, I am still hooked. Where does it go? I ask myself. What if I took a chance? Could this be my very own Yellow Brick Road, disguised as a leaf-strewn path hidden between hedgerows? Those signposts always look welcoming. The English *want* people to use their paths. Walking in England is a national pastime, and everyone zealously guards public rights-of-way on these paths, rights that may date back to the Middle Ages or earlier.

Last summer, I read with approval in the *Times* about a small group of protesting ramblers who were determined to liberate walking paths on a section of northern moorland. It was part of an estate that had been bought by a sheikh, and the sheikh, seldom in residence, had posted No Trespassing signs on his moor, supposedly to protect his hunting preserve. Led by a veteran rambler in his eighties, the English group had announced a series of "walk-ins" to force the sheikh to reopen his footpaths. The *Times*, I thought, made it quite clear whose side it was on.

Not every footpath involves a long hike or even a ramble. One of my favorite walks takes perhaps ten minutes, along the Winyard's Gap path, through a thicket that lies undisturbed between the A356 and the minute Dorset village of Chedington. Few people ever enter this thicket, which seems to exist mainly so that Philip and Hilary Chapman, who run Chedington Court as a country-house hotel, can let Wally and Gemma, their two dogs, take an evening run among the enticing scents of deer, rabbits, mice, and other rustling small animals.

After a five-course dinner at Chedington Court, James and I like to pretend we are walking off floating island, trifle, and summer pudding by a determined ten minutes on the Winyard's Gap path. The wood feels as if it is part of a world that has not changed since 1644, when Charles I led his troops through the Gap. Not far from the path is a monument to a Dorchester regiment that distinguished itself in the Battle of Normandy in 1944, three hundred years later. Our walk is a salutory reminder of more than nature's pleasures.

Sometimes a path looks short and predictable, but once I place my foot on it, it carries me much further than I had intended to go. Staying for the first time in Lynmouth, James and I decided one morning to take what we thought

would be a fast walk up the Glen Lyn Gorge. This narrow
gorge is cut by the West Lyn River as it tumbles down
from the high moors to meet the sea. Although on one
terrible night in 1957, following torrential rains, the Lyn
turned into a raging flood, thundered through the village,
and swept away thirty-four lives, on this sunny June morning the river looked like a harmless mountain brook. We
could see it fell steeply down the gorge, splashing over
rock ledges, but we thought it probably vanished into the
hillside not far above us, where it was soon hidden from
sight by thick ferns.

Before long we had left all signs of the village behind,
and we were edging cautiously up stone steps and along
stretches of mossy, slippery path that were bathed in
spray. We could barely hear each other over the deafening
crash of water. Every time we reached a new ledge or
turned a corner or reversed ourselves on a switchback
slope, the path turned sharply again and led us further
upward. Trees and giant ferns bent over the path and river,
making us feel as if we had entered a green watery king-
dom, hidden and insulated by the sound of water from
everything below.

Eventually, just as I was wishing I had a scone in my
pocket, another turning struck into a pine woods. Here,
high above the village, the path widened into a lane. We
followed it until it deposited us at the beginning of another
path, which we could see led rapidly down into the village
again. It cut past the front gates of hillside cottages until we
reached our own front door. We had been gone little more
than an hour, but I felt as if we had made a distant journey.

An hour's walk, of course, is not a serious outing. In

England, thousands of ramblers take to the footpaths for an afternoon, a weekend day, or weeks of backpacking vacation. Walking tours have played as important a role as the Grand Tour of Europe in many an English education. Stories abound about legendary English walkers, like the famous historian G. M. Trevelyan, who is supposed to have left his wife on their wedding day because he could not bear to miss his daily "little walk," which in this case was a tramp of forty miles.

Walkers are also among England's contemporary heroes. Alfred Wainwright made a career of walking in the Lake District, which he then chronicled in an astonishingly detailed series of authoritative guides. Mention a walk in the Lakes, and almost anyone in England will refer to Wainwright.

Ask in any respectable English bookstore for walking guides, and you will be confronted with shelves of books and pamphlets. Walking guides will carry you up hill and down dale, around a few miles of local countryside, through every county, across England coast to coast. In his *National Trust Book of Long Walks*, Adam Nicolson blithely outlines a series of walks that run from a mere ninety miles (the Ridgeway) to five hundred and twenty miles (the South-West Peninsula Coast Path). England is fringed by long-distance paths: the Pembrokeshire Coast Path, the Cornwall Coast Path, the Devon Coast Path, the Dorset Coast Path, and so on.

I first discovered the lure of coastal paths one summer morning in St. Agnes, Cornwall, in 1978. My recently widowed mother had come to stay with six-year-old Jenny and me as we neared the end of our difficult seven-month saga in London. None of our little family was very happy that spring. After several weeks of closeness in our two-bedroom London flat, I decided the three of us needed a break. I proposed a long weekend in the country. Since I had never been to Cornwall, I picked St. Agnes for its remote seaside location, its inexpensive bed-and-breakfast accommodation, and its relative accessibility by train. "A holiday by the sea! Wading and castles in the sand!" I promised Jennifer. "Quiet days just watching the tide!" I promised Mother.

But it rained. A cold spring rain hung implacably over St. Agnes all weekend, falling hard at first and then dwindling into a stop-and-start drizzle. Our bedrooms were small and chilly. After her first wet outing, Jenny did not want to go to the pebbly beach below our house. The village was a depressingly damp distance away, and it did not offer much except a few shops for provisions and souvenirs.

The second day Mother and I took turns reading to Jenny. Then I tried to interest Jenny in coloring or jigsaw puzzles. Nothing worked. Before long, all three of us were feeling out of sorts. I was increasingly restless and irritable. "Look, Mother," I finally said, "tell you what: I'll go out now for a walk somewhere, even if it *is* raining, and when I come back, then *you* can go out for a while."

"Why can't we all go for a walk together?" Mother asked, somewhat plaintively.

"Yes! Yes! I want to come, too!" cried Jenny, who just a few minutes ago had declared loudly that she did not want to go back to the beach, ever.

"Of course you want to come, dear," said Mother soothingly to her. She turned to me. "Susan, I think it would be a good idea if—"

I interrupted her. "No!" I said sharply. Mother tightened her lips but said nothing. By this time, I was struggling into my flapping raincoat. As I left, I promised I would be back within an hour.

Although I wasn't sure where I was going, I walked quickly out the door. I didn't want to go into the village and I didn't want to descend to the beach, so I thought I might as well try to find a way to the cliffs that edged the cove. I turned on a path that led in front of the house and up the hill behind it. The straggling overgrown footpath was almost impossible to follow, but I kept straight on, listening nervously for the sound of any mother or daughter coming behind me.

After a few minutes of fast walking, I found myself almost on top of the hill behind the house. There my route merged with another, slightly wider, and much more heavily traveled path. A sign on this larger path pointed toward the horizon. COAST PATH, it said, and I almost felt as if it had spoken aloud in a heartening voice. Feeling suddenly lighthearted, and forgetting the rain, which was now almost imperceptible, I set out to see where this coastal path would take me.

It is many years since I explored that small section of the Cornwall North Coast Path, and I do not remember exactly where I walked. I cannot say what kind of flowers were blooming at my feet or even what kind of terrain lay to my landward side. All I had eyes for was the sea. It was everywhere. The path ran close to the edge of cliffs that plunged suddenly from a level grassy edge into gray-green water. All along the coast a wind was whipping up rings of white feathery surf, which endlessly hurried into small bays, vanished into out-of-sight coves, and broke against the misty gray-green headlands.

After I had been walking for some time, the rain stopped. Minutes later the clouds parted, and the sun shone brightly enough so that I took my raincoat off, threw it over my arm, and unbuttoned my cardigan. I knew enough about English sunny intervals to enjoy them while they lasted. Now the water transformed itself, changing miraculously into an intense blue green, a jewellike color that shone in the sunlight. I kept walking. The air felt fresh and clean, the sea sparkled, and everything was shockingly green.

As I stretched into a longer stride, I felt the tension in my neck, shoulders, and backs of my legs beginning to dissolve. When after some time I looked at my watch, I was startled. An hour had already passed, and I would be very late getting back. In fact, I would have to turn around immediately.

Before I did, I looked wistfully ahead. The coastal path continued, wandering briefly inland in the distance but then returning to the cliffs and finally disappearing over a fold of the highest hill on the horizon. I did not know how far it went, and I could not conjure up a mental map of Cornwall. I could only think of more cliffs, more sea, more cloudy sky, more gulls crying as they soared through the rainwashed sky toward nests in the unseen rocks.

I return to England for paths like that. Anytime James and I are in easy driving distance of the coast—which is almost anywhere in England—I anticipate a long walk within sight and sound of the sea. Besides the long-distance coastal routes, many other paths lead to the water's edge and along it. Some appear unexpectedly, on the way to somewhere else. I usually feel they are a private invitation it would be impolite to refuse.

Once, as James and I were driving to Barnstaple in North Devon, we decided to take a break for some hot decaf from our thermos and buttery scones from our cottage pantry. I looked for a picnic place. Although our road ran along the coast, we had not been enjoying much view of the sea. On English roads it is often hard to see over intervening hills, hedgerows, or steep roadside banks. Many lanes lie in centuries-old beds that have long since sunk below the level of the surrounding land.

But this morning we were in luck. I saw a place to pull off the road right onto the slope of a high heather-covered hill that stood between us and the sea. Once we had stopped, I saw that a stony path had been worn through the low purple heather to the top of the hill. I quickly consulted my map: this was Holdstone Down, it informed me.

After coffee, James and I grabbed our walking sticks and began to climb. It was a sunny September day, with only the faintest wisps of clouds in the blue sky. As we approached the crown of Holdstone Down a panoramic view opened before us. Behind lay the familiar patchwork of Exmoor, the glowing green of fields and pastures separated by the darker green lines of hedgerows, with other irregular shapes of shimmering moorland. The heather was in full bloom, an ever-changing palette of lavender turning into a brownish mauve, touched with the gold of gorse.

Ahead of us was the sea, an empty bright blue that made us blink, blending into the only slightly paler blue of the sky.

As a brisk breeze blew over the top of Holdstone Down, we listened for sounds of something besides the wind. We were too far above the ocean to hear the surf breaking on the rocks, and almost no traffic moved along the minor road we had left. James walked on for a while, following the path and disappearing over the brow of the hill. I sat down on a large stone. When I turned my head away from the sea, I could see miles in every direction, an unimpeded sweep over what looked like a green, blooming, but almost uninhabited world.

During all this time, we saw no one. As we left, another car did turn tentatively into the parking area, but then it pulled out again. Like most English paths, the route across Holdstone Down evidently did not attract more than an occasional walker.

Not all walking paths are deserted, of course, nor are they all in the countryside. James and I also seek out the boardwalks at England's seaside resorts. Many of these resorts flourished in the eighteenth and nineteenth centuries, but in recent years they have lost their clientele to the lure of packaged Mediterranean tours with guaranteed sunshine. What is left at towns like Sidmouth in Devon or Cromer in North Norfolk are rows of fancifully ornamented small hotels now, alas, often rather run-down, and a few grand establishments in the old style, perhaps surviving with business from corporate meetings, passing tourists, and families who probably came decades ago with their parents to these same resorts.

Most of these towns still have long planked boardwalks running the length of the seafront. On an early morning, when James and I take the morning air on these board-walks, we can watch a rare hardy swimmer taking a plunge in the icy water (nowhere in England is the ocean really warm), listen to the insistent tide breaking on pebbles just below (many English beaches are short on sand), and study the aging pastel-stuccoed hotels on the front. (What would that one be like inside? Knobby brass bedsteads to match its Victorian cupolas and gingerbread? Or a stripped-down pallet with flabby mattress?)

By midday, we might pass a scattering of balding over-weight men and their stolid wives leaning back in rented deck chairs under the fitful sun. The men have unbut-toned their shirts and loosened their belts, and if the sun has been out long, we can see warning red splotches spreading on those whitish chests and drooping bellies. They look sun-starved, those middle-aged men and women on a rare holiday, and as if they would like to lie in those chairs until their holiday ended, their eyes closed, their spirits flown somewhere out to sea.

At Sidmouth, the Esplanade leads eventually uphill to the Connaught Gardens, a series of walled outdoor rooms, where, protected from wind blowing off the water, older men and women sit dozing on benches or walk slowly among the terraced roses. Just beyond the Connaught Gar-dens, the path begins again, this time turning onto the chalk downs and once again following the sea. On a clear day, standing on top of Jacob's Ladder, an ingenious high staircase that leads in three flights down to the beach at the end of the gardens, I can look along the dark red rocky cliffs and remember how the path runs up and down the edge all the way to Cornwall. In the distance I can just make out a solitary hiker, pack on his back, trudging toward Torbay. The young and fit do not stay long in Sidmouth, I think, and instantly aging, I find myself wondering whether it might be time to think about an afternoon nap.

But even as I turn back to town, my heart goes with that solitary hiker. The joy of most English paths is how quickly anyone can feel alone on them. Just being able to disappear from a busy road between high green hedgerows is wizardry. One moment, a straight cement line, whizzing cars and thundering lorries, acrid fumes and oily smoke. Another moment, a quick turn of the path, violets poking up through a hawthorn-and-hazel hedge, the gray flash of a disappearing rabbit, and the tantalizing scent of unseen wild roses.

The best paths usually lead to the most remote places. After negotiating the hairpin curves of Hardknott Pass in the Lake District, James and I decided to unwind by taking a walk to Devoke Water, a small mountain tarn not far away. We had followed a tortuous train of cars through the pass, and I expected that we might also find other tourists on this side trip. But I always forget how few holidaymakers really want to walk very far from their cars. We parked at the signpost and began our walk by ourselves.

Our path turned out to be a rocky track, an easy half-mile walk, that took us gradually over a slight incline and then down to the shores of the lake. The track cut across the top of a moorland that seemed absolutely deserted, not even any sheep drifting over its barren slopes. It was late September, and under heavy gray skies, the grass looked almost brown, and the empty fells as if they had already fallen into a winter sleep.

Devoke Water lay in a shallow bowl formed by treeless gray-green fells. The surface of the lake was absolutely still, a steely gray that seemed a mirror image of the lowering sky. An old stone boat house, which seemed abandoned but was securely locked, looked as ancient as the landscape to which it now belonged. We stood for a while on a stone ledge jutting out into the lake and listened to the gentle lap of the barely moving water against the wooden boat-house door. It was so quiet that the lulling liquid sound seemed almost as loud as surf.

Since dusk was just beginning to shadow the hills, we did not try to walk around the tarn. It looked forbidding, hidden away from the ordinary world among these treeless fells, bereft of any living presence. Slowly we followed the rutted lane back to our car. We did not talk much. Devoke Water had cast a spell, and neither of us wanted to break it.

A week later we had left the Lake District for London and then for home. Back in Minnesota, Devoke Water seemed like a dream. But it was a haunting dream, one I remembered the first morning we were home, on another lakeside path. Whenever I return from a long trip, I walk the next morning around Lake Harriet. A deep, spring-fed lake in the heart of Minneapolis and just minutes from my door, Lake Harriet is bordered by trees and wide asphalt walking and biking paths. On a three-mile jaunt around its shores I can glimpse, in different seasons, the high splashy leaps of mating carp, a wavering parade of ducklings, the white whir of migrating arctic swans, and the blinding gleam of snow-covered ice under a bright January sun. Like all of us who live near it, I love Harriet.

On that morning of return, I looked from the lake up at the Minnesota sky and breathed deeply. I belong here, I thought contentedly, under all this sky. So much space, so much room to move. Surely I would feel cramped if I had to live in a small country, one layered with history and subdivided into minutely mapped spaces. Beyond the lake, I could picture the Twin Cities stretching out to their flat suburbs and finally, after the last scattered outposts, fading into the prairie farms that in their turn disappear into the horizon. I was born and raised in this country, and I am always glad to come home.

That first morning home, as I looked at Harriet's rippled surface, I thought of Devoke Water. Even as I rejoiced in Minnesota's sunlit sky I was aware of the noisy muffler from a passing car only a few yards away. Walking Harriet's shore, I admired the fall color on trees I know almost by heart, but they seemed sparse, shorter, and thinner than I had remembered. Although I was exhilarated to be back in the Midwest prairieland, I could not help noting that everything was open to the glare of day.

I was glad to be home, but already I knew that before too long—next spring, summer, or perhaps the spring after that—I would need to return to England. Perhaps more than anything else, I would want to set foot on an English path. I would long for those suggestive signposts, those disappearing meandering lines, those hints of detour and surprise.

When I first read Tolkien's *The Hobbit* as a young girl, I knew that I wanted to follow its winding roads among misty green hills, clear brooks, and distant mountains. Like me, Tolkien clearly loved English paths. In *The Lord of the Rings*, which I read much later, he captured their seductive music. "Still round the corner there may wait / A new road or a secret gate," sings Frodo. And on every footpath I take for the first time, I hear Bilbo's mysterious refrain: "The Road goes ever on and on / Down from the door where it began. How far ahead the Road has gone, / And I must follow, if I can. . . . And whither then? I cannot say."

Bugles over Bodmin

We had not planned to stop at the Duke of Cornwall's Light Infantry Regimental Museum in Bodmin, Cornwall. But our car developed brake trouble, and only a factory-authorized dealer in Bodmin could install new linings. Faced with two empty hours on the outskirts of Bodmin, we strolled by a heavy stone fortress with a sign announcing that it housed the Duke of Cornwall's Light Infantry Regimental Museum.

"Why not?" James asked. I sighed, envisioning dusty, untended rooms filled with a disorganized assortment of rusty cannon and old uniforms. The very name of the museum seemed musty. But the sun was warm, the building looked cool, and my new walking shoes pinched. We went in.

At first I was mainly surprised by the immaculate, up-to-date efficiency of this regional museum. A brisk and enthusiastic young lady sold us tickets and pointed us into a large, well-lit, subdivided room filled with shiny glass cases. Glancing around, I could see a vast, intricate, and highly organized collection, including some uniforms and weapons, but also maps, letters, sketches, and diagrams. An introductory placard informed us that this room traced the history of the Duke of Cornwall's Light Infantry from its formation as Fox's Marines in 1702 to its amalgamation with the Somerset Light Infantry in 1959.

With over an hour to fill, my husband and I set out to follow the regiment's footsteps. The first wars were illustrated by old engravings and maps from which the fierceness of battle had long faded. Here was a naval battle at Gibraltar in 1704, with a painting of high-masted English and Spanish ships harmlessly puffing clouds of smoke at each other.

"What war was this?" I asked James, slightly embarrassed at the blanks left by my college history course in European Civilization from the Roman Empire to the Present. He didn't know. "Ah," I said a few minutes later, having moved up to 1741, "The War of the Austrian Succession. I've heard of that."

As I moved on through the eighteenth century the wars became more familiar: the conquest of Canada (1760), the siege of Havana (1762), troubles in Ireland (and this war, I realized, I was still reading about). I paused at the American War of Independence. The redcoats were, of course, the heroes: "On the night of 20th September 1777 a British Force which included the Light Company of the 46th surprised an American detachment under General Wayne, killing and capturing 400 with a loss to themselves of only 8 killed and wounded. The Americans vowed they would give no quarter to the British troops engaged, so the units employed in the attack dyed their hat feathers red in order that they might be more easily distinguished in the future! This is the origin of the red backing on the cap badge of today."

Now the wars began to come into focus. As I read about those four hundred Americans I felt a quick surge of patriotic anger. Then I was both startled and a little ashamed: after all, I think of myself as a peace-loving woman. This museum was bringing out something in me I didn't like.

As I looked around the crowded room, I could see how the displays rolled on and on: the wars seemed continuous. As soon as the eighteenth century ended, the regiment entered the Napoleonic Wars, fighting in the West Indies and Spain, distinguishing themselves at Waterloo. ("Their casualties were greater than any other regiment of the Army, amounting to 685 of all ranks killed and wounded.") On they went, through the Second Sikh War in India (1848–1849), the Crimean War (1854–1855), the Indian Mutiny of 1857. ("During the great siege, the Regiment lost 15 officers and 364 other ranks killed, and 11 officers and 198 other ranks wounded, as well as scores who died from sickness. Many of the women and children also perished.")

The regiment continued to police the British Empire. I drifted past case after case of mementos—letters, daggers, memoranda, medals, citations—and took in campaign after campaign: the Egyptian Wars (1880s), Burma (1891), another action against tribesmen in India (1897), the South African War (1899–1902).

Although I was beginning to lose my ability to distinguish these wars, sometimes a particular artifact cut through my glazed trance. An ornamented sword gleamed in its case; a card noted that during the Defence of Lucknow in India, Captain Bernard McCabe had died with it in his hand. With the help of a vivid painting on the wall,

McCabe's Last Sortie, I could picture the slaughter on both sides. Once warm with blood, this shiny sword was preserved now as an object of veneration. Into whose skin and muscles had it sliced? Who had wiped the blade clean?

Another small but eloquent memento was a scrap of paper covered with microscopic writing, a message in code that used French, German, and Greek characters. A typed explanation informed me with undisguised complacency that the Indian mutineers were uneducated, but no matter what British hands the message fell into, "some British officers would *always* know Greek."

Leaving India and Africa, I arrived at World War I. As I walked along the rows of display cases, I sank into a depression that deepened as I realized that this war, hideous as it was, would soon be followed by another. With the invention of the camera, battlefields did not look quite so glamorous: enlarged photographs brought into the embalmed room some of the churned-up mud of Flanders Field and a few of the grim-faced, filth-covered soldiers in the trenches. Yet the celebratory mood of the displays continued. One showed an iron helmet with a huge rent in it. This had belonged to a German dragoon who had died from the first shot fired by the infantry in World War I. I stared for some moments at the jagged hole. I wondered how the dragoon's son or daughter might feel on visiting this museum.

Why does it go on and on and on? I wondered, studying scattered pieces of the answer. One case held propaganda memorabilia, such as a boldly lettered disk stating: NO ONE AT HOME. This disk was hung in windows during World War I to shame those who hadn't volunteered. I thought of our late-twentieth-century presidential campaigns in which nominees' military records were waved like banners. Near the drab photographs of trench warfare were cases filled with medals hung with variously colored ribbons and models draped in handsome red-and-gold uniforms with braided decorations, an array that would make even the soberest man strut.

James, who had left the room some time ago, returned for me. "Across the hall is another exhibit," he said. "But it's time to leave."

With some relief, I stepped out into the hall. Behind me the fluorescent lights shone steadily on the glass cases and framed maps. During our visit, no other tourists had wandered in. The room seemed meant to be empty of life.

I had been chilled by the past hour, and I thought I had had enough war. But passing the souvenir desk, I saw some tapes of marches recorded by massed British regimental bands. "What do you think?" I asked James, who loves rousing band music. We bought a tape.

We left Bodmin to the bright, brassy sounds of military music, floating from our car into the quiet streets. Caught up in catchy rhythms, I rocked back and forth to the marches. As the bands cheerily piped us along, I was reminded of the slipperiness of moral judgments. I knew this music was part of the deadly glamour I had just finished deploring. Under its stirring influence, young men had rushed into war. But I could not bring myself to eject the tape.

Driving away, I was strangely disconnected by the music from the hedged green fields around us. The museum was set on the edge of the beautiful heathland of

Bodmin Moor, part of the English countryside I love, with its rolling hills, quiet villages, and wooded walks. And yet what we had seen in those glass cases was England, too: a violent country, with a record of centuries of war.

Then I remembered how I had felt in front of the case extolling the American massacre. "It isn't just the English, you know," I said suddenly to James. "We've had the Gulf War, Panama, Grenada, the Vietnam War, the Korean War, World War II, World War I, the Spanish-American War, the Civil War. . . ." He nodded. I looked out the window at the tranquil Camel River and the pastures high above it, where sheep were peacefully grazing in the sunshine.

Bugles blaring, the regimental bands swung into "No More Parades Today." In thrall to tunes of glory, we drove on.

1978: A Shady Patch

"S ince you love England so much, do you ever think about living there?" someone occasionally asks me. "Oh no," I say quickly. "I once taught in London for seven months. That was long enough."

It was, in fact, more than long enough. It was forever. Although London's weather from January to July 1978 undoubtedly had its normal quota of *sunny intervals*—the lukewarm phrase English forecasters offer as good cheer—I remember those months as one long, cold, damp winter. I must have seen the daffodils bloom in March, and I recall a summery dress with a white lace petticoat I bought at Peter Jones. But I lived most of the time under a prolonged shady patch that did not lift until I checked in at the airport in July. When I left London that summer, I did not return for six years.

That seven-month stay was probably a healthy dose of realism, the way a brisk whiff of camphor cures the vapors. Now, on my shorter trips to England, if I am dazzled by too many grass-edged gardens overflowing with extravagant peonies and old roses; if I sit an hour in the soft light of a medieval church and wish I could return again and again;

or if I am saddened as I take one last long walk through a meadow by the sea, I remind myself: 1978.

When I think of those seven months, they are linked in my mind with another teaching assignment, the January of 1971 when I traipsed around England with ten students. At one end of that continuum, I see myself at thirty, in a shaky marriage, childless, new to teaching. Young and eager, I enjoyed sharing my love of England with my students. Then England was an escape and an adventure. At the other end, I seem much, much older: thirty-eight, divorced, with a six-year-old child. I had been teaching for nine years. Recovering from a brief but disastrous love affair, I had decided I needed a new setting, new experiences, something close to a new life. Why not London?

Looking back, I can see how I managed to convince myself that everything would work out. My job was to serve as director of the London segment of "The Arts of London and Florence," a well-established semester program during which two different groups, each with about twenty-five Midwestern college students, spent half their time in London, half in Florence. I would devise a curriculum, find and rent classroom space, plan day trips, supervise all arrangements, and teach two of four courses. One of my courses was specified as Theatre and Related Arts, for which I would attend plays and dance and musical concerts with my students two or three nights a week. I could choose my other course. Resident British experts taught the history of English art and architecture. Weekends we would take occasional day trips to Brighton, Stratford, Oxford, and other nearby landmarks.

It all sounded so feasible. I could teach a standard literature syllabus in something I knew well. Naturally I'd enjoy going to the theatre, and I'd hold lively discussion sections after each performance. Easy. To help with Jenny, I was sure I could find a live-in baby-sitter who'd jump at the chance at a free semester in London. Jenny would be in some kind of kindergarten, anyway, so she'd be away much of the day.

That was just my organizational outline. What I saw beyond its edges was much less focused but full of possibilities. In fact, I pictured the semester as a kind of upbeat early-Fifties movie, something like *Sunshine Peeking Through a Foggy Day in London Town* or *Susan and Jenny Singing in the Rain*. Renting a flat and living in London, I'd be an insider, shopping, making friends, going to parties. At the butcher shop, or news agent, or perhaps through my teaching, I might meet a slightly older, tweedy, Cambridge don, newly divorced.

In my free time, I could be a jollier mother. I'd take Jenny to watch toy boats sailing on the Round Pond in Hyde Park. Maybe we'd even see the Changing of the Guard at Buckingham Palace. We could go to the zoo on Saturdays. We'd ride on the top of a big red bus—I was sure she'd love that—and afterward we'd stop at a bakery and buy jam tarts and mince pies to take home. Then, while I made tea, she'd sit at the kitchen table and quietly color with her new pastels from Galt's Toy Store.

It was hard to hold on to this vision during our first week in London. While I hunted for a suitable and affordable flat, I had rented, unseen, a self-catering one-room apartment that turned out to be in the dark basement of a hulking Victorian house near Earl's Court. It had one small grated window, a two-burner hot plate, a miniature refrigerator, and a sofa bed for Jenny and me. Our live-in baby-sitter, Laura, joining us at the end of the week, would sleep on a roll-away cot.

It was late December, just after Christmas, and London was not in a celebratory mood. Dark fell early in the chilly streets, and lights did not sparkle in Harrington Gardens. Jenny, who had a nasty cough, refused to explore much beyond our front door. After our first top-of-the-bus ride, she showed no interest in another. Under gray, rain-soaked skies, no one was sailing boats in Hyde Park, and I was too busy to go all the way to the zoo.

Anxious to get settled, I began reading ads, following leads, and searching agencies for the perfect flat. I towed Jenny unwillingly with me to visit a host of estate agents, none of whom looked on us with much enthusiasm. "*How* much did you say you were willing to pay? Seventy pounds a week? No, I don't think we can help you." "A child? No, I'm sorry, the owner doesn't accept children." "Too bad. We have just the thing, but it requires a year's lease." "No, I'm afraid we don't have a lavatory here your daughter might use. You might try the Underground station at the corner."

At the end of the week, just as time was running out— Laura had arrived and it was instantly clear we three couldn't live comfortably in Harrington Gardens—we had a stroke of luck. We met Camilla. About my age, Camilla was definitely U: well educated, crisply spoken, dressed in cardigan and pearls, though just a touch shabby at the heels. She confided that she had taken up work at the St. James Agency as a temporary measure, following her recent divorce. Oh, was I divorced, too? Ah yes, it wasn't easy, was it? She smiled at Jenny, who surprisingly smiled back. Only six? Just had a birthday? Her own daughter was twelve. Not easy, was it? Yes, of course, we needed something with a bit of space. Actually, she might have something. Perhaps, just possibly, if she spoke with Mr. St. James, and we could put down a substantial damage deposit, we might be able to look at the Bingham flat.

That was how we came to live under the shadow of an unsolved murder. As Camilla elliptically told us the story in the taxi on the way to South Kensington, it was a nasty business. The flat we were about to see belonged to a Mr. Bingham, brother of "Lucky" Lucan. Did we remember the Lucan scandal? No? Well, best not to mention it to Lady Lucan, Mr. Lucan's mother, who was letting the flat in her son's absence. He had had to make a very sudden trip abroad. No, she didn't know why.

Laura and I pressed Camilla for details. Several years ago, Lord Lucan—Lady Lucan's son, she was the dowager countess, really a remarkable woman, once an active socialist, quite shocking at the time—anyway, Lord Lucan was unhappily married. Attractive woman, though, and two children. They had a nanny, also young and attractive. Lord Lucan, nicknamed Lucky, was something of a bad lot. Wild, gambled a lot, sold the family silver. He and his wife separated. One night someone broke into her flat in Belgrave Square. After some kind of terrific row, the distraught, bloodstained wife ran into a local pub for help. Back at Belgrave Square, the young nanny was dead, bludgeoned by a series of maniacal blows.

And Lucky Lucan? He disappeared that night. His car,

with telltale bloodstains, was discovered several days later near the pier at Newhaven. No body was ever recovered. But rumor said that Lucky had fled the country, covering his tracks well, possibly with help from his rich friends and family. Some said he was in Indonesia, others in Patagonia. Various sightings had been reported, one in South Africa as recently as six months ago. No one knew what had really happened, either at the Lucan home that night, or afterward. "Of course, if you should ever meet her, you are not to mention any of this to Lady Lucan," Camilla said anxiously.

As I looked through the flat I could see signs of Mr. Bingham's hasty departure. His clothes were stuffed in bundles in the upper cupboards, a few shoes still lurked in the back of a closet, all his books were on the shelves. We noted several textbooks on forensic medicine. Had Mr. Bingham, a loyal brother, been summoned suddenly to South Africa? Would he return, just as suddenly? Would Lucky perhaps be with him?

Despite these speculations, I thought the flat was perfect. It was half the second floor of a dignified building only a few blocks from the South Kensington Tube station. After looking at many tiny, dingy apartments, I was delighted with this one: a large front bedroom, with a bed for me and a camp cot for Jenny. A smaller back bedroom for Laura. A generous-sized sitting room with a dining table under a window that overlooked an enclosed garden. What Camilla called an American-style kitchen, very large, with old but full-sized refrigerator and stove, many cabinets, a gaudily patterned if stained linoleum floor, and a 1950s dinette booth, complete with a flecked Formica-slab table and benches. All this for seventy pounds a week and an indefinite lease: "Lady Lucan isn't sure when her son will be returning."

How could we not be happy here? I thought with relief. But I was about to learn that it is quite different to think what fun it might be to live somewhere—and then to move in. After seven months in what I came to think of as the Murder Flat, I began to develop a different perspective. Take those charming thatched-roof English cottages, for instance. Charming to look at, yes, but probably quite dark inside. Cramped. Damp. Hard to heat.

Heating is something one thinks a lot about in an English winter. The Murder Flat had electrical storage heaters, Camilla told us reassuringly, very efficient and low-cost. They were large metal cases, the size of radiator enclosures, with ceramic bricks inside. At night, the bricks accumulated heat; in the daytime, they released it. That way we paid for cheaper nighttime rates. We also got heat in the day, when we were up and about, instead of at night, when we didn't need it. Quite marvelous, storage heaters, Camilla said.

Unfortunately, one of the two heaters in the large, drafty sitting room didn't work. Although Camilla eventually summoned a repairman, he did not appear for three weeks. The necessary part wouldn't arrive for four more weeks. Then he'd have to see when he could install it. Meanwhile, the cold wind blew in through the loose single-glazed windows, ruffling papers on the dining table. I called Camilla again. Lady Lucan, gray-haired, tweedy, and gracious, appeared a few days later with two old portable electric heaters. Laura and I gratefully gave her tea, poured from her son's tea service.

The term *central heating* took on new significance for

me that winter. It means, I quickly realized in London, a heating system that distributes an even amount of heat in each room. It means that you can take off your outdoor jacket when you come inside and still stay warm. It means that your feet are not always cold. It means that you do not have to brace yourself before sitting down on an icy toilet seat.

One portable heater went in the front bedroom, whose storage heater, even operating full blast, could not dispel the clamminess of winter mornings. At night, I slept with my down bathrobe on the bed as an extra blanket. Sometimes I wore long johns under my flannel nightgown. In the daytime, we moved the heater to the sitting room and huddled around it. The kitchen had no heat at all. Until spring brought a faint warmth to the flat, Jenny quite sensibly refused to sit at the kitchen table and color with her Galt's pastels.

The second heater became Laura's portable property. Sometimes she kept it in her small room. Sometimes she took it into the bathroom. There it hummed and rattled while Laura lay in the cavernous old bathtub for an hour, perhaps two, even more. She took candles with her, too. "I like having a bath by candlelight," she explained. She preferred to stay up until the early morning and then sleep until noon. Sometimes, if I came in from a late theatre performance, I saw a light under the bathroom door. Except for the muffled hum of the heater, all was silent. I did not call through the door, although I often wondered if Laura was all right.

The London winter was especially hard on Laura. At least I was from Minnesota, where we rather prided ourselves on our subzero stretches, our blizzards, and our mountainous drifts of snow. I was used to boots, gloves, sweaters, and warm tights. Laura was from southern California. She had grown up in sandals, shifts, and swimsuits. Most of her life she had lived outdoors, under sunny skies, on playgrounds, patios, and beaches. Already her tanned face was slightly weathered from so much sunshine.

I had met Laura the previous summer, when I enrolled in a seminar at the University of California at Irvine. Jenny and I lived for two months in an apartment over a converted garage owned by Laura's parents, and Laura had an apartment below us. Then thirty, Laura was a gentle, slow-moving, and affectionate woman who had worked for some years with emotionally disturbed children. A vegetarian, she now had a part-time job in a Newport Beach health-food store. Sometimes she brought me samples of strange medicinal-tasting herbal teas.

Feeling the need for a change in her life, Laura had moved back to her parents' house while she planned what to do next. A stay in London sounded appealing to her, a respite from decisions and a chance for adventure. She liked Jenny, Jenny seemed to like her, and she was clearly experienced at dealing with children. How could this possibly *not* work out?

But I had underestimated the effect of London weather. "Doesn't the sun ever shine here?" Laura asked wistfully at first, then with increasing bitterness. She bought a large black umbrella so she could walk Jenny back and forth to school. Although she wanted to go out to museums, theatres, and movies, she was short of money, and often the gray cold rain seeped into her spirits and kept her home. She did not like the Underground, with its subterranean tunnels, and buses often took too long. As I watched in dismay, Laura slowly sank into increasing gloom, as if reflecting long dark hours in the candlelit bathroom and only slightly brighter hours under her black nylon canopy.

Frenetically busy with my teaching and supervisory duties, I did not have much time to spend with Laura. With almost thirty students and a six-year-old daughter, I had my hands full. Then one rainy day, walking under her giant umbrella, Laura suddenly found a young man from India walking beside her. "May I share your umbrella?" he asked with a smile, and Laura, though startled, laughed and agreed. They introduced themselves, soon decided to dash inside a pub to escape the rain for a few minutes, stayed several hours, and parted with plans for a date that night. When Laura came home, she was thrilled and happy.

"Ahmed is wonderful," Laura said. "So interesting and nice. Very polite. He insisted on buying my drinks. He wanted to hear all about me. He says he would love to come to California and enroll in UCLA. Can you imagine?" I was skeptical; I had been brought up to be wary of the sort of men who appeared under umbrellas. But, Laura reminded me, I had not met Ahmed. She knew I would like him.

I did not see Laura until late the next day. When I returned from taking Jenny to school that morning, she was still asleep. Before dinner, as Jenny sat in front of our rented television set, Laura finally joined me in the sitting room. We talked in low tones, afraid to attract Jenny's attention.

"Ahmed's a spiritual person," Laura told me earnestly,

"but he's really mixed up." Ahmed had made a serious pass. Laura had not expected this. She had told Ahmed she wasn't that kind of woman. They had argued. Though Laura continued to see him, off and on, for several weeks, Ahmed finally disappeared. For a while Laura occasionally stopped in at the pub where Ahmed had first taken her. It attracted many Indian and Pakistani men, and Laura met some of them. But none of these friendships ever flowered.

At least, I thought to myself, Laura *has* had a fling. Certainly no Cambridge don had yet appeared under *my* umbrella, and I had begun to realize that I had almost no way of meeting anyone, anywhere, anytime. Dashing between classroom and theatre, Jenny's school and home, the butcher and the delicatessen, I was unlikely to make a new acquaintance unless I happened to run someone down in my rush. I wanted to blame my isolation partly on English reserve, but I wasn't sure that was fair. Did I expect a stranger in the butcher shop to comment on my excellent taste in pork chops and then ask me home to tea?

At first I thought I might meet some other mothers at Jenny's school. After consulting with last year's program director, I had sought out the only school within walking distance that would take Jenny for a half year. The Stanhope School was a small private establishment for young ladies, run by an elderly Miss Stanhope and her few assistants. Although it occupied rather drab rooms in a modern office block, its general tone and curriculum seemed to harken back to halcyon days before the Great War. Once Jenny had been properly outfitted in her tailor-made red school blazer with the Stanhope crest, red pleated skirt, and navy raincoat, she would study French, ballet, music, art, handwriting, reading, and arithmetic. What more could I ask for?

I could have asked, I realized later, for a school closer than a long half hour's walk. A half-hour walk with a lagging six-year-old easily becomes forty-five minutes, then fifty. In a London drizzle, one can become quite damp within a half hour; in a downpour, one gets drenched. Although a bus stopped in front of our flat, it did not go to World's End, the appropriately named location of Miss Stanhope's school. If we walked five blocks to Redcliffe Gardens, we could take another bus, which came close to World's End, but it ran irregularly and, in the rain, seemingly not at all.

What I remember most about Jenny's school is walking back and forth to it. Occasionally I arrived in the afternoon as a class was ending and glimpsed a bit of handwriting practice or beginning ballet, but mostly all I saw of Miss Stanhope's was its vestibule. I smiled at other mothers who were hustling their daughters into blue raincoats, but no one ever had time to chat. The class day was unexpectedly short: half nine to half one. No sooner had I returned home from walking Jenny to school than suddenly it seemed I had to turn around and walk back again. Living in London, I was learning, took time. Lots of time.

Early in the morning, we set off together, Jenny with her schoolbag and me with a *shopper*, a carryall I soon learned to take everywhere. Although Jenny looked like a bright little bird in her red beret and matching uniform, she was seldom as cheerful as her plumage. Shy with strangers, she had not made any real friends at school. During the entire term, no one asked her home to play, and she never felt confident about inviting anyone back to our flat. Each morning she left home with a glum reluctance.

Gently tugging, encouraging, and trying to cheer her on, I led her by the hand through Kensington into Chelsea, across the busy Fulham Road, and down to World's End. I looked for cats we might pet or a red postbox where Jenny could mail letters, which she enjoyed. As much as possible, we kept our eyes on our feet, watching carefully for the countless dog turds, scattered everywhere as if the sidewalk were a randomly seeded mine field.

Once, toward the end of our stay, Jenny was invited to a birthday party. I was delighted, but the birthday girl lived in a distant part of London, off the edge of my *A-Z* map. Although I discovered we could travel most of the way on the Tube, the journey would take at least an hour. The party itself would only last two hours. I had to return to South Kensington during that time to meet with students. Laura had a ticket to a concert. How would Jenny get home? Finally I decided that, expensive as it was, she would have to take a taxi. But alone? At six? All the way across London? With a driver I didn't know? Remember, I told myself, this is London. My city. It would be okay. I would ask the birthday girl's parents to take the driver's name and number and then call me so I would know she was on her way.

When the square black taxi pulled up in front of our door, both Laura and I were waiting anxiously at the curb. The driver got out and opened the rear door. "Here you are, miss," he said. I looked inside the cab.

Jenny, smiling happily, was sitting with great aplomb on

the little jump seat, facing backward. "Hi, Mommy," she said. "Look where I got to ride!" Then she hopped down.

I looked at my little daughter, and at that moment, I had a sudden startling premonition. Someday, before too long, Jenny would be coming and going in taxis by herself. London was teaching her something it had taught me long ago. I was both pleased and a little sad.

That moment of independence did not last, however. Part of the claustrophobic feeling in London that winter came from Jenny's increased reliance on me. Without any playmates, my daughter did not turn, as I had hoped, to Laura. In fact, she turned defiantly away. Having lived alone with me since she was two, Jenny soon resented Laura's constant presence in our little household. After repeated rebuffs, Laura in her turn began to develop a certain resentment toward Jenny.

"I've dealt with seriously disturbed kids," she said to me in agitation one day, after Jenny had adamantly refused to go for a walk with her, "and I've never had this kind of problem." At supper that night, Jenny fussed unpleasantly, and Laura finally took her own plate and stormed off to a chair in the corner of the room. "From now on, I'm going to eat here," she said, and began to cry.

The garden behind our flat came to symbolize to me the frustration of our life in London. We could look down into the garden, through tree branches and tangled greenery, from our sitting-room window. It was an inviting little square, with several paths that wound among flower beds and shrubs, stone benches, and close-trimmed bits of lawn. Like many of London's garden squares, it was strictly private, fenced and locked, and reserved for occupants of the surrounding flats. The first time I opened the wrought-iron gate with a large antique-looking key, I felt a little like Mary Lennox in *The Secret Garden*.

"What a wonderful place for Jenny!" I thought when I saw this tiny park. But Jenny almost never went to the garden. From high up in our flat, the garden looked enticing. From Jenny's ground-level point of view, it did not. Once there, she had no one to play with, no one to take turns in hide-and-seek, no one to share giggles out of sight of the grown-ups. Of course it had no play equipment, no sandbox, swings, or jungle gym.

Nor could Jenny go there alone. Even on the rare bright days when she wanted to be outside, either Laura or I had to accompany her. To get into the garden, she would have had to walk by herself down busy Old Brompton Road, around the block, and up another narrow street. Then she could not have managed the locked gate, whose mechanism was stiff and difficult to turn. Once she was inside the garden, we did not feel easy about leaving Jenny there alone. It was mostly hidden from our window, and we knew nothing about the other visitors who came and went through the gate. So the garden remained a tantalizing possibility, never fully explored or enjoyed.

When I was not trying to be a good mother, I was immersed in the Arts of London and Florence. Almost at once, I saw that most of my time as director would be spent on logistics. What space could I hire to hold my classes? Where could I order books for my students? What performances of theatre or music or dance should I schedule, on what dates, and at what price? What out-of-town excursions should we take, and which coach company should I contact? What money would I need to disburse to students this week for expenses? Was it time again to trek to the bank in Berkeley Square that held the program's accounts? I quickly learned that the subtle differences between English and American speech and customs meant that I needed to go in person to make all these arrangements.

It was not as easy to do anything in London as it was at home. In 1978, the director of the program had no secretary. Earlier directors, I'd been told, had always used their (unpaid) wives. There was no money for anyone else. What I collected from a rented storage cubicle in January was my nonexistent secretary's equipment: a recalcitrant typewriter, stacks of old syllabi and excerpts from texts I wasn't using, letterhead stationery, and a hand-run antiquated duplicator.

When I think of my tenure as director of the Arts of London and Florence, I immediately see two images: a battered gray ditto machine and the cold cement steps in front of the Aldwych Theatre. "Oh, you once taught in London?" a young colleague of mine enviously remarked not long ago. "I'll bet that was exciting."

"Well," I said, "actually, not exactly."

Since I had no desk or study, the ditto machine sat permanently on our dining-room table. Cranking that stubborn machine, I ran off assignments, brief texts, and weekly schedules. Without those twenty-seven copies, my students would not know what to read, where to go or what to do. ("Be at the Wyndham Theatre Tuesday *promptly* at 7:30 P.M.; Wednesday, 9 A.M., field trip to Greenwich, meet in front of Harcourt Terrace.") On Sun-

day evenings, I stood grimly over the machine, as it stut-
tered and stopped, clogged and spilled fluid, and sometimes simply jammed for no reason at all. *Crank, crank,
crank*: the handle jerked, the paper (sometimes) slipped
through, the next week of my life squeaked and rattled
onto the table.

Once I had decided what plays we would see, I had to
purchase blocks of tickets. For the Royal Shakespeare
Company, my favorite, that meant lining up on the first
day of a booking period at the Aldwych Theatre so that
we could get low-cost group seats. Those seats sold out
quickly, and I had not arrived in London soon enough to
get a place on the group mailing list. So one early winter's
morning, in a cold drizzle, I armed myself with umbrella
and book and took the Underground to the Aldwych. For
two hours I sat on the cement steps, waiting for the doors
to open.

No one in the line spoke to anyone else. Everyone in
London, I thought, always seemed to be looking over my
shoulder at something I couldn't see. As I hunched against
the wall, feeling the stony chill penetrate through raincoat,
skirt, and tights, I did not feel like reading. I nibbled at a
damp croissant left over from breakfast and wished I had
a thermos. Soon I fell into a kind of daze, occasionally
shaking off accumulated droplets of rain from my umbrella, and hoped I'd arrive home for a cup of hot tea
before I had to meet my students for class.

Two or three evenings a week, my students and I went
to the theatre. Now, when I search my memory for sus-
tained impressions of those forty-some plays, I can barely
trawl to the surface a few actors, scenes, or fleeting mo-

ments. I remember Susan Hampshire, whom I had loved in *The Forsyte Saga*, looking anachronistic in a modern play. Also, a much-lauded performance of *Macbeth*, at which I spotted Lauren Bacall in the theatre foyer. A murkily lit and verbose drama, whose title I forget, labeled by *Time Out* as the best of current fringe theatre. Long high-strutting legs in *A Chorus Line*. A startlingly sensual Julian Glover, straddling the Aldwych stage. I went home and asked the unemployed young actress who lived in the flat above ours if, like many actors she'd mentioned, Julian Glover was gay. "Hardly!" she said, and laughed. I was irrationally pleased. Perhaps one rainy day, when I was walking down the Haymarket under a large black umbrella . . .

These are not notes, I know, that readily indicate a professor who taught a credit-bearing course in Theatre and the Related Arts. But something happened to my love for the theatre during those seven months. It is one thing to choose to go to a play. It is another to *have* to go. Exhausted at the end of the day, I would rush to make an early dinner for Laura, Jenny, and myself so that afterward I could sink for a few minutes into a comfortable chair in front of our sitting-room space heater—and then rise again to hurry to the South Kensington Underground for a seven-thirty P.M. curtain in the West End. I seldom arrived in a receptive frame of mind.

The London theatre, however, intervened in my life in a sidelong and unforeseen way. Toward the middle of my stay, I was invited to a casual party given by a friend of a friend of mine back home at Macalester. There I talked briefly in the kitchen with an American, a tall, lean, and somewhat gray-looking man who had been working for ten years in London at IBM. I barely registered Dan Cummings, but he called three weeks later to ask me to a lunchtime theatre.

That early afternoon at the Institute of Contemporary Arts was intricate theatre, both on the stage and at our lunch table. Although I have forgotten the name or subject of the play, it was presented in a way I'd never seen before, with shadow puppets before a backlit screen. Dan's passion, it turned out, was acting in amateur theatre, and he knew the director, with whom he'd done a show the year before. It seemed strange to think of Dan, who seemed so quiet and reserved, as an actor. Over quiche, chocolate gateau, and coffee, we tentatively probed into each other's private lives.

Dan was forty-two and separated, I quickly learned, although he and his wife had not yet decided whether to get a divorce. They now had a purely platonic relationship, he said. Sex had gradually disappeared, and neither of them was really interested in it anymore. But they had stayed friends. They still shared an allotment, a small garden space just outside London, where they both grew vegetables. Gardening was Dan's other passion.

I in turn told Dan about a brief love affair from which I was recovering. I did not enter relationships easily or lightly, I said, and in any case, I seldom had time to explore them. I described my life in London, the courses I was teaching, and my daughter. I talked about my writing, sandwiched into tiny pockets of leisure. One of my stories had just been reprinted in a British magazine called *Woman*, and Dan asked to see it. He said he'd like to meet

Jenny, and maybe we could all go to the park together.

Within a few weeks, Dan and I had dinner, went for walks, and attended several plays. It was wonderful to be treated like a woman, not a teacher or a mother. Without family nearby and evidently with few friends, Dan was probably almost as lonely as I was. He was startled to find, he soon told me, that he had not in fact lost interest in sex altogether. In fact, he wondered if perhaps I would like to drive that Friday to a quaint inn he knew just outside London, where we could have dinner together, stay the night, and drive around Henley-on-Thames the next day. He was sure I'd like Henley-on-Thames.

Like everything else in London that winter, this tryst did not turn out quite as I'd imagined. In fact, far from being a scenario for an American movie of the Fifties, it was more like London fringe theatre: lots of talk, fretting, complications, and not much action. The complications came from Laura and Jenny, both of whom, in different ways, were angered by my temporary defection from our tight little threesome. Although Laura agreed to take care of Jenny on Friday night and Saturday, she was cross about it.

Jenny sulked more openly. "Why do you have to go, Mommy?" she asked plaintively. "I don't like that Dan. I wish he'd go away. I want you to stay home with Laura and me. Besides, I don't want Laura to take care of me."

I finally slipped away with as much furtiveness as if I were eloping with a riverboat gambler.

In post-1950s movies, lovers usually dive into bed, hurled by waves of tempestuous lust. Alas, Dan and I found ourselves stranded on the beach. Dinner seemed long, as we awkwardly made conversation, but then not quite long enough. When we arose to go upstairs, I remember feeling—at thirty-seven, divorced, and head of a family—as if people might be staring.

The Puddle Inn, though advertised as certifiably antique, had been renovated to meet modern standards of plumbing. Our room was small, just large enough for a double bed, with a bathroom clumsily carved out of a closet. The bathroom opened virtually onto the bed, with only a thin—a very thin—door between. I remember the sound of water running from faucets turned on full, never quite loud enough, more than anything else about that night.

After that weekend, Dan's and my relationship went rapidly downhill. His wife, he informed me, was furious to discover that he had embarked on a love affair. She had thought they had a gentleman's agreement: no sex for either one of them. He felt guilty; he hadn't meant to betray her. He spent even more time at his allotment. I suffered from hurt feelings and made rash statements. Within a month, Dan disappeared.

But my abortive romance had many consequences. It was perhaps the last straw for poor Laura. The spring was a long time in coming, and even the blossoming daffodils in Hyde Park were not enough to dispel her depression. At about that time, my stepfather, long ill from cancer, died at home in Ames. Laura asked if I could possibly find a replacement for her so she could go back to California, and I urged my mother to leave as soon as she could and join me in London.

When my mother arrived, I thought perhaps I would

now have one last chance at recapturing my dreams of an exhilarating life in London. Would Jennifer welcome her grandmother instead of a baby-sitter? Would we sit happily at the dinner table together? Would Jenny and Hazel play together in the garden? Would I now have time to visit all those museums I'd not yet managed to get to? Could I yet recover my old love of London and see it once more as a city of adventure, excitement, and high times?

Well, no. Jenny didn't want *anyone* living with us, not even her grandmother. In deep mourning, my mother needed my attention as much as Laura had. Sometimes we hired a baby-sitter from Universal Aunts so we could go out together, but that was expensive, and since I went to the theatre several nights a week, I usually preferred staying home when possible.

What I remember most from the end of that unhappy spring is the increasing strain of trying to feed everybody. Since I did not have a car, I had to do all my shopping on foot. In the morning, after dropping Jenny at Miss Stanhope's, I usually stopped at a sizable all-purpose grocery store. As I tossed items into my cart—oh yes, we're out of sugar; maybe a can of oxtail soup? and certainly a pound of coffee, two cans of tuna fish, a box of laundry detergent—I never quite estimated their weight properly. At checkout, I was appalled to discover that I suddenly had three or four white plastic carriers, loaded to the top, each feeling like forty pounds. Lugging them home, I stopped at every street corner, and sometimes in between, and rested. As I struggled down the long blocks, past the elegant Georgian doorways with black wrought-iron knockers, I felt like a bag lady.

Shopping in our neighborhood also took time. Waiting

in line at the butcher, baker, fruiterer, and deli, and some days the fishmonger and wineshop, I learned patience and a deeper understanding of the traditional Londoner's instinct to queue up. Marketing did have a few compensations. Eventually the butcher smiled pleasantly at me, the young Arabs who ran the deli made jokes as they wrapped my croissants, and the white-haired, red-faced old woman who ran the Laundromat across the street stopped glowering when I came in the door. This, I found, was the closest I was going to come to making new friends in London.

For I did, in fact, have two old friends. One, a woman I'd known as a girl in Ames, had recently moved to London with her husband and daughter. Although our separately busy lives did not give us much time together, Faithe listened, consoled, and laughed with me. She reminded me, if I had ever needed reminding, how critical a good woman friend was to my ultimate survival. Graceful, ash blonde, and gray-eyed, Faithe also caught the attention of my other old friend, Rich Huntington. Though he only met her once, Rich often asked me hungrily that spring, "And how is that blonde friend of yours?"

Rich was leading the kind of London life I had planned to have. When I had first known him years before at Macalester, where he'd taught for a term, he was married with three young children. Though clearly a rising young scholar, specializing in Shakespeare, he was also surprisingly domestic. In the early 1970s, a man who liked to cook was still unusual in my academic circle. Once, at a department potluck, he had distinguished himself by bringing an entire turkey he had boned, reconstructed, and stuffed.

When I met Rich again in London, he had been divorced for some time. The years had settled well on him, and now in his late thirties, quick, knowing, and sardonic, Rich had assumed a kind of reckless authority that would have seemed presumptuous in someone younger. He was tall, with laugh lines and craggy features just beginning to blur a little, perhaps, I later decided, from too much booze. But though I almost always saw him with a glass in his hand, he kept fit with tennis and jogging.

While I was dashing around London buying theatre tickets, arranging excursions, and distributing dittoed schedules to my students, Rich was spending a pleasant semester doing preparatory work for a new London program his Massachusetts college was planning. Mostly, however, he was cozily ensconced at the British Museum, doing research on *Richard III*, for which he was preparing a new set of annotations. When he grew tired of his scholarly work, he wandered through the museum or set off for other museums and galleries. "You've got to get to Sir John Soane's Museum," he told me. "I stop in there whenever I can. And have you seen the new exhibit at the Tate? Great! Just great!"

Rich had no trouble meeting people. At least, meeting women. He already had several friends in London, who introduced him to *their* friends, and I didn't see much of Rich. We were old colleagues, respectful but wary of each other's private lives, and I was not his kind of woman. "The problem is," he said to me one night, when we'd managed an early supper, and he'd already had several drinks, "you're just about the only woman I can talk to like a man. Wouldn't want to jeopardize that, would we?"

Rich lived in a flat near Sloane Square, not too far from

me, and one late afternoon, I stopped there for a proffered glass of sherry before going home to fix supper. Rich wanted me to meet Les, a friend from graduate school, who was staying with him for a week or two. Les had left his wife and children home in Kentucky. "God, I suppose I should say I miss them," Les said, "but the fact is, Rich has been setting me quite a pace. Last night, we went out to Wimbledon and met Marcia after work. Didn't realize they had such good pubs in Wimbledon. Do you know Marcia?"

Rich had mentioned her. I gathered she was wildly attractive, barely thirty, very bright, a history teacher at some girls' boarding school.

Yes, I said, I had heard of Marcia. Rich and Les began to talk even more quickly, bouncing funny stories off each other, laughing at escapades they did not entirely explain. "And the shoe! I mean, what a gesture!" Les said, reaching for the Scotch. "Only Rich could get away with that, don't you think, Sal? It is Sal, isn't it?" Rich raised his eyebrows at me and smiled.

I looked inquisitive. The shoe?

"Well," said Les admiringly, "we'd had several drinks. Rich ordered some champagne. And Marcia—well, my God, she is gorgeous. I mean, *really* beautiful. I envy Rich, you know. What luck. *I* never had a woman in my life like that. Class, real class. Anyway, Rich proposed a toast to Marcia." Les began to laugh again, and Rich looked at the ceiling, still smiling. "And do you know what he did?" Les looked at me. I shook my head. "He drank champagne out of her shoe!"

Not long after that, I went home. I had to find time to

crank up the ditto machine after supper so I could print out next week's schedule before meeting my students at an eight P.M. concert. I did not think I would see Rich again before he left London, and that was probably just as well. Hazel, Jenny, and I would be leaving soon, too. When I had planned my seven-month trip, I decided to stay on in London a few weeks after my students left in June. I had made a plane reservation for the Fourth of July, a date that seemed fitting for a return to America. I had thought that would give me even more time to revel in London's pleasures.

Now I wished we were departing sooner. I no longer cared about trying to go to Sir John Soane's Museum, I didn't plan to visit Kew Gardens, and I even wished I hadn't gotten Mother and me tickets for that series of concerts at Royal Festival Hall. I just wanted to go home.

As I was hanging up my raincoat in the bedroom closet, I glanced down at the floor. Stacked in a row were my few pairs of shoes, low-heeled, sensible, good for walking. After seven months of hitting the London pavements, they looked wrinkled and worn. No, I thought, no one would ever drink champagne out of one of those. I closed the closet door and went in to make supper.

Walk Softly and Carry
a Hickory Stick

O n my first trip to England, I desperately wanted
to look like a native—though the proper London look, whether Burberry mac or wool Jaeger
suit, was not one I could easily afford. What I eventually
acquired to transform myself was a long beige nylon ladies'
umbrella with a plastic fake-bone handle. I loved that
umbrella. Although it was undeniably useful during London's drips and drizzles, I really treasured it because I could
tap it so smartly on the pavement as I walked. When I
swung up Regent Street or along the Embankment, its
brisk rat-a-tat was an assurance that I knew where I was
going—and that I could take care of myself.

Not only did I mark my steps, defiantly claiming each
inch of foreign territory as if I were a patrolling cat, but I
was unobtrusively yet effectively armed. As a freshman at
Smith, I'd had a brief and inglorious career as a fencer; now
I carried a disguised rapier. On late nights, as I left a West
End theatre for my room at the University of London, the
four-inch steel tip on my umbrella rang out with ominous
sharpness. "Don't mess with me," it said, tapping a little
faster down the dark tunnel at a Tube station. "I belong

here," it remarked confidently, heading into Cartwright Gardens.

That steel-tipped umbrella was my first walking stick. When I board a plane for London now, some thirty years later, other passengers glance curiously at my husband and me as we maneuver down the aisle with what appear to be thick wooden canes awkwardly protruding among our coats and carryons. Neither one of us is young, but neither is yet lame or infirm. Yet we both refuse to travel abroad without our favorite sticks, James's of ash with a real (not plastic) bone handle and mine of slightly warped hickory. We would not feel quite right on our country walks without them.

I acquired my first walking stick eight years ago on an impulse that often overcomes me in National Trust shops, those determinedly tasteful emporia of wildflower stationery, little jam jars wrapped in sprigged fabric, Portmeirion bowls, and wipe-clean folders with William Morris covers. (A writer in a recent *National Trust* magazine wryly claimed that as soon as she and her husband sailed their small boat into the harbor of St. Michael's Mount, they could smell the NT's bars of lavender soap.) On this particular afternoon, my attention was caught by a handful of walking sticks casually displayed in a white china umbrella stand decorated with colored birds. James and I had just begun a two-week exploration of West Country coastal paths, gardens, and country-house parks. The previous day, on a water-soaked path, I had noticed a couple striding along with sticks in hand, avoiding particularly soggy spots with a judicious poke. I had been intrigued.

"Me use a cane? Are you kidding?" James said when I tried to nudge him toward the umbrella stand. James does not ever intend to act as if he were old. "But of course, buy one if you want," he added kindly. "Just don't expect me to carry it around for you when you get tired of it. I'll wait for you outside." I made him wait quite a while, for I did not know how to choose. What height? What wood? What kind of handle? An elderly Englishman browsing near me saw my dilemma and offered polite advice: I should be able to rest comfortably on my stick for support and fit my hand around its handle without cramping my fingers. I settled for an inexpensive (eight-dollar) cane of varnished dark hickory with a simple curved top.

The rest of the afternoon I concentrated on becoming acquainted with my new companion, turning it in my hand, swinging it back and forth, and hooking it over my arm. I tested it on pebble-strewn walkways, dirt paths, and close-cropped turf. I liked it. It reminded me of my long-gone Marks & Spencer umbrella. No longer a would-be Londoner, I now coveted the image of a member of the Ramblers' Association. My stick made me feel sporty, tweedy, and—well, almost English.

During the next week, I soon found that my new walking stick, like my old umbrella, was more than good-looking. Climbing on a narrow, rocky path, I could lean a bit on my stick as I pulled myself upward. Edging my way down, I could quickly check the path for shifting or loose stones. On boggy or spongy ground—which includes most ground in a rainy English summer—I could locate firm tussocks. When James once unexpectedly sank up to his ankles in mud, I quickly probed for the nearest solid footing. I gave my stick the slightest twirl as I sauntered past him.

Approaching a nasty patch of stinging nettle, I could

push it aside without risk. I could lift and inspect a folded wildflower, or point in the direction of a camouflaged bird's nest, or knock down an apple from a high branch. When we covered long miles of open country, I took possession of the land with every firm stroke of my stick, just as I had once claimed the crowded streets around Piccadilly. I learned that a walking stick is an unobtrusive aid to meditation. It makes its owner mindful; it urges her to pay attention to her walking, to measure her steps, and to notice precisely where she is going.

James observed all this. At our next National Trust shop, he marched straight inside. He emerged with the bone-handled stick that he still prefers to all others. Yes, we now have others. On a recent trip, spending a pre-Gatwick night in the tourist-oriented town of Arundel, we wandered late in the day past a store that specialized in walking sticks. When I spied an antique store at the end of the street, James decided to stay behind and browse. Although he loathes redundancy, half an hour later he presented me with four new walking sticks. One, of shiny walnut, had a round brass knob for a handle that conceals a hidden compass. Another, faded and pitted, was a vintage stick that spoke eloquently of long-gone idyllic walks. The other two, James added a touch defensively, were for guests who might visit us at our Wisconsin cabin.

For we now have walking sticks at home. Most souvenirs that seem eminently sensible in England turn out later to be flops: silver toast racks, for example, or padded tea cozies, or china egg cups. Admiring them in a stall on Portobello Road, I forget that we eat our toast fast and hot, always brew tea in individual mugs, and usually scramble our eggs. But we do keep our English sticks handy by our Wisconsin cabin door, ready for rambles down seldom-traveled gravel roads, across fallow pastures, and through the tangled woods.

I have even found a new purpose for my walking stick. Our bluff on the Mississippi River above Lake Pepin is one of the last refuges of the timber rattlesnake, and although I have never seen one, during summer months when the snakes are out, I wield my stick with considerable energy. I do not really imagine three feet of hickory would discourage a six-foot snake, and I would undoubtedly trip over the stick in panic, but at least its swish through the tall grass would offer a wary snake some advance warning. He might, I reassure myself, just decide to slither away.

In our part of rural Wisconsin, pickup trucks are more common than walkers, and we attract some attention on the roads just by being out in all kinds of weather. But what mainly causes pickups to slow down are our walking sticks. Since we are visibly hale and mobile, those sticks probably look like an eccentric affectation. I wish I could reassure our neighbors. I'd like to tell them what happens when I set out for a walk with stick in hand.

As I swing my length of hickory along a dusty Wisconsin byway, I am connecting myself not only to the ground beneath me and the countryside around me but also to my own history. My walking stick prods my memories. Today, I find my footing on a firm bed of gravel; a few months ago, it was on a springy moor of blooming heather. Tapping down a dead-end road near Maiden Rock, Wisconsin, I am also rousing the echoes of a young girl's footsteps down marquee-lit Shaftesbury Avenue.

Among the
Alchemillas

Running barefoot on damp grass at eleven o'clock in the morning was not exactly how I'd planned to start this English holiday. But the plane from Minneapolis had arrived at eight A.M., and by nine-thirty James and I had cleared customs and picked up our rental car. We knew we could not check into our bed-and-breakfast in nearby Lamberhurst until at least noon. Groggy, stiff, but restless, what could we do for an hour or two in the vicinity of Gatwick?

Digging into my carry-on satchel, stuffed with essential maps and guides, I quickly consulted *A Guide to English Gardens*. "Yes," I said to James, "of course there are lots of gardens around here. I've found one that opens at ten. Take the A23, we're off to Wakehurst Place."

Although my guide had tersely noted that this "interesting large garden" was a branch of the Royal Botanic Gardens at Kew, I could not have foreseen its extraordinary variety or size. As James and I stood before the imposing Elizabethan house now used as the garden's headquarters, we studied our pamphlet. "Do you think we should take the lower path through Westwood Valley and the Himalayan Glade, or turn off through Horsebridge Wood, or go through Bloomer's Valley and Bethlehem Woods, or do the Pinetum, or the Heath Garden, or just head in that direction over there?" I asked, pointing.

James looked over my shoulder at the map. "They call this a garden?" he said. "At home, we'd call it a national park."

After an hour's walk through a woodland, into a deep valley, past a lake and up a path among rhododendrons and foxglove, we came to a dazzled stop in front of a bed of seven-foot-high white lilies, each stalk covered with many trumpet-shaped blossoms. The rich musky fragrance of these giant Himalayan lilies was so strong it felt dangerous to stand before them too long.

When we emerged once more onto the lawns that surrounded the house like a moat, we were tired and sleepy. The sun was shining brightly on this July morning, although the air was pleasantly fresh and cool. Only a handful of people were wandering over the grounds of Wakehurst Place, and we felt quite alone at the far edge of acres of lawn. James flopped gratefully down on the grass, studded with tiny white daisies and as thick and closely cut as if it were a plush green carpet.

I suddenly wanted to walk barefoot on that grass. I sat down and took off my walking shoes and socks, peeling off the long hours on the plane, the stale air, the cramped seats. For a moment, as I stood up and felt my bare toes sink into the unexpectedly crunchy grass, I felt a little foolish. After all, I was not exactly a kid. And I usually prided myself on being the sort of unobtrusive tourist who follows local customs and tries to fit in. Everyone else strolling around the garden had shoes on, including the toddlers, and English women didn't even seem to wear athletic footwear, only suitable pumps or unstable wedgy sandals.

But my feet felt heavenly. Usually I don't think much about them. I suppose I vaguely picture them as sort of a shifty filling for socks. But now, bending blades of cool damp grass underfoot, I could quiver each individual toe. I curled, stretched, and pirouetted. Half jogging a few steps, I resisted an urge to run full tilt across the lawn.

James opened his eyes. "What are you doing?" he asked.

"Going barefoot," I said. "At home, I don't get to do this." Since James hates yard work, he has filled both the front and back yards of our city house with dense honeysuckle. And if I were to walk barefoot on the grassy verge of our nearby lake, I would have to watch for occasional dog droppings, bottle caps, and bits of glass hidden in a tough sparse turf that is only a distant frontier relative of an aristocratic English lawn.

James watched me padding to and fro. "Come on," I urged him. "This feels great. Why don't you take your shoes off?" He shook his head. I wiggled my toes and mimicked ecstasy. He sighed, sat up, and began to unlace his Reeboks.

Before long, we were both walking back and forth on the grass. One or two passersby glanced at us curiously but, with typical English politeness, they quickly looked away. "I don't know when I last did this," James admitted, with a touch of sadness. He doesn't always like to be reminded that his childhood is behind him. When we left Wakehurst that noon, he took my arm and said, "Let's be sure to come back here again before we leave. There's no other garden like this."

On a chilly, overcast morning a week later, we were walking—shoes on, jackets buttoned—down the narrow paths of a very different garden. The flowering haven at East Lambrook Manor, a fifteenth-century stone-and-brick house near South Petherton in Somerset, is the legacy of Marjorie Fish, a onetime journalist known as the dean of modern cottage-style gardening. She came here with her husband Walter in 1937, to a derelict house and unkempt grounds, and after he died in 1947, she continued until her own death in 1969 to turn East Lambrook into a national gardeners' resource.

Though its two and a half acres are not much larger than some American suburban lots, the garden seems to expand. It is subtly divided into distinct sections separated by walls, low hedges, and curving stone paths. To keep each walk private, these paths are often bordered by topiary or high shrubs.

The East Lambrook garden is crammed with flowers. They spill over paths and stepping-stones, cluster around trees, crowd down the banks of a tiny rivulet, and casually intertwine leaves and blossoms in deep borders along the paths. Entering Mrs. Fish's garden is like plunging into a tumultuous sea of flowers. Walking on the almost invisible paths among rising and falling waves of rainbow color, I felt a miraculous staff might be striking open the way before me.

But East Lambrook is far from intimidating. Although Mrs. Fish cultivated many rare and endangered plants, she also filled her garden with familiar and old-fashioned flowers—hydrangeas, salvias, achilleas, poppies, alyssum, lavender, iris, geranium, and daisies. Despite its complex design, it is both welcoming and cozy, as an English cottage garden should be. After our first visit to East Lambrook, I turned to James and said, "We will have to come back here. There's no other garden like this."

That is perhaps the most obvious but incredible fact about English gardens. Not one of them is just like any other. They vary in size, age, design, plantings, and, most important, in atmosphere. Not far from Marjorie Fish's lively, cheerful, and overflowing garden at East Lambrook are the moody, melancholy, and haunting terraces of Mapperton. Since Mapperton House is seldom open to the public, its garden is almost unknown. To find it, a determined visitor has to consult a detailed map of western Dorset, watch for an unobtrusive signpost near Beaminster, and then follow, mainly on trust, a high-hedged lane that seems to sink into the countryside. When a tree-lined drive opens toward Mapperton, it is as unexpected as a drawbridge.

Mapperton's garden lies behind and to the side of the golden-stone Tudor house, in a wedge-shaped valley not obvious from the front. When a visitor has circled the house and crossed its wide green lawn, the garden appears below. With its formal Italianate terraces cut into the soft blurred contours of Dorset pastureland, it is a startling vision. Filled with carved yews, geometrical plantings, long rectangular stone ponds, summerhouses, and cavelike niches in high stone walls, the garden moves in a stately fashion down the valley. Gradually it becomes less formal, then wilder, until it disappears at last into the surrounding hills.

First created in the 1920s, Mapperton now has an air of age and decay. Although the flowers and topiary are obviously tended with great care, the old stonework is slowly crumbling. Moss-edged ponds brim with murky water, roses twine over faded brick walls near a disused summerhouse, and flowers spill over the edges of great stone urns pitted by weather. Parts of the garden are old enough to have acquired bits of historic legend: down a steep, moss-covered, slippery staircase, in an alarmingly dark stone-roofed cistern, Queen Elizabeth I is supposed to have once taken a bath.

On rainy days, mists often hang over Mapperton. Silent stone creatures—lions, eagles, cranes, mythical griffins—watch anyone who pauses in the orangery or slips in and out of the stone shelters. On such a day I once wondered if I were playing hide-and-seek with ghosts wandering under the dripping trellised roses. At the far end of the garden, the pebble-paved avenues turn into an overgrown path edged with tall grasses, wild foxglove, and Queen Anne's lace. Standing there, looking back at the formal garden as it disappeared behind foggy curtains of rain, James and I felt as if we were the last survivors leaving a lost world.

Gardens like East Lambrook and Mapperton have turned me into an obsessive garden visitor. On recent trips to England, James and I often divide our days among different gardens. At first we stumbled upon them, almost by accident, whenever we stopped to see a country house. Then, as our interest grew, I began noticing signs for gardens like Wisley, Stourhead, and Wakehurst, that didn't even involve houses. Finally I bought an inexpensive paperback guide, *A Guide to English Gardens*, issued by the English Tourist Board, that astounded me by listing more than five hundred gardens open to the public. Each one was given a purple rosette on a sketchy map, with one or two sentences of description. With some maps almost frantically covered by rosettes, I quickly realized that I needed more information, both about how to select a garden and precisely how to find it.

So a year or two later, I was pleased to acquire *The Ordnance Survey Guide to Gardens in Britain,* which listed only two hundred gardens, but gave each a full page, including photograph and map coordinates. Surely, I thought, I was now well equipped for a lifetime of garden visiting. But not long afterward, we were privileged, through a letter of introduction from a mutual friend, to be shown through Sissinghurst Garden by Nigel Nicolson. Mr. Nicolson responded to my enthusiastic comments about English gardens by asking what guide I usually followed. "Is it *The Good Gardens Guide?*" he inquired. When I told him what I used instead, he visibly sniffed.

So the next day I hustled into a bookstore and demanded *The Good Gardens Guide.* Quintessentially English, it is a briskly assured, opinionated, five-hundred-page tome that not only lists more than one thousand gardens— "the best gardens"—but ranks them. Class consciousness in England obviously extends to gardens. "Readers will appreciate that direct comparisons cannot be made between a vast estate like Chatsworth with its staff of professional gardeners and a tiny plantsman's garden in a terraced house," Graham Rose and Peter King remind us, adding, with a certain noblesse oblige, "although that having been said, both may be excellent of their kind."

Ranking in *The Good Gardens Guide* follows a star system. The crème de la crème—some eighty gardens— have been marked with two stars, "to indicate that in our opinion these are amongst the finest gardens in the world in terms of design and content." Slightly further down the scale, removed from royalty but still definitely aristocratic, are the one-stars: "of very high quality, though not perhaps as unique as the * * ones." And then there are the worthy masses, who are lucky to be issued a rather patronizing invitation to the ball: "The bulk of the gardens in the *Guide*, though not given a mark of distinction have considerable merit and will be well worth visiting when in the region."

Messrs. Rose and King make sure that everyone keeps up to the mark. On the back cover of my 1991 edition, they promise: "All the gardens have been revisited and their grading reassessed. Some gardens have been excluded and some new ones added. There is a new list of the best gardens." I am debating with myself about whether I need to upgrade my guide each year so I don't inadvertently miss a best-dressed garden newly risen from the ranks, or, conversely, waste my time on a garden that has sunk into reprehensible sloppiness.

But even this list of one thousand top-rated gardens is not enough for a true addict. To supplement *The Good Garden Guide*, I also consult the homely but invaluable *Gardens of England and Wales Open in Aid of the National Gardens Scheme.* Issued yearly, this inexpensive handbook lists more than 2,500 private gardens, normally not open to the public, which occasionally admit visitors, though perhaps only one day a year. Gate receipts are donated to several charitable organizations, especially the Queen's Nursing Institute, for the relief of nurses in need.

Although I like the notion of contributing my pence or pounds to good causes, I am drawn to these particular gardens through unadorned curiosity. When else could I walk around the grounds at Long Barn, Vita Sackville-West and Harold Nicolson's famous first garden? Although I had often read about Long Barn, I still had not been able to imagine it. Striving to be informative, writers on this garden left my mind's canvas covered with plant names, not pictures. "A planting of double peaches, walls patterned with ceanothus, arches of honeysuckle," "low retaining walls clothed with rock plants like aubrieta and helianthemum," "long grass walks, a hornbeam hedge, rows of Irish yews and an avenue of poplars, walls thickly latticed with climbers"—all this told me much, but showed me little.

So on a hot July Sunday afternoon, one of the only two days in 1991 Long Barn was open, James and I joined several hundred other visitors in strolling up and down its slopes and terraces. The garden I had read so much about came instantly alive. Now I could see for myself the dramatic contrast between formal dark rows of yews and the rich luxuriance of crowded cottage-style plantings. I could easily picture Vita arm in arm with Virginia Woolf as they paused, chatting happily, in front of the Dutch knot garden. I thought of Harold, returning from London, passing beneath white climbing roses as he entered the medieval gabled and half-timbered house. Beyond the borders of the garden, I could see the open fields and clustered woods of the serene Kent countryside.

On a rainy Saturday afternoon that same July, James and I drove to a very different garden, not as large, not at all famous, but as *The Good Gardens Guide* had promised, well worth the visit. The listing in our National Gardens Scheme handbook sounded irresistibly English: Major and Mrs. Cave, owners of Crown House, Eridge Green, East Sussex, would open their one-and-a-half-acre garden on this weekend, with a share of profits to multiple sclerosis. Full-size croquet lawn. Produce stalls.

After loading up on homemade jams and carry-away pies sold by a lady in a rain-soaked tent, and then refreshing ourselves with hot tea and scones at the house, James and I raised our umbrellas and set out to explore. The mildly sloping flat lot had little intrinsic interest, and the house itself, built in 1912, was not compelling. But within their limited space, Major and Mrs. Cave had created a splendid series of small gardens, including a heather bed, an herb garden, an alpine garden, and a rose garden, complete with ponds and even an aviary.

I think of Crown House Garden sometimes when I drive through American suburban developments or past isolated houses in the American countryside. I cannot help feeling their yards are often depressingly bare. Would it be possible, I wonder, to transform one of these dull flat rectangles? Could the owners of that three-bedroom bungalow plant evergreens, arrange paths, erect trellises, build benches, dig shallow ponds? Would this have to cost a fortune, or even a major's pension?

My obsession with gardens developed over many years. On my first several visits to England, I noticed them, of course, because they burst out everywhere, from London parks to city window boxes to the doorsteps of tiny cottages. Staring out a train window, I could see white and pink lupin, blue delphinium, and purple iris waving gaily in the backyards of the dreariest row houses. Almost everyone in England seemed to have a rosebush somewhere, gracefully bending over a front walk or climbing a trellis or rambling along a wall. At any great country house, I found a landscaped park or flowering terraces or enclosed gardens or perennial borders.

As I absorbed all those gardens, I began to think of England in brilliant Technicolor—bright greens, soft pinks, deep scarlets, shocking blues, blinding yellows. London a gray city? Not with red tulips and golden daffodils springing up all over Hyde Park. The English dull? Not if they could mix plate-sized blossoms of red, white, pink, and purple in a ten-foot-high tangle of rhododendron. Unimaginative? Not when they thought of training lavender clematis or yellow roses around twisted tree trunks or planting hundreds of crocus under a row of pleached lime trees or creating white-and-silver gardens that sparkle in sun and glow in moonlight. Lacking in humor? Not when they could clip and trim box and yew into the shapes of a fox being pursued by hounds.

What impressed me most about English gardens was their generosity of spirit, an exuberant lavishness that could not always be contained within strict squares or rectangles. This was a kind of garden design new to me. For years, the only gardening style I knew was string-and-stake: pound a stake in the ground, tie a string around it, run the string to the end of the garden, fasten it to another stake, plant seeds in a straight row under the string, and slip the empty seed packet over one stake to identify the seedlings when they come up.

As I was growing up in Iowa, the first garden I remember was my father's victory garden, with carrots, lettuce, beans, peas, corn, and tomatoes planted in close rows in a rectangular plot. Zinnias or cabbages, marigolds or beets, everything marched in identical rows up and down ours and our neighbors' gardens. Only weeds grew outside of lines. In England, I discovered cultivated flowers that soared on trellises, curved along winding paths, tumbled over walls, popped up between stones on a terrace, clustered in hidden corners like gossiping friends at a tea party, and crowded each other to show off their colors in mixed borders. In Ames, only dandelions blossomed in such abundance.

I was also amazed by the incredible variety of flowers in English gardens, many of which I didn't recognize or whose names I had never heard. Although rarer cultivars were often signposted, I discovered early that some plants were evidently so commonplace that the head gardener didn't bother labeling them. I would peer hopelessly into the foliage trying to learn what that white buttonlike flower was called or whether that shrub was a sort of hydrangea. Once, visiting Heale House Garden in Wiltshire, I was struck by the careless beauty of a low, burgeoning, yellow-green flowering plant that had been allowed to seed itself all over the cracked and uneven stones of the terrace. In vain I looked for an identifying marker. Finally I stopped another visitor, who, in her bulky tweed skirt, cardigan, and dampish dark felt hat, looked distinctly English. "Can you tell me, please, what that lovely yellow plant is?" I asked her, and pointed.

She looked disbelieving, as if I had asked her what was the name of the short green stuff that covered the lawn. "Why, that's alchemilla," she said, barely resisting the impulse to shake her head.

After that morning, I began seeing alchemilla everywhere. Now that I could identify it, I realized it was almost as common in English gardens as hardy geranium, a plant I had already learned was very different from the strong-smelling, bright red flowers we grew at home in window boxes. "Geranium?" I once said hesitantly to the gardener I had briefly captured at East Lambrook. "But how that can be a geranium? It's *blue*!"

For years, if someone said "flower garden," I thought of zinnias: long straight rows of stiff-stalked zinnias in brazen colors, red zinnias, orange zinnias, yellow zinnias, bright pink zinnias. I certainly did not picture soft drifts of lavender catmint over rosy brick paving stones, creamy white water lilies floating in a grass-edged pond, pale yellow tassels of laburnum hanging from a shady wooden pergola, or banks of purple foxglove scattered in a woodland clearing. It is no wonder I came to regard England as a giant conservatory without glass.

When I eventually became an avid gardener myself, I began to focus more closely on English gardens. It was not that I was searching for specific ideas in design or plantings. Much of my gardening is simply a struggle to discover what will survive a forty-below-zero night or a freeze-and-thaw cycle that lasts for weeks. Once, at Hadspen House in Somerset, I asked the head gardener about a showy pink mallow that lit up one corner of the garden. "Oh yes, it does quite well here," he said, "but do you ever get any ground frost?" He could probably guess why I laughed.

As for design, I am always in a hurry, frequently changing my mind, and prone to unpredictable disasters. So I cannot pretend I visited English gardens in order to learn how to group roses or naturalize iris along a stream or clip box hedges or construct a maze.

But when I became a gardener, I noticed more. I began to glimpse what complex planning went into a perennial border so that, for example, the foliage of a silver-leaved artemisia would contrast properly with green-and-white spears of iris and plumes of ornamental grasses. Although I could barely imagine how anyone could lay out an extensive garden, let alone a small one, I could savor the geometry of viewpoints. I could see why the sealing-wax-red Japanese bridge at Heale House Garden draws the eye to the thatched-roof teahouse hovering over the River Avon, or why an arch in Sissinghurst's famous White Garden invites a view of the surrounding Kentish Weald, or how ascending and descending steps modify an almost level site at Tintinhull.

I admired yew hedges more closely, not only because they sometimes looked like oversized pieces of cushy green furniture, abstract sofas, or bumpy room dividers, but because they held a secret. Almost hollow, many tall hedges concealed a half-lit cavelike corridor, hollowed out among smooth trunks and roots. Soon I became a connoisseur of secret places in English gardens, from a brick-walled orchard behind a latched gate to an unadorned circular lawn surrounded by fifteen-foot-high hedges. I sought out follies, pavilions, summerhouses, and grottoes.

At Killerton House in Devon, I was enchanted by the Bear's Hut, once the nineteenth-century home of a black bear, a family pet. A thatched rustic summerhouse, it had lattice windows, one ceiling of matting and pinecones and another of deerskin, and a floor made, astonishingly, of deer knucklebones.

Each garden has its own surprise. At Blickling Hall in North Norfolk, I vividly recall its ha-ha, a deep ditch, invisible except at the rim, dividing the house and garden from grazing animals in the landscaped park. When James and I took what we thought would be a relatively short loop around Blickling's reed-lined marshy lake, we did not know that the ha-ha circled the estate. Since the ha-ha had been fortified with barbed wire and electric fencing, we had to continue hiking for an hour around the entire perimeter.

When I try to explain to anyone the sheer impossible magnificence of English gardens, I invoke Leonardslee. One May morning a few years ago, James and I visited Leonardslee Garden in West Sussex for the first time. It is a spring garden, open mainly from April through June, famed for its hybrid Loder rhododendrons, azaleas, camellias, and magnolias. I was expecting a spectacular display, but I could never have been prepared for what I saw. Hovering near seven lakes, what seemed like (and perhaps were) thousands of shrubs had burst into bloom. Clouds of pink, white, purple, red blossoms floated above the water. Every turn on a petal-covered path unveiled a new set piece: a hillside of flaming orange and apricot azaleas, masses of white and pink rhododendrons higher than some trees, mirrorlike water filled with reflected color. It was less garden than fantasia.

Yet I knew Leonardslee was real. When James and I reached the far side of the garden, we could see where the dire hurricane of 1987 had swept through, ravaging slopes now littered with stumps, half-sawn logs, and churned-up roots. But it was not hard to imagine regeneration. As I stood at the edge of the garden, I realized that even here I could not actually see its exact borders. Where the land turned rough and the azaleas grew spotty, open fields and a fringe of undeveloped woods took over. This corner of the garden was part of the growing green countryside.

The profound pleasure I find in English gardens may be partly due to my awareness that they are part of something larger. Each is a refinement or concentration or artful arrangement of a natural world that still exists beyond their fences, gates, walls, or ha-has. At home, once I turn my back, many gardens seem to disappear. They are swallowed up by the other houses on the block, by city streets, by freeways leading out of town, by the vast spaces waiting at the edge of every settlement. In England, gardens belong and remain. I think of them forming a linked community, marching across the country in restrained luxuriance.

Walking in an English garden, I feel connected. At Knightshayes, a forty-acre garden in Devon, James and I stopped one late afternoon for the briefest of visits. We had been driving for several hours, and we needed to thread many more miles of narrow, winding lanes before reaching our cottage in Exmoor that night. I was exhausted, bleary, and out of sorts. James, still energetic, went off to explore. I walked under an arch cut in a high yew hedge and found myself before a circular pool. It was set in the middle of a grassy enclosure and protected by hedges carved as if they were battlements. I looked down into the clear dark water, admiring the floating flowers of white, yellow, and a brilliant red among the glossy green lily pads. I had never seen three colors of water lilies before.

Feeling better, I left the pool and followed a path toward "The Glade" and "The Garden in the Wood." Soon I found myself passing innumerable fall-blooming crocus, scattered like stars in the grass under tall murmuring trees. I sat down again on an open patch of turf. Nobody passed by, and I looked out at the rolling countryside beyond the woods. I was no longer so tired.

When I knew I had to leave, I walked reluctantly back along the path. Knightshayes Court rose from a high hill. Now, my eyes clear, I could see how the terraces in front of the mansion billowed with roses among the clipped lawns. These semiformal gardens stepped down slowly, with a thoughtful grace, to the lower level of parkland. The park in turn blended into the Exe Valley, which opened before me. It was a familiar Devon landscape, rising and falling downs, dark green hedgerows dividing lighter green squares of pasture, dots and splashes of woodland, white moving specks of sheep. Gazing into the distance, I felt as if the garden went on forever.

Notes of a
Non-Bird-Watcher

*A*s I stared at a rain-misted bog through a rectangular slit in the wall of a rough shed, I thought
briefly of the signalman in Cromer. Although I
did not realize it at the time, he had been an introduction
to my afternoon of bird-watching on Hickling Broad.

Several days before, James and I had driven from our
rented apartment in nearby West Runton to the rail station
in Cromer, a Victorian resort on the North Norfolk coast.
We had planned to meet Leonard, an old friend from
Minnesota, who was arriving after a London vacation to
join us in this quiet corner of England. But Leonard's train
had been delayed in Norwich, and we wanted to get word
to him that we'd still meet him at Cromer two hours later.
On this September morning, off-season for coastal resorts,
the tiny Cromer station was closed. Walking far down the
deserted platform, we stopped below the high-perched
signal box. I called to the man inside. He stuck his head
out, listened sympathetically, and promised to call Norwich with a paged message.

After his dispatch, he returned and stood in the door of
his box, chatting with us for some time. We spoke about

trains, England, world events in the news, and different cultures. He wondered if we would like to see the machinery housed beneath his signal station. He descended from his box to take us below, where we studied an intricate array of levers, switches, and cables. The metal parts were lovingly polished. "All of it about a hundred years old," he said admiringly. "Look at that workmanship. The engineering. It's all out-of-date, of course, they don't make them like this anymore, but it still works."

Back on the platform, he invited us to see his signal box. High above the tracks, reached by a narrow outside stair, it was a surprisingly domestic little room, tidy and furnished with a sink and a "nice little cooker" (hot plate). Was he lonely? No, he said, it was just the sort of life he preferred. "I like the quiet. I've got lots of time to myself. Only five trains a day now. I've got my bits of things to do." He showed us some neatly sanded woodcarvings. "I don't make much money, of course, but I'm single. I don't need much. I don't understand the people who seem to think they'll do anything for money." When we left, he stood at the top of the staircase that separated his tiny world from the one below and waved goodbye to us. We did not see him again.

For the first two days of Leonard's visit, we hurried around North Norfolk, stopping at medieval churches and touring country houses and gardens. Both architects and professors used to full schedules, James and Leonard set a daunting pace. On the third day, I announced that we were going to Hickling Broad. "This is going to be a rather different day," I said. I did not know how different.

I had chosen Hickling Broad because one guidebook

had informed me that it was the least spoiled of all the Broads. Once peat bogs, the Broads were excavated in medieval times. The resulting low-lying depressions eventually filled and turned into shallow lakes, a patchwork threaded together with streams, channels, and rivers. In recent years the area has become increasingly popular for pleasure boating and windsurfing. Several commercial companies take tourists on small excursion boats to view parts of the Broads, but none operates on Hickling Broad. It is part of 1,400 acres maintained by the Norfolk Naturalists' Trust. Twice a week, on Tuesday and Thursday, my guidebook alerted me, a naturalist escorts small groups, up to twelve people, on a Water Trail Bus around Hickling.

I wasn't sure what we'd see on Hickling Broad, but a Water Trail Bus sounded promising. I envisioned a placid hour or two, gliding through canals and across the open water. I could bask in the sun on an outdoor deck, or I might even snooze a little, snugly under cover, if it happened to rain. We'd enjoy panoramic views of shining water, perhaps some wildlife, and lots of Norfolk sky.

Our day's outing on Hickling Broad did not begin well. My guidebook had not said exactly how to reach Pleasure Boat Inn Staithe, the starting point of the water bus, and I had miscalculated how long it would take us on winding country roads. After many wrong turns and misleading directions, we finally pulled up to the dock shortly after ten A.M., the scheduled departure time. We saw no sign of a boat. I inquired at the inn. No one knew anything. The boat might have come, it might have gone, or it might not be operating in off-season. One other couple waited stolidly on the dock, middle-aged and rather dour looking, heavily dressed in woolen pants and sweaters, mackintoshes slung over their arms. When they spoke low to each other, I could detect a marked accent. Somewhere in the north? I tried to engage them in conversation. They answered my questions brusquely and did not ask any in return.

The Yorkshire couple turned out to be well prepared. As we waited for another half hour, a cold drizzle began to fall. I had a rain jacket but nothing to cover my thin jeans. Leonard had a trench coat but no hat. James had a leather jacket. For all three of us, I had brought only a small thermos of decaf. I hoped the water bus would have a concessions stand.

Suddenly a shape appeared on the horizon. It moved slowly but surely toward us, a low flat boat with a small outboard motor, piloted by a man in a dark green oilskin. When he pulled up to the dock, I hurried to the edge. "Are you the water bus?" I asked, hoping my voice didn't sound too incredulous. He nodded. I looked at the ancient open boat, rough and weathered, rather like a larger flat-bottomed version of an old wooden rowboat my grandfather had owned on a Minnesota lake in the 1940s. Then I looked at James and Leonard, both of whom already seemed a touch grim. A wind was beginning to ruffle the dark gray water.

We had come too far to draw back. Gallantly, Leonard handed me into the water bus. It had several wide flat planks for seats. David, our guide, introduced himself and told us how to arrange ourselves for proper balance. Our trip would take two and a half hours, David said, and I lost most of his other remarks as I hastily began to calculate the amount of rain it would take me to soak through, the probable rate of heat loss, and the level of hot liquid in my thermos. I did not even hear David's explanation about the boat, which was evidently a prized artifact, the last of its kind left on the Broads.

As the rain dripped, paused, and settled into a blanket of suspended mist that seemed to envelop the boat, we set off. Through the mist I could see flat banks edged with high reeds, openings that were evidently channels leading to other banks of reeds, and long stretches of gray water in every direction. Although I peered cautiously over the side of the book, the water was so dark I could not see the shallow bottom.

The boat moved at such a slow speed it seemed almost as motionless as the hanging clouds of moisture. We inched along, heading away from the inn and out onto the open water. Leonard pulled his mackintosh more closely around him, and I fastened the tabs of my hood tightly under my chin. Some twenty minutes later, I could see that we were edging toward a very short dock that jutted out from the reeds. Beyond it, on a slight rise that seemed like a hill in this flat landscape, stood a small wooden shed on stilts. "This is the first observation station," David announced. The Yorkshire couple pulled out binoculars.

Of course, I thought to myself. They're bird-watchers! This is a bird-watching expedition! David cautioned us to be quiet and to move slowly. We got out and waited while David unfastened the padlock on the shed and motioned us inside. "Are you a bird-watcher?" I whispered to Leonard, although I was sure I knew the answer. Leonard, a cosmopolitan and dashing man, would be at home on yachts or in symphony halls or at art museums, but I did not think he had probably ever spent much time in a bird blind. He shook his head but, following David's instructions, took his place dutifully on the long plank bench that was the hut's only furniture. We all sat in a row in front of a board flap fastened down at eye level. Carefully, with almost no noise, David unlatched and lifted the flap. We all stared out the slit, a long narrow window perhaps eight inches high, at a marsh in the near distance.

"Here," David whispered, handing me a spare pair of binoculars. He gave another to James. I motioned to Leonard, who indicated I should look first. David raised his own binoculars. The Yorkshire couple had already trained theirs on the marsh. "Two red-shanks at the right," David whispered. "A black-ringed plumer. Three, no, four—no, five fluff-tailed grebes on the far side. Eight slider ducks."

I looked. I looked harder. I could indeed see several birds, most of whom seemed absolutely identical, some perched on wood stumps, others sitting in the swamp. I had no idea what they were. Nor did I recognize the names David was calling out in whispers. I had heard of Canadian geese, mallards, swans, wood ducks, and mud hens, but these English waterfowl were all distinctly foreign.

As I tried to refocus my binoculars I was reminded of the summer night on Dartmoor when our English host had taken us to see badgers. As a spotting expedition, that had been a resounding success, partly because a large badger on a hillside is hard to miss. It is also instantly recognizable as a badger. At least on Dartmoor, it does not come in different varieties.

I handed my binoculars to Leonard. He looked out the

slit at the marsh. I glanced at David, who was riveted to the view, and at the Yorkshire couple, binoculars raised, who were muttering softly to each other. Chin on hand, James had put down his binoculars and was gazing serenely at the sky over the marsh.

Neither James nor I had ever gone on a bird-watching expedition. It was not that we were indifferent to birds. At our vacation retreat on Lake Pepin in Wisconsin, we eagerly watched for migrating bald eagles, soaring hawks, and vultures, and we listened happily to the recognizable songs of Baltimore orioles, robins, and red-winged blackbirds. We could also identify crows, cardinals, blue jays, bluebirds, rose-breasted grosbeaks, and three kinds of woodpeckers. But despite our bird books, neither of us had advanced beyond this elementary list. Birds moved so fast and hid themselves so well. When we gazed up into greenery, we could barely make out their forms, let alone their markings. Though we both enjoy quiet pursuits, we had never wanted to spend much time tracking birds.

But today, on this chilly English afternoon, I was grateful for the chance to be a bird-watcher. Any time spent inside a hut was time I would not have to huddle in the open boat. "Well, I suppose we should move on," David said after a quarter of an hour. "We have four more stops to make." My spirits rose. Four more shelters, at least fifteen minutes each.

As we pushed off from the dock, which almost immediately disappeared into the waving reeds, I felt increasingly cheerful. The rain had almost stopped, the wind had died down a little, and I turned my head to the stern so I could talk to our guide. Perhaps because I had been rather gloomily preoccupied at the beginning, I had thought David seemed taciturn. But when I asked him about the Broads and his work in the preserve, he answered my questions with ease. For some years, he had been the full-time warden of Hickling. But he was also a passionate sailor, and now he had decided to work only part-time so he could be away for long periods on the sea.

"I'm single," he said, "and I'm of an age when I don't need a large income. I make do with part-time work so I can live the life I want."

I glanced surreptitiously at David for a few moments, wondering what his age was. Outdoor life had weathered and wrinkled his face, and his hair was thin, but he looked lean, healthy, and tough. Forties? Early fifties? It was as hard to tell as it was to guess the age of his oilskin slicker, a dark green with crackled pigmentation as if it were a prehistoric but well-preserved scroll.

As we motored almost silently toward our next stop, David spoke feelingly about the plight of the Broads. They used to be clear, he said, so clear you could see to the bottom, only three or four feet down. But agricultural runoff, phosphates and nitrates, and unfiltered drains had polluted and clouded the water. Some fish were still alive in the lakes, but the vegetation had changed. In his lifetime he had seen the reeds markedly retreat from the water's edge. The Norfolk Naturalists' Trust was doing its best to protect the life of the broads, from insects, including the rare swallowtail butterfly, to stoats and deer. But sometimes it seemed like a losing battle.

Soon David pulled up at what looked like a small island. Leading from the island was a minuscule drawbridge, connecting to the mainland. The drawbridge had a padlock.

This part of the preserve fronted on the Weaver's Way, David told us, a major English long-distance hiking path. The drawbridge kept hikers away from a special part of the preserve that lay beyond. After David unfastened the padlock, James, Leonard, the Yorkshire couple, and I all walked across the few feet of drawbridge. It was like leaving one enchanted world to enter another, even more private, one.

Once across the bridge, we walked for a few minutes through a hardwood forest, an entirely different environment from the watery one we had just left. The path led to a towering oak tree with a metal ladder affixed to it. Looking up, I could see several wooden platforms at different levels high above us. Leonard thought for a moment and then said firmly, "I think I'll stay down here." James was already on the ladder, climbing upward. Although I'm often uneasy about heights, and my palms were already a little clammy, when else would I ever climb to the top of an oak tree? "Wait for me!" I called to James, and I pulled myself up the metal rungs, hand over hand.

When I joined James on the uppermost platform, I caught my breath in delight. As we looked out through the branches of the oak tree, we could see far beyond the glade. The sky carried us over the surrounding flat countryside and finally across distant sand dunes to the sea. We were sixty feet high, David told us. He took out his binoculars and helped the Yorkshire couple search for birds. James and I tried to wave to Leonard below, but we could not see him through the thick foliage. We were adrift in a magical treehouse, removed from the ordinary world, among leaves, birds, and sky.

After we descended and walked back through the glade

and across the drawbridge, David locked its gate behind us.
Back in the boat, everyone became unusually chatty. I
began to talk to the Yorkshire couple. Husband and wife,
they were on a bird-watching vacation, celebrating his
recovery from cancer surgery. I had thought they looked
dour. Now I realized that, like David, they were merely
reticent, valuing their privacy and unwilling to intrude on
anyone else's. We spoke about the weather, and I told
them how much James and I had loved Yorkshire.

When we stopped at the last observation post, I didn't
even make a pretense of trying to identify the birds that
David called out so quickly and accurately. I put down my
binoculars and simply let my eyes sweep over the wild
marsh, its grasses and reeds, its murky pools and hillocks.
I felt extraordinarily peaceful. "Look!" I heard David say
with excitement. "I think that's the black-toed water hen
I saw yesterday. And do you see the russet hawk to the
right?" His voice was low but vibrant. I thought of how he
loved the Broads and its creatures.

Then, by a connection so swift and natural I did not
need to trace it, I thought of the signalman at Cromer.
Both of these men had something to teach me, nothing I
could reduce to aphorisms, about priorities, simplicity, and
tranquillity. Of course, I knew I could not survive long days
in either a signal box or an open boat on the Broads, and
I did not think I could reduce my needs to the minimal
level these two men had achieved. But I was glad to be
aware they had done it.

When I returned to my crowded and often hectic life,
I would remember them both. I would think of the signalman, perched in his box above the tracks, brewing himself

a cup of tea on his cooker. I would picture David, quietly guiding his boat through a passage in the reeds. I might even hear the sound of feet on a wooden drawbridge and feel the wind through the branches at the top of an oak tree. Surprising vistas can open to a non-bird-watcher from a chink in the wall of a bird-watching hut on Hickling Broad.

A Pilgrimage
to Culbone

Climbing beneath the delicate green fretwork of thick woods, I could sometimes glimpse the sea far below through a break in the foliage. Luxuriant ferns grew on the steep hillside along which the path was carved, and regal purple foxglove flourished in sunny intervals among the green darkness. Pausing to catch my breath, I leaned gratefully against a cushion of emerald moss, listening to the quiet. Except for a rustle of leaves and a whisper of wind blown up from the sea, James and I walked in total silence, wholly removed from the world below.

That silence was fitting, for I was on a brief pilgrimage. Vacationing in nearby Lynmouth, a seaside village on the edge of Exmoor, I had heard about St. Beuno's at Culbone, the smallest complete church in England, and realized I had to go there.

After visiting and admiring many medieval country churches in the West Country, I knew upon reading a brief description of Culbone that it was special. My guidebook mentioned that Culbone Church lay four hundred feet above the sea in an Exmoor combe, or valley, approachable only by a path deep in Yearnor Wood. When the rector conducted services, he arrived in a Land Rover. Everyone else walked. Culbone's remoteness, difficulty of access, and the foreboding tone of the phrase *deep in Yearnor Wood* acted as inducements rather than obstacles. Not every church needed to be in the heart of a bustling village or town, I thought; I liked the idea of one that had been set apart for prayer and contemplation.

Our trip to the West Country this particular June had been unusually full of activity, with little space for reflection. Every day I thought of another garden I wanted to see, a new footpath I needed to follow, a part of Exmoor I had never explored, a nearby picturesque town where I could do our marketing. But I was aware of something frantic in all my comings and goings. A few weeks before we'd left for England, a dear friend just my age had died after a long and excruciating illness. She had never wanted to talk about her approaching death, so we had talked of almost everything else instead. But much—too much—remained unsaid.

Now in England I dreamed of her sometimes at night and woke with tears in my eyes. When Culbone beckoned, I felt the tug of postponed mourning. Perhaps here was a place where I could release some of it. James volunteered to go with me.

The first stage of our pilgrimage was easy. James drove us to Porlock Weir, a snug harbor with tearoom and seaside hotel, about ten miles from Lynmouth. A few tour buses stop next to the Old Ship Inn, for Porlock is a local attraction. A famous sea rescue took place here in 1899 during a terrible storm. When the Lynmouth lifeboat could not be launched in heavy waves to save a ship wallowing in Porlock Bay, the coxswain declared, in words now legendary, "We launch from Porlock!" Through torrential rain and darkness, his men dragged the twelve-oar heavy boat up hills with a 1:3 gradient and across fifteen miles of difficult terrain—and saved the stricken crew. Now, when something looks quite impossible to either James or me, one of us is apt to whisper encouragingly to the other: "Never mind! We launch from Porlock!"

Although one trail begins at the harbor, it is also possible to drive up the hill a half mile to the Manor House, now a tollgate for a road through the adjoining Worthy Wood, and walk from there. I wanted to assure enough energy for the final hike, so I decided we would start from the Manor House. With its stone walls covered with climbing roses, thatched roof, and enclosed arch over the road, the Manor House is just the right entrance to the Culbone path. After parking behind the house, we rang a bell at the white picket gate, a woman emerged from a low curved door to collect fifty cents, and we were on our way.

For almost an hour, we toiled upward, sometimes beneath overhanging ilex trees and evergreens, sometimes in the shade of sweet chestnuts, oaks, and sycamores. The route passed through a dark tunnel and stone arch, part of crumbling ornamental masonry that once belonged to the great house. Landslips had caused a temporary deviation in the path, diverting us to a stony track. But even this seemed almost part of the forest, finding a hidden way between green walls, winding up and up, and then up again.

It was a hot day, I had not thought to bring any water,

I had not counted on such a steep incline, and I had slept poorly the night before. Stinging flies buzzed around my face whenever the sun broke through onto the path. Just as I thought I'd have to turn back, I suddenly saw the church below me, nestled into the side of the narrow combe. It was in a small clearing, surrounded by a sloping churchyard and terraces of shrubs and flowers. Scrambling downward with new energy, I soon found myself in open sunshine, sitting on a bench in the churchyard next to a noisy stream that hurried over rocks and short waterfalls to the sea. The sun, gurgling stream, and bright flowers added to the sense of peace in the clearing.

Evidently one or two families still lived in this tiny enclave. Not far from the path a woman was hanging out clothes near her home, an ancient tumbledown stone building. Someone had established an enterprising refreshment stand in a new shed where the path turned into the woods. Inside, I found an ingenious arrangement of electric pot, cups, and tea bags—fix your own, said a sign, and leave money in a cup—together with a table of homemade marmalade, hand-knit baby booties and mittens, and some books on meditation, all inexpensively priced. It was a modest pilgrim's way station.

Walking back to the church, I slipped into half-light, the soft tones of filtered sun on stone. Although St. Beuno's at Culbone was indeed small, thirty-five feet in length with "seating for 33 in great discomfort," according to a cheerful pamphlet by the door, it did not seem an anomaly. Like many other country churches, its architecture was a comfortable mix of ages and styles, with—the pamphlet told me—rubble walls dating at least to the twelfth century, a

Saxon window, a thirteenth-century porch, a fifteenth-century screen, and a short spire, or spirelet, added about 1810. In one window recess was a fresh bouquet of lavender, and the church had a feeling of being used. I noted with regret that I had missed by a day the biweekly Sunday evensong.

A visitors' book told me that I was not the only pilgrim. Culbone derives its name from a Welsh saint, St. Beuno, or Kil Beun, who was a healer, and his church sits on an ancient Celtic religious site. More people than I could imagine had probably prayed at Culbone, and the woods through which I had walked had once held a colony of lepers. They, too, had known the tranquillity of this place.

Although I am often suspicious of shrines, mostly those that are overpublicized and exploited, I wondered if any of the lepers had been healed here. For me, healing is always a very slow process, but perhaps it could begin in this unassuming place. James sat quietly for a while on a nearby bench and then walked outside to the sunshine, tactfully leaving me alone in the church. I remained in my narrow pew, letting the silence do its work, until I began to feel the chill of the stone as a shiver along my spine. It was time to go.

Walking back to our car was an easy downhill trek, and I could sometimes hear the sea breaking against the far-off pebbly shore. To my pleasant surprise, my pilgrimage wasn't quite over. Driving away, we followed another stream through the green darkness of thick woods that seemed impenetrable, despite the narrow slice of road. No other cars appeared, which was fortunate, since we couldn't have passed. Eventually the road emerged into a land banked with high hedges, with occasional breathtaking views of faraway sheep on heather-covered hills. As I twisted around and looked back, I could see how the hills swept down to the sea.

Even when the road ended in a main highway, the A39 that runs along the coast of Exmoor, the spell of Culbone seemed to linger. At a turnoff, we parked the car and got out to bask again in the shifting sunshine. Scrambling over a low hedge and through tall grass, we sat down in a clearing among the bracken only yards from the road, but hidden from it, and listened to the wind in a plantation of nearby pines. Ahead were the bleakly beautiful hills of Exmoor, patched by cloud shadows and outlined by wandering hedgerows and wind-stunted trees.

"Take your time," James said gently. "There's no rush." So we sat for a long time and soaked in the warmth of the sun. I thought of the afternoon and of St. Beuno's at Culbone that lay behind me. Soon it would be dark in that narrow combe, and the church would return to unbroken silence. I was glad to remember it was there.

1984–1992
On the Sunny (If Wrong) Side of the Street:
Travels with James

*B*oy, this left shoulder is *tight*," Peg said sympathetically as she expertly kneaded and eased my muscles. I grunted assent. Lying under Peg's skilled hands in the relaxing darkness of the massage room at the Y, I sometimes lose the power of speech. "I can't remember this being so tight. Do you know why it's all knotted up?" Peg went on.

"Mmm-hmmm," I murmured, and then made an effort at coherence. "I told you James and I just got back from our month's trip to England. Well, it was a driving trip. I wasn't driving, of course. But I was sitting on the passenger side of the car. I had my left shoulder hunched for twenty-nine days."

I sank back into my pleasant stupor. I didn't have the energy to explain to Peg what it is like to drive in England—or rather, to sit mesmerized by oncoming motorway traffic, or brush against flowers and branches in the hedgerows that edge most minor country roads, or squeak past stone walls as I wait for the sound of scraping metal.

With James at the wheel, I know I should not worry. "Just remember, Susan, I'm the son of a rural mailman," he assures me with his usual good humor as we suddenly leave what I thought was the narrowest high-banked road anywhere in the world and turn onto another that is even narrower. Willing to venture almost anywhere, he is a confident but careful driver. In our eight trips together to England, he has not yet even scratched one of our rental cars, although he always confesses as we drive into the airport at the end of our journey, "Okay, let's give thanks! We made it one more time!"

I should not worry, but I do. I am not very flexible. I have discovered that part of my brain is permanently frozen in a driver-on-the-left, passenger-on-the-right position. Ignoring this flaw, James has assigned me a critical task. From the moment we pull away from the airport, I am supposed to shout loudly at every stop sign, intersection, and roundabout: "Think *left*! Think *left*!"

As map reader and direction finder, I sometimes get a little giddy trying to remember which lane James ought to turn into. Underneath my bravado, I am still thinking *right*. So to reassure myself, I hold my fingers together and stick my arm out as if it were a signpost, pointing for James with body language, "This way!" (Right?) "That way!" (Left?) On some days, filled with constant maneuvers involving motorway exits or obscure routes on unmarked country byways, my arm flutters back and forth like a loose semaphor. No wonder my left shoulder twitches into knots.

"Obscure routes" may sound relaxed and low-key, as if we merely meandered down the equivalent of Minnesota's wide gravel roads (nearly always at right angles to each other, punctually dotted by farmhouses, and inevitably leading to a well-marked highway). But leaving England's

A roads—supposedly just a step below the murderously fast M motorways—is an uncertain adventure.

We take this leap into the unknown for several reasons. Sometimes I think we'll make better time on minor roads (although James, rightly, is usually dubious): the M road is hopelessly clogged, for instance, or the A road leads through the center of town. England's ancient settlements developed around coaching roads that did not foresee the need for bypasses. Once we spent almost an hour crawling through Tunbridge Wells (population 45,000), because we had to traverse a main street that ran for what seemed like miles with stops at every corner, and then we lost the turning out of town. Such towns have only a few directional markers, small, polite, and seldom visible until a driver has zoomed right past both sign and necessary turnoff.

Sometimes we look for atmosphere. After twenty minutes in the seamless line of traffic on the crowded A35 from Sidmouth to Bridport, I might study the thinnest spidery lines on our detailed map of Dorset in order to figure another route home to Chedington. "Now, if we turn at Morcombelake, and take the second right, just past Whitchurch Canonicorum, we could watch for a little road that goes by Plenty House and Cutty Stubbs, and that would bring us out at Shave Cross, where we could get a road that would join the B3162 and then cross over past Stoke Abbott to the B3163 above Beaminster, which will connect us up with the road to Chedington," I suggest, trying to sound as if all this will be quite simple. James, who loves me, usually does not point out that he wants to get home the most direct way possible. He knows that I

have once again given in to the elusive promise of undiscovered villages, quaint farmsteads, and green hills far from
the sound of lorries and caravans.

He also knows that I resonate to English place names.
How could anyone who relishes language *not* want to visit
Whitchurch Canonicorum? Or Stoke Abbott? Or Shave
Cross? Even aware from long experience that a town seldom reflects the romance of its name, I still thrill to the
siren call of Sparrow's Green, Cricket Hill, Upper Slaughter, Bashall Eaves, Cockley Cley, Pinchbeck, Old Wives
Lees, Rising Bridge, Sheepy Magna, Fortuneswell, Nemp-
nett Thrubwell, Edge End, Dingley, and Sutton-under-
Whitestonecliffe. Doubtless to my loss, I have never
wanted to explore the plainly named cities of Plymouth,
Portsmouth, Bristol, or Birmingham, but I am always delighted when we drive once again through Piddletrenthide.

These excursions into the unknown are often fun but
seldom easy, either for driver or map reader. I keep my
index finger tracing our route on the map and glance up
and down constantly, obsessively scanning the landscape
for signposts, side roads, and turnings. Signposts are not
always entirely reliable. Many times, following a clearly
marked route, I will note a sign that says, for instance,
MOSTERTON, 7 MILES. We drive on for five, ten, or fifteen
minutes. Another signpost. MOSTERTON, 8 MILES. Feeling a
little like Alice in Wonderland, I hypothesize that after
World War II, during which the English deliberately
removed or falsified many signposts in order to mislead any
invading Germans, someone forgot to change the signs
back.

Of course, sometimes such a signpost tells me that we

have unwittingly taken a wrong road. Since so many country lanes are not marked at all, they can intersect, join,
bend back upon each other, and in general hopelessly
confound my sense of direction. Once, trying to guide us
from West Runton in North Norfolk to Mannington Hall,
a mere six miles away, I pointed James down roads that
kept us circling what looked like the same countryside.
Once we left West Runton, none of the roads on my
highly detailed (1 1/4 inch to 1 mile) map was named or
marked. It was not a question of watching for the B4982;
there *was* no B4982 or Shady Lane Road or anything but
squiggly lines. I was reduced to muttering, "Now, one of
these three roads that turns off here leads to Little Barning-
ham, but I'm not sure which one, except probably the one
that seems to be more leftish than the other."

Traveling cross-country in England means many one-
lane roads. One-lane roads provide a certain excitement.
Often we veer around a corner with steep banks and see
a car imminently approaching at breathtaking speed. Actually, it might be doing twenty miles an hour, but on a
one-lane high-banked road, any approaching speed seems
breathtaking. Then someone has to find a turnaround or
backing place, usually a sort of deliberate dent in the
hedgerow where one car is supposed to pull off when
confronting another car on a one-lane road.

Fortunately, the English are used to fast braking and
implicit negotiations, and someone always backs up
quickly and politely, usually following the general rule that
whoever is going downhill gets to proceed first. As the car
who *didn't* have to back up passes the car who did, it is
de rigueur to raise a right hand or wave ever so slightly in

acknowledgment of yet another potential crisis met and defused.

On rare occasions, the opposing driver does not want to give ground. Once, returning from Hunter's Inn in Exmoor to a more or less main road, we were inching between rocky walls and hedges on a sunken lane that seemed like an enlarged footpath. Needless to say, it had been my idea to take this undeniably uncrowded route. The road was deeply shaded by overhanging trees—"any moment it will become a tunnel," pronounced James with uncharacteristic pessimism—and it curved so sharply every few feet that we could not possibly see more than a car length ahead. We were almost to the top of a very steep hill when suddenly a large tractor appeared at the top.

The day was dark and rainy, the trees formed an almost impenetrable ceiling, and in the gloom the tractor looked like a hellish creature, belching smoke and blocking the way before us. James quickly threw on the handbrake and waited. I knew we were pointed upward at an untenable forty-five-degree angle and might slip backward at any moment, right into a stone wall or gnarled hedge. The tractor honked and belched again. He wanted us to make the first move. Even James, who has driven fearlessly over mountain passes in Crete where I had to close my eyes, did not want to back up on this squeezing-shut road.

We waited. I wondered what would happen if the tractor decided to hurtle down the hill toward us. But after several tense minutes, its driver relented, the machine rumbled and grumbled, and it slowly edged back into the farm drive from which it had come. When we passed it, nobody waved.

Most of our days on English roads have been sunnier, however, in spirit, if not in weather. When I met James, he took me into parts of England I had never been able to visit before. When I traveled alone, it was always by a combination of train, bus, and foot. This was not a bad way to see England; I could take a train from London to Lyme Regis, for example, walk to a small hotel, and circle from there several miles in any direction by foot. A timorous driver at best, I never even considered braving English roads in a car. But only by car—or by determinedly long-distance hiking—can one really reach so many of the un-spoiled and tranquil places that for me remain the heart of England.

For us, that heart has often meant the West Country. "The west" in England means something more than a di-rection. It has an aura about it, a blend of magic, mystery, and enticement, qualities associated with the ancient cul-tures of the southwest peninsula. The West evokes the brooding moorlands of Dartmoor, Bodmin Moor, Exmoor; deeply carved, craggy coastlands that once sheltered pi-rates; sheltered beaches; unexpected sunny warmth and near-tropical gardens. The West Country, which usually is understood to include the counties of Devon, Dorset, Somerset, and Cornwall, is a traditional holiday destination for the English. Still retaining its old allure, it has not yet been reduced to a terrain of leisure centers, caravan parks, and tourist-oriented villages.

Perhaps my complex feelings about the West, like many of my attitudes toward England, stem partly from literature. Some thirty years ago, when I read Tennyson's "Ulysses," I was moved by its hero's longing for a last voyage, an exploration into an "untravelled world, whose margin fades/For ever and for ever when I move." At the end of this haunting poem, Ulysses summons his old comrades-in-arms: "My purpose holds/To sail beyond the sunset, and the baths/Of all the western stars, until I die."

In England, the West is often synonymous with myth, legend, and the land of faeries. At the end of *The Lord of the Rings*, Bilbo and Frodo, the hobbit heroes, accompanied by the great wizard Gandalf and other lordly elves and fairies, depart for the West. Tolkien's conclusion is reminiscent of Tennyson's elegy: "And the ship went out into the High Sea and passed on into the West, until at last on a night of rain Frodo smelled a sweet fragrance on the air and heard the sound of singing that came over the water. And then it seemed to him that as in his dream in the house of Bombadil, the grey rain-curtain turned all to silver glass and was rolled back, and he beheld white shores and beyond them a far green country under a swift sunrise."

It is little wonder that the very sound of *the West Country* raises such seductive echoes. The North and the South have their meanings in England as well, usually in contemporary references invoking specific social and economic comparisons—heavy industry versus agriculture, coal mines versus computers, poverty versus increasing wealth. Neither North nor South, however, has the added mystique of *Country* attached to it.

To an American used to looking at highway maps that cover hundreds of empty miles, the West Country may seem quite small. But the same American who thinks to *see* the West Country in a week or two will soon be surprised. No casual visitor, not even someone who finds a corner of the West Country in which to settle for a long while, can begin to explore all its towns, villages, dells, dales, woods, churches, stately homes, gardens, twisting roads, high-walled lanes, and footpaths.

When James first drove me into the West Country, he also introduced me to life in English country-house hotels, a worldly romance of its own. For several years, until the falling dollar and rising English inflation turned us elsewhere, we slowly motored down leafy drives toward quietly sumptuous hotels that made us feel as if we'd just arrived as welcome weekend guests of the resident squire. The typical English country-house hotel, converted from one of thousands of stately private homes set in secluded countryside, gives its guests an idea of what it might have been like to be a member of the leisured upper classes in, say, 1895—or 1925, or 1935, or, for the fortunate few, even in Margaret Thatcher and John Major's England.

At home, when I am grimly domestic, scrubbing a broiler pan or pouring bleach into the washing machine or brewing coffee for breakfast, I sometimes think wistfully of our sojourns at Chedington Court. This unpretentious but luxurious country-house hotel, where we still try to return almost yearly, represents the best of its kind. It is so removed, located in the West Dorset countryside a few miles outside the market town of Beaminster, that when we first tried to find it, we had to stop three times to ask for directions.

Built high on a slope overlooking three counties (Dorset, Devon, and Somerset), Chedington Court is an 1840 version of Jacobean domestic architecture, a dignified house with ten ample bedrooms, a library with fireplace, sitting room, dining room, conservatory, miscellaneous small warrens of rooms, and halls so vast that the few guests easily disappear in them. The house has a long close-cropped side terrace occasionally used as a putting green, a front terrace with tables and chairs looking over miles of fields and meadows, a velvety croquet lawn, and ten acres of gardens, complete with summerhouse, duck pond, stream, flower borders, and giant yew hedges.

The first time I walked onto the soft green carpet of "Rhododendron," our spacious guest room, I felt as if I had just discovered the kind of cosseting I'd obviously been missing all my life. "Rhododendron" not only had beds with satin coverlets, but antique inlaid-satinwood furniture and comfy chairs upholstered in deep rose velvet. From a cushy window seat I could look out through leaded panes of glass in stone casings onto the conservatory and garden. On a linen-covered table sat a tea-making set with a little jar of biscuits, so I could fortify myself while watching television, listening to the radio, or thumbing through an intelligent assortment of books on the mantel. Mostly what I wanted to do was lie down on the satin-covered beds and pretend I was going to stay for months.

Sometimes at Chedington Court I ask if I can keep one of their handwritten dinner menus. Then, when I'm back in Minneapolis, I can always remind myself that I once ate like this: smoked duck and sliced ripe avocado on lettuce with raspberry vinegar dressing for an "opener"; next, scallop mousse with a sweet-pepper-and-ginger sauce; then roast loin of Wild Blue (a cross of wild boar and Camborough blue pig), served with a grain-mustard sauce; cheese, coffee, and the sweet trolley. Ah, the Chedington

Court sweet trolley! On the night of September 6, 1990, it included raspberry delice, honey ice cream with brandy snaps, apple-and-ginger fool, apricot dacquoise, chocolate-mint mousse, and fresh fruit. Sitting in my own dining room and dipping into an occasional splurge of nonfat vanilla frozen yogurt, I can hardly bear to recall the sweet trolley.

Of course, not every country-house hotel is run like Chedington Court. Some are even grander. Many are less cushiony. When I heard that the Lake Vyrnwy Hotel had recently been extensively renovated, I was rather sorry. Without James at the wheel, we would never have come to this Victorian hotel, tucked into a fairy-tale setting high in the Berwyn Mountains of Montgomeryshire in mid-Wales. It overlooks a majestically wooded thousand-acre reservoir, and views from the main rooms and most bed-rooms are staggering.

Inside the hotel, advertised as "a country house and sporting retreat," we discovered an endearing shabbiness, a let-it-all-hang-out feeling, which indeed some of the upholstery did. At some hotels, I have taken snapshots of terraced gardens or baronial public rooms; at Lake Vyrnwy Hotel, I commemorated a chair. Valiantly trying to hold its own on wobbly legs, it stood in our bedroom, sagging to one side, while one arm listed in the other direction. Its faded brown-striped slipcover hung loosely, as if the chair had recently lost weight, and the stripes swerved into queasy waves. Squashed into the back of this armchair was a lumpy green cushion, which could be moved about in a hopeless attempt for back support.

I also kept a menu from the Lake Vyrnwy Hotel: prawn

bisque (a salty soup the brownish color of our bedroom carpet), fried fillet of sole with tartare sauce, chipped potatoes, spring cabbage, beans, and, of course, a sweet trolley, which featured a heavy sherry-soaked trifle, followed by a savory, "devils on horseback"—prunes wrapped in bacon on fried bread. Everything seemed to be of a piece: the dark brown chenille bedspreads, the bound volumes of *Shooting Times*, the calendar advertising the Injured Jockeys Fund, the stuffed and mounted fish on the walls. We were given hot-water bottles to take to bed, and at the end of our corridor I found an empty large room with a gilt placard on the door: AIRING OUT ROOM.

But we were happy in our brief stay at Lake Vyrnwy, and we have often talked of going back. Now, however, I have noticed that, under new owners, it currently appears in a glossy high-priced guide, which lauds its individually decorated bedrooms, four-poster beds, Jacuzzis, and lounge suites. I rather liked the hotel as it was, a vintage memorial with fringed lampshades.

We probably would not go back, anyway, because in recent years, James and I have preferred weekly rentals of a "holiday flat," which means a fully furnished apartment or cottage complete with cooking utensils. We like the extra space, the privacy, and the freedom of preparing our meals how and when we want. Tending to rise at alarmingly early hours, we can then fall into bed when everyone else is just sitting down for the first course in a country-house hotel. And, of course, we like saving money. Self-catering, as the English call this kind of travel, cuts our costs at least in half, perhaps more.

Staying in a cottage, we can live in the heart of a com-

munity and pretend for a week or two as if we belonged
there. In Padstow, Cornwall, we once rented two upper
floors above a tearoom on the quay. From our door, we
could walk everywhere in the old part of the village. Each
morning I strolled to the local newsagent for a paper, to the
baker for fresh bun rounds, to the butcher for the day's
chicken or chops, and to the fruiterer for carrots, lettuce,
and oranges. At almost every stop I chatted briefly with
either customers or shopkeeper. After we had discussed
the weather, where I was from, whether Minnesota was
anywhere near Detroit, Chicago, New York, or Denver,
whether I might know someone's friend or relative in any
of those cities, comparative American and English prices,
if I was enjoying my holiday, what I thought of Padstow,
and where we were staying, I returned home with a heartening sense of having acquaintances and neighbors.

In a little-known village in western Dorset, we felt like
visiting royals when we rented York Cottage, a guest cottage occasionally let by the local lord of the manor when
his own friends were not using it. It was named for the
Duke and Duchess of York, who once made it their base
in the West Country while Prince Andrew was on training
maneuvers. The owner invited us to roam his three-
thousand-acre estate and one evening gave us a tour, after
cocktails, of his antique- and art-filled house.

In the Lake District, our small stone cottage sat next to
a wide path used by a neighboring farmer to drive his cows
and sheep from pasture, past our cottage, across a road, and
back to their barn. Our first afternoon, we were startled by
a bellowing moo that was as loud and constant as a fire
alarm. Rushing to the door, we saw the farmer guiding a

cow down our lane—"bloat," he glanced up and said with irritation, not at us, but at the cow, who had evidently just gorged herself on too much sweet clover—and we watched as, still bellowing and swaying her head, she moved reluctantly toward her threatened massive dose of castor oil. Once, when James had stepped outside in the early evening, he was easily pressed into service to help our neighbor herd his sheep across the busy road. This kind of experience does not happen at a country-house hotel.

For one-night stays between cottages, we often look for farmhouse accommodation, a category that does not mean sleeping in a hayloft or behind a wood-burning stove. Many English farmhouses are handsome, venerable, rambling structures, now owned not only by farmers but also by commuters or by retired city people who want to live in the country. An increasing number of these farmhouses offer bed-and-breakfast rooms, sometimes in the house itself and sometimes in a separate purpose-built annex.

What a farmhouse virtually guarantees is a quiet location, surrounded by fields, woods, and/or water. To find Great Wapses, for example, we started from the West Sussex town of Henfield, took country lanes that seemed increasingly unused, and finally bounced down a very long, deeply rutted track that passed one remote house (Little Wapses), then some distance later, another (Middle Wapses), and finally dead-ended at a mellow old house that is now a country home and hobby farm. Although we were only thirty-five minutes from Gatwick, Great Wapses lay undisturbed among cultivated fields and horse pastures.

Our hostess recommended a pub in Henfield for dinner

that night. We bounced back along the lane, and in twenty minutes, we were sitting before a fire in a half-timbered, slanting-roofed inn, where we ordered fresh poached salmon with hollandaise and finished with raspberry pavlova. When we returned to Great Wapses, we strolled in the fading evening light on its green lawns past iris, primroses, and delphiniums planted around a small tree-shaded pond. This was not the kind of farmhouse living I remembered from growing up in Iowa.

Whether we stay in a farmhouse, cottage, or country-house hotel, James and I use our lodging as a base for daily explorations. We subscribe to the thumbprint school of travel, which commits us to spending at least a week in one spot no larger than my thumbprint will cover on a standard folding road map of England. Within this small space of a ten- or fifteen-mile radius, we take daily excursions, limiting them to a half-hour drive each way, which always seems quite long enough on narrow, winding, and high-hedged roads. In almost every few square miles of England, or at least the parts of it we choose to visit, we find more to see and explore than we can ever manage in our allotted time.

Our daily itinerary usually includes at least one English country house. They seem to abound everywhere—one popular annual tourist guide, *Historic Houses, Castles and Gardens Open to the Public*, currently lists more than 1,300 properties in Great Britain and Ireland—and they are increasingly thrown open to visitors who can help share the spiraling costs of maintaining these works of art. Each country house in England is unique, often added to and adapted over the centuries. The blending of radically different building styles sometimes results in a harmonious whole, sometimes in a startling conglomeration.

After ten years of traveling with an architect, I am now much more sensitive to what is happening in houses. I notice the noble proportions of a staircase, the generous width of an upstairs hall, or the bewitching effect of filtered light from a high stained-glass window. I can sense a change in mood when we walk from the dark crooked rooms of a Tudor wing, paneled in smoke-blackened wood and murkily lit from narrow-paned small windows, into an expansive Georgian dining room, with pastel-painted walls, elegant Classical ornamentation, and tall windows flanked by gilded pier-glass mirrors.

We critically assess each house. "Now, we could live here, I think," says James, musingly, as we pace together the length of a sunny room in, say, Killerton, Dalemain, or Pencarrow, perhaps a sitting room laid with age-softened Oriental carpets and furnished with comfortable-looking brocaded chairs placed near polished tables and desks of inlaid fine woods. "With the right number of servants, of course, and I'd have to put a bell on you so I'd know what part of the house you were in."

Although James views country houses with an architect's eye, I look at them as a romancer. In every house, I try to picture life as it was once lived there. Sometimes I find a few leading facts in guidebooks or on placards. At Blenheim, I was shocked and saddened to realize that Consuelo Vanderbilt was forced into a marriage with the Duke of Marlborough when she was only seventeen—a year younger than my own daughter just then. I imagined my Jennifer weeping as she picked out her trousseau, waiting fearfully for the duke at night in one of these grand drafty bedrooms, pacing these vast halls, staring out the windows at the endless sheets of winter rain.

Yet I wondered whether as a mother I, too, might have been swayed by all this opulence—Blenheim is as mammoth and richly furnished as a palace—and the aura it confers. I hoped not, of course. But I wasn't entirely sure. When the ticket taker at Blenheim's front doors had seen our walking sticks, she had insisted we leave them in the umbrella stand, since their metal tips might damage the flooring. "The duke is around today, and he'd have a fit if he saw them," she explained. The duke is around today! I might see him at any moment! Would he look different from anyone else? Should I keep an eye out for a haughty gray-haired man with aristocratic cheekbones and a monocle? Even when I later saw from his portrait that the middle-aged duke was quite ordinary looking, I gaped unashamedly with the other tourists when, after concluding a BBC televised interview, the duke and his current duchess slipped through the far door of the room we had just entered.

The great country houses provide me with a walk-on set, in which I can imagine myself transformed. What might it be like to awake in the master bedroom at Parnham House, in the super-sized four-poster contemporary bed carved from a single yew, and gaze out the window at the stark rows of fifty topiaries carved like cones that march down the terrace? Would my mind be sharper or clearer after months or years of contemplating those severe abstract shapes?

Would I find more time to read in a library like the one

at Stourhead House or Felbrigg or Blickling or Blenheim? Many of these private libraries seem larger than the Carnegie public library I grew up with; they are ornate rooms that often run the full width of the house, with carved or frescoed ceilings, little bays with fireplaces, satin-covered armchairs, and massive gleaming tables. At Arundel, home of the Duke of Norfolk, the library is a Gothic-style room, one hundred and twenty-two feet long, entirely fitted in carved Honduras mahogany. It resembles a church, with clustered columns supporting a vaulted ceiling, and stately stone chimneypieces like chapels carved into the walls. This room houses a collection of more than ten thousand volumes.

"I'll be in the library until bedtime, dear," I imagine myself saying to James after dinner, first making sure that a servant had lit one of the fireplaces and set a tray of hot chocolate and biscuits on one of the inlaid tables. At Stourhead, I especially admired a Chippendale library staircase, a sort of fancy stepladder on wheels used to reach the uppermost books. What fun, I thought, to sit on top of that high staircase, pushing myself along the rows of books, browsing here and there, and not coming down to the everyday world for hours.

Sometimes the sheer scale of living in these houses defeats my ability to put myself in the picture. I can uneasily see myself immured in a priest's hole, one of those tiny secret spaces behind false walls or tapestries in which Catholics were once hidden for their own safety. But I cannot envision myself in some of the high-ceilinged bedrooms. What kind of nightmares would I have if I woke up in the dead of night under a dark dusty canopy, surrounded by heavy damask curtains, and facing life-size portraits of long-dead grim-faced ancestors?

Although I admire the grand rooms of great houses, I seldom wish I could live in them. How could I make myself cozy in a sitting room filled with Japanese screens, silk-embroidered footstools, carved-back sofas, and tables covered with carefully arranged Ming vases and Fabergé eggs? How would I feel about a nightly bath if I had to climb the portable steps into the enormous mahogany-encased bathtub at Llanhydrock House in Cornwall? Without central heat, the room would cool off very quickly, as would the hand-carried jugs of water. No wonder a sign in front of the tub said that THE LORD PREFERRED HIS SAUCER BATH IN FRONT OF THE FIRE.

But I would certainly have loved walking every day in the gardens and pleasure grounds of these great country houses. Even outdoor life had its accustomed amenities. At Rievaulx Terrace, near Helmsley in Yorkshire, I looked longingly inside a little temple, an eighteenth-century garden "folly," built on a half mile of clipped lawn overlooking the remains of medieval Rievaulx Abbey in the valley below. The colonnaded temple was a viewing point for the picturesque ruins. Inside, a table was still laid with sprigged china for the Feversham family, who had once owned this terrace and used the temple as a picnic spot. In the dark basement below the temple, a National Trust sign told us, the servants would have waited to serve the next course.

Although I enjoy dreaming my way through these stately homes, I seldom want to stay too long in them. Like museums, they demand a kind of intense attention that is very tiring. At the start of a tour my intentions are always commendable. I buy a guidebook at the front door or pick up in each room the informative pamphlet sometimes pasted to a hand-held board like an old-fashioned primer. In National Trust houses, volunteer guides, often elderly gentlefolk, are posted in each room with thick notebooks of even more detailed information on the room's objects, so it is possible to ask, and they will promptly look it up, "And just what is the date of that ebony-and-ivory cabinet?"

Actually, I do not usually want to know the date of an ebony-and-ivory cabinet. With only an amateur's passing interest in antique furniture and minor portraiture, I glaze over quickly in room after room of ancestral mementos, urns, tea services, china settings, and tapestries. Although I can almost always remember each house's distinctive garden, most of the interior furnishings tend to blur together.

If pressed, I would probably describe every large country-house interior as one long great hall filled with gilt mid-eighteenth-century needlework-covered chairs, Italian rococo tables, Dutch chairs of walnut inlaid with turkey bone, English *verre eglomisé* looking glasses with blue-and-gold borders, Venetian red-and-gold rococo armchairs, an important series of continental sixteenth-century tables, Italian tables with tops of various rare marbles, painted satinwood pedestal cupboards, Gobelin tapestries, seventeenth-century Boulle clocks, German green-dyed marquetry cabinets, suits of armor, Russian sleighs, sedan chairs, and stuffed owls. And even these simple identifications are not ones I have committed to memory. I lifted them from a guidebook I brought home from Arundel Castle.

It is instructive for an American used to casual dispersal

of unwanted household goods—we are a nation addicted to estate, tag, and garage sales—to realize how many families in England not only cherish furniture for generations but also know the exact provenance of each piece. England also seems to have a number of highly specialized authorities in decorative arts who tour country houses sharing their arcane knowledge. Anyone who spends any time in one of these houses probably acquires some of this expertise; indeed, it is an evident hobby among country-house aficionados, who collect data on china teapots and oak dowry chests as some Americans collect box scores. This is an impression I gleaned last year, when, by special arrangement, James and I were able to see the interior of Mapperton House.

Mapperton, near Beaminster in Dorset, is a Tudor manor, enlarged in 1660, built of softly glowing rose-tinged Hamstone. Like many of the smaller country houses in England, it is still privately owned, lived in, and loved. The owners of some of these houses generously share both their time and their homes with occasional visitors who write in advance and request an appointment. The few pounds they charge is a very modest contribution to the enormous upkeep of these centuries-old buildings.

We were shown around Mapperton by Mrs. Valerie Dalton, who lived nearby in an estate cottage. A gracious guide, Mrs. Dalton claimed she was not deeply versed in Mapperton's furnishings and history, but she in fact knew the approximate date of the Tudor chest, the characteristic curl of the master carpenter who had carved the staircase, where the Jacobean overmantels had come from (Melbury, not far away, and someone wanted them back), and which chair Charles II had allegedly sat in (though an expert had recently authenticated the chair at fifty years later).

As she pointed out one object after another, Mrs. Dalton kept mentioning various experts who had come and gone at Mapperton, authenticating this or that. This Augustus John drawing was a late one, because someone visiting from the V&A had noticed that the chin of one model was sketchily drawn, with rough strokes. That tapestry, unfortunately falling to pieces, is now thought to be at least one hundred years older than previously assumed, according to a friend of Mrs. Dalton's who restores tapestries and who had been here recently.

An extensive network of experts is obviously needed, and available, to help even a smaller country house like Mapperton maintain its treasures. Mapperton has a prized collection of ship's models. When a ceiling fell in not long ago because of high winds and heavy rain, and as Mrs. Dalton deftly put it, a rare model ship did indeed "go to sea," Mapperton's caretakers knew enough to call the National Maritime Museum. "They said to use a hair dryer, but from a distance," Mrs. Dalton said, a suggestion that proved eminently practical.

Thinking of someone at Mapperton aiming a hair dryer, from a distance, at a damp ship's model, I was struck by the kind of personal hands-on attention (and expense) such houses demand. When we left that day, impressed by Mapperton's well-proportioned but not overwhelming rooms, fine workmanship, and general air of comfortable living, I think both James and I were also a little relieved that we did not have the responsibility for such a place.

When I recently decided we had to fix a partially clogged kitchen faucet in our twelve-year-old Minneapolis house, it took both of us an hour, with mutual discussions, bordering on acerbity, about how to proceed. Though I am glad the water now runs freely (James still feels we could have managed with a halfhearted dribble), it was not an hour we regarded as well spent. Our marriage would be strongly tested in a four-hundred-year-old house with a leaky roof and smoky chimneys.

After our tour of Mapperton, we decided to walk once more through the enchanting 1920s Italianate garden, with its crumbling summerhouses and fish ponds, even though a soaking rain had been falling all day. As James nosed our car down the tree-lined drive, I reflected gratefully on the afternoon. "You know, I would never have seen Mapperton at all if it hadn't been for you," I told James. I say this often during our trips, and James, who enjoys the results of my planning, says it right back. We are usually quite pleased with each other, except when repairing a kitchen faucet.

It is not merely that James is a superb chauffeur, driving cheerfully down roads I cannot quite believe are navigable by anything larger than a dogcart. He is an indefatigable and entertaining travel companion, someone I never imagined I'd find during the eleven years I was living alone with Jennifer after my divorce. When I first met James, I was a little worried about the fifteen-year gap in our ages. "Don't do it, Susan," a well-meaning friend advised me, before our marriage in 1985, "or you'll end up pushing a wheelchair." What I've ended up doing is panting along in James's high-speed tracks, trying to keep up with his energy and enthusiasm.

When I think happily about my last eight years of travel in England, I think about James as well. He has opened doors—or, more usually, gates—to many paths that have led us ever deeper into the English countryside. "I've spent lots of time in England already," James told me doubtfully, when I proposed our first trip there in 1984. "I don't know whether there's much more I really want to see." Fortunately, our excursions have proved to be as revealing for him as they have been for me. He never tires of medieval churches, country houses, or footpaths, and he now complains if a day passes when we don't stop at an English garden.

During the months before our trips, I immerse myself in maps, travel material, guides, and books that range from *English Topiary Gardens* to *The National Trust Handbook* to *Holy Waters: Ancient Wells in Britain.* I am a compulsive planner, a traveler who enjoys making up an itinerary almost as much as taking the journey itself. James plans for our trips only by casually packing his bag two hours before the plane leaves. So when I suggest that we try to find the last bit of virgin heath in Hardy country, or the healing well at Patrishaw Church in the Welsh hills, or the oldest clapper bridge on Dartmoor, he almost always says, "Sounds great! Let's go!"

Without James to encourage and support me—and to drive there, while I call out, "Think *left!*"—I never would have discovered the Yorkshire village of Lastingham, where one early evening as we walked back from the moor that began just outside our door, we saw a ewe and her lamb ambling peaceably down the main street.

I would not have bought tickets to a Coffee Morning in Aid of the Royal Lifeboat Association held on the back lawn of a house in St. Merryan, Cornwall, where we joined perhaps twenty local residents in coffee, cookies, and polite conversation, followed by a jumble sale in one of the upstairs rooms.

James has taken me to the Cotswold Farm Park, a zoolike set of enclosures high on a green hill, where rare breeds of sheep, cattle, and other farm animals graze undisturbed in their pastures as if they did not know that they belong to disappearing species. We have spent a morning dazzled by beating white wings at the Abbotsbury Swannery in Dorset, where we could see nesting mute swans and their goslings in marshy reed beds, an ancient colony first cultivated here by medieval monks.

High in the fells of the Lake Country, James and I have wandered among the fog-shrouded monoliths of the Castlerigg Stone Circle, where a nearby farmer's cows graze among the mysterious markers. We have climbed Pilsdon Pen in the early morning, a Dorset Iron Age earthwork still used for occasional ceremonies by a local white witch. There, straining in vain to see through a faint rain the view that is supposed to extend all the way to the English Channel, we finally decided that we were just as impressed by the haunting atmosphere of the rainy mist.

Although James wanted to get on the road again, he has patiently stood with me in a small crowd in the grounds of Sudeley Castle in Gloucestershire, where I wanted to watch Sid, a falcon, perform for his trainer. Once loosed, Sid rose high in ever-widening circles but then swiftly landed in a nearby thicket, where he staunchly refused all the trainer's pleas to emerge. Eventually the crowd dispersed. I do not know what happened to Sid.

James also has taken me without complaint to Compton House in Dorset, home of Worldwide Butterflies and Lullingstone Silk Farm, so I could see how silk, a fabric I favor, is actually made. We looked at lots of butterflies, moths, and silkworms behind glass cases and then walked through a wire-mesh cage in a hot humid room so we could experience tropical butterflies in their native habitat. When we left, James said placidly but firmly, "Now I don't think we'll ever need to do that again."

When I wanted to make a return pilgrimage to out-of-the-way St. Beuno's at Culbone, James not only agreed but pushed me until we did it. That Sunday afternoon, as we hiked our way to vespers, the sun shone so hotly that biting flies clustered around his head, which has a certain distinguished bareness. I insisted on tying my silk neckscarf behind his ears, babushka style, and although he prides himself on a dashing appearance, he did not even flinch or attempt to explain his gypsy headdress when we met two other walkers on their way to services.

At Lydford Gorge, a dramatic chasm in Devon that runs for a mile and a half in a deep ravine scooped by the River Lyd into a series of potholes, James encouraged me to hold tight to a thin rope railing and edge my way above the Devil's Cauldron, a tumultuous boiling mass of white water so dangerous that several reputed ghosts haunt its slippery ledges. I am proud of the picture he took of me, poised and smiling above chaos. No one can see my quivering knees.

When I did not think I had enough stamina one weary afternoon to climb to St. Michael Brentor, a church perched precipitously high on a Dartmoor tor, James handed me my walking stick and promised we could turn around at any time before we reached the top. We kept going, and the view over miles of moors was worth every slow step.

At Betwys-y-Coed, a Welsh village where we drove for my birthday lunch one June, I was dispirited by the heavy crush of tourists in the shops and streets. I had wanted to go somewhere special on this day, but the town was not it. James took the lead, almost dragging me along, and found a sign for a footpath leading straight up a hill from the main street. Although, not in a hopeful mood, I told him the path probably didn't lead anywhere in particular, I followed dutifully. We kept going up, through tangled shrubbery, then broken woods, and finally from the top of the hill into a wild forested back country unimaginable from the road below. After an hour's climb we arrived on the shores of a small pristine lake, shining in the sun.

Although we love good food, James and I both care just as much about where we eat it as what it is. So I remember not only restaurants but picnic spots, like the shaded cowpath leading from Llanthony Abbey in Wales along a rapidly moving brook. We sat on large flat stones by the side of the brook and listened to the music of the water as we ate our lunch. At Chawton, Jane Austen's last home, we picnicked as neatly as possible in her small old-fashioned garden, filled with the kinds of flowers she would have known, primroses, daisies, and larkspur, and we tried to picture the author, whose novels we both cherish, walking across an adjoining field on her way home from a charitable visit.

Although I have never kept daily journals at home for

more than a week or two in my whole life, I do make brief notes when we travel. Too much happens each day and I'm afraid I won't remember it all. If I had not jotted it down, I might not so easily recall another picnic, this one in London, that perhaps explains why I have so loved my travels with James. My old friend Faithe, still living in London, and I had left James that morning so he could run in Hyde Park while we searched for finds at Camden Passage Market. James loathes shopping. We promised to be home by eleven-thirty A.M. so we could all three eat at a highly recommended French restaurant in nearby Beauchamp Place.

After a long and expensive taxi ride, Faithe and I arrived at Camden Passage only to find all the shops shut tight for *closing day*. So we decided to tube to Portobello Road. But we were gossiping so furiously—we had not seen each other for a year—that we didn't pay enough attention when we changed at King's Cross, took the wrong line, and ended up, to our astonishment, aboveground at Royal Oaks. When we finally backtracked on the Tube again to Portobello (it was now close to noon), I was determined not to leave empty-handed. Discovering a little shop that sold antique clothing at very reasonable prices, I acquired several old linen-sheeting nightgowns and, for James, a somewhat frayed, stained, but genuine polka-dot silk Sulka bathrobe. I decided to forget that James, who does not share my passion for bargains, also does not much like clothing that bears obvious signs of former owners.

When Faithe and I finally raced into the hotel room where James was waiting, it was past two o'clock. The French restaurant was closed. James had not yet eaten. He did not look happy, but he waited for my story. I hurriedly explained what had happened and then triumphantly showed James his new (old) silk bathrobe. I insisted he slip it on over his turtleneck and jeans. "Well," he said, gingerly sliding his arms into the sleeves, "I suppose you can probably get those stains out." Then he took it off quite quickly, laid it on the bed, turned to us, and grinned. "Okay, ladies," he said, "I don't know about you, but I'm starving. We'll stop at that deli down the street and load up on some cold meats, rolls, and salads and have a picnic in Hyde Park. I saw the perfect spot by the Serpentine when I was running this morning. Quit fussing about being late, Susan. Come on, let's head out!"

And so we did.

You Can Go
Back Again

*E*ven the staid *Times*, which usually avoids strident headlines, seems worried these days. CRIMINALS DAMAGE GROWING NUMBER OF CHURCHES drew my attention last summer to an alarming statistic: as many as half of Britain's sixteen thousand Anglican churches could suffer arson, vandalism, or theft this year. "An Anglican church is attacked every four hours, according to the Ecclesiastical Insurance Group, which insures ninety-five per cent of them," the *Times* glumly reported. The story described thieves who strike the country's rural churches and seize brass crosses and candlesticks, empty offertory boxes, and even remove stained-glass windows. These isolated and often empty churches, left open for passing tourists and visitors, are easy targets.

LONDON'S BURNING FOR DECISIVE ACTION—NOW! URGENT: DELIVER US A SOLUTION TO THE CAPITAL'S CRISIS, demanded the *Sunday Times* a few days later. For anyone unaware of London's dire plight, the *Times* laid out a bleak scenario: dirty streets, immobilized traffic, a public transportation system close to collapse, outrageous housing costs, failing schools, rising crime rates. "Dirt, crime, squalor, expense—Londoners grin and bear it, as there's nobody in charge to complain to," said the *Times*, and proceeded to complain at length.

It all sounded depressingly like the ritualized hand wringing I glimpse from a Midwestern distance in my weekly copies of *New York* magazine. After I had fallen in love with London, I used to compare the two cities with a certain sense of smugness. "I'd be afraid to go to New York by myself," I told friends, when, as a single woman, I planned my vacations in London. Besides extolling London's art, architecture, theatre, and historical associations, I authoritatively assured everyone that it was cleaner, cheaper, and much safer than New York. Now the *Times* and *New York* mournfully carol together: Can This City Be Saved?

Even the Underground, once a symbol to me of London's civility, has lost its crisp confidence. The chairman of London Transport, the *Sunday Times* reported, recently declared that "the Tube was suffering from thirty years of neglect and it was 'a daily miracle' that it ran at all." Last spring, a friend of mine, once a London maven, announced, "No more. A former student of mine who's lived there for ten years got mugged on the Underground last month. In daylight. With her boyfriend. They knocked her down and grabbed her bag. She wrote me all about it. This summer I'm going to visit my sister in Duluth."

Not long ago, James and I followed a sketch map in a walkers' guide to a grassy parking area from which we could hike to the Golden Cap, a high bluff on the Dorset coast. When we pulled into the secluded clearing, which had room for only a few cars, no one was there—but we did see a prominent sign: WARNING! CAR THIEVES OPERATE IN THIS AREA! LOCK YOUR CAR AND TAKE YOUR VALUABLES WITH YOU!

Yes, I nod when people ask me, in thirty years England has indeed changed. Most informed Anglophiles know something about socialism, the Labour Party, the National Health, Margaret Thatcher, the Docklands, and the resurgence of the City. I notice other changes. When my college friend Joyce and I hitchhiked together, we ambled along major roads that seemed almost deserted, listening for the rare passing car as if it were a weekly stagecoach about to rumble by. Now James and I resign ourselves to halting progress in stop-and-go lines on the A35 along the Devon coast; we add an extra half hour of driving time if we need to weave through the streets of any town larger than a village; we know we may sit for a fume-filled hour or more during frequent tie-ups on the M25 circling London.

On my first trip to England, I packed every possible convenience I might need for the summer, including three tubes of toothpaste. "You'll certainly find something in the stores to brush your teeth with," my stepfather mildly noted. But I wasn't sure. In 1960, England was still recovering from the war, and although I didn't take any packages of nylon stockings or ballpoint pens to give away to the natives, I confess I thought about it. Now I can find almost any consumer item on an English shelf—or in a market stall. A few years ago, James bought a pair of Nikes from the weekly market in Tintagel, the legendary stronghold of King Arthur and now an outpost for four brands of athletic shoes in three colors.

The Nikes weren't a bargain, but James needed them.

Otherwise we would have waited until we returned home. England used to be cheap. Even a penny-pinching single-parent college teacher like myself could once afford to travel there, staying for a few dollars in bed-and-breakfast houses and spending less than the price of an American movie for a good seat in a London theatre. When the dollar was higher and the English standard of living was lower, I returned to America with cashmere sweaters, wool tweeds, stacks of books from Foyle's, china vases and bowls, handwoven aprons, padded tea cozies, and irresistible oddments—silver-plated fish knives, heavy cotton nightgowns, sequined Indian cushion covers—from antique markets. At an antique stall I visited in Covent Garden last fall, I saw a rather attractive china commemorative plate for fifteen pounds (twenty-seven dollars), almost exactly like one in my favorite odds-and-ends store in Stockholm, Wisconsin. But Lucy at Stockholm Antiques sells her china plate for twelve dollars.

In 1960, I was awed by some of the bomb craters still left in London from the war. "American, are you?" Englishmen and women asked then, glad to show their friendliness. Americans were allies. Now the war is a distant memory, and the English have seen too many American tourists. America is no longer even very foreign. "I've been to Chicago," they say, or "We went to California last year, then Salt Lake City, of course the Grand Canyon. And a rodeo at Cheyenne; have you ever seen a rodeo?"

When I was twenty, I thought I knew England. It was a tradition-bound, quiet country, where the lord still lived in the manor and the villager in a thatched cottage. The villages themselves had little shops as predictable as their names: A. Jones, Butcher; J. Collingworth, Baker; Chemist, Ironmonger, Tea Shoppe. Although I myself did not attend Sunday services in the local Anglican church, I assumed that everyone in the village did. Nothing had changed much, I thought then, from Dickens's day, perhaps even from Samuel Johnson's.

Now when James and I vacation in England, we usually look for a supermarket where we can shop quickly and thoroughly for a week's housekeeping. Last summer, staying near East Grinstead, I inquired about a fishmonger, but before we could find his shop, James pounced upon some reasonably priced fresh cod in the Safeway. I didn't bother to inquire further. Even in a sleepy North Devon village, I can find a natural-foods store with several brands of soy milk and herbal teas. The beachfront café at Brighton advertises burgers, hot dogs, and "do-nuts."

Other cultures have left their mark on England as well. Driving through the main street of Chard, a venerable market town in Devon, I recently caught a glimpse of a converted shop—once, perhaps, a *shoppe*—that now housed the Chard Sufi Centre. It probably has more adherents than the local church.

The landscape is not as pristine as it once was. Many English men and women believe, in fact, that it has been devastated. Caravan parks sprawl along many scenic stretches of seacoast, ugly new housing encircles many venerable villages, and high-speed highways cut through otherwise pastoral countryside. Standing on a hilltop at Killerton in Devon, in the midst of its landscaped park, I was startled last July to hear a muffled roar. Although I could not see it through the trees, I quickly realized that

I was close to the M5, which was carrying a ceaseless flow of traffic to Exeter.

What once seemed removed has moved closer to urban centers. On a recent trip to Exmoor, where James and I have often returned for the pleasure of long walks on the bracken-covered moors, I found I needed to rush a copy-edited manuscript to New York. With one phone call to Exeter, I located an express delivery service. Undaunted by my obscure location, the expediter had no trouble setting up a pickup four hours later at a designated gas station a few miles from our tiny village of Lynmouth.

But despite its changes, England has not yet been hopelessly Americanized. Houses have not sprouted helter-skelter, billboards do not clutter the approaches to towns, and malls have not yet emptied most main streets. Developers have been surprisingly ingenious. One recent afternoon in the Kent countryside, James and I followed an English Heritage signpost down an almost hidden lane to Bayham Abbey. I had never heard of this monument, and I assumed it was perhaps the tracing of a foundation in a field.

Bayham Abbey turned out to be a magnificent ruin, giant fragments of stone buildings rising over startlingly manicured green lawns. Three towering arches, still intact, framed a stunning perspective of bright blue sky. No one else had evidently been tempted to explore the abbey on this sunny weekday, so James and I walked in companionable silence down its grassy aisles and over its tumbled walls. At the end of the cathedral, whose shape was still discernible, a huge tree sprang out of the cracked high altar, its roots clinging to the stone while its branches reached toward the vanished vaulted ceiling.

Overlooking this ruin, high above a valley now given over to pasture, was a sprawling country house, with several wings, stories, and towers. It looked as if it were part of a movie set, ready for women in Edwardian gowns to sweep across the front lawn, greeting guests in full evening dress. I could picture its ballroom and servants' quarters, state dining room and endless bedrooms, its innumerable windows opening onto miles of corridors.

As we stood among the ruins of Bayham Abbey, the scene seemed so removed from the real world—the twisting lane that had led us here, the massive stone arches of the fallen church, the ivy-covered blocks of stone, even the impeccable lawns—that I wondered what storybook aristocrat lived in the great house. So as we left I paused at the ticket taker's office and inquired.

"Oh, it used to belong to the Earl of Something-or-Other," she said, "but it was sold three years ago and now it's been converted into flats."

"Flats?" I asked incredulously. The very word seemed incongruous. Nor could I quite envision who would choose to live in a flat in such a remote section of countryside. It seemed unimaginably far to commute to London, or indeed, to anywhere. "How many flats?" I asked.

"Twenty. Twenty-five. I'm not sure," she said.

I glanced back at the house, its ample proportions, its spreading wings. Still, twenty-five flats? Was it subdivided into bed-sitters? Was it now filled with loos in jerry-built cabinets and indoor-outdoor carpeting? I strained my nearsighted eyes, peering into the distance, trying to catch telltale signs of twenty-five flats. The house, gazing over the green valley, looked unperturbed.

Of course, even on my first visit in 1960, I knew that

historic stately homes, burdened by maintenance costs and inheritance taxes, were rapidly disappearing. I read about the Duke of Bedford's transformation of Woburn Abbey into a combination of museum, playground, theme park, and zoo, and I rather admired the duke's enterprising spirit. Nor have I been alarmed in succeeding years at the many great houses that have been remodeled into hotels, since our stays at several of them have given us a rare chance to sample something of the country gentleman's ambience.

I also know that village life has changed. When we drive past immaculate village greens surrounded by thatched-roof cottages, I am aware that the butcher, the baker, and the candlestick maker probably no longer live there. They have retired, sold up—at a tidy price, I would imagine—and moved away. Many of those cottages are now week-end retreats for London stockbrokers. Some are rental holiday homes, and here, too, James and I have gratefully taken advantage of new opportunities. Much that might otherwise have fallen into ruin or disrepair has been rescued by such transformations, and while I understand those who are saddened by this process, I am glad that the cottage roofs are freshly thatched, that those great houses still stand, and that someone—even twenty-five someones—still uses them.

Perhaps the reason I am not unduly depressed by most of the changes in England during the past thirty years is that my England, the countryside I love, is still there. I can still seek out its gardens, walk its seacoast, and retreat to its medieval churches. For me, England remains a refuge. Although James and I may encounter other walkers when, for example, we stroll along the Dorset Coast Path at the height of the summer season, we can always find paths where we will be alone.

Last July, on a sunny Sunday, returning from a rather crowded shingle beach a short distance from Brighton, we stopped to see a manor house that was scheduled to open at two P.M. But it was now only one o'clock. What should we do for the next hour? James reminded me of a shady parking area we'd passed five minutes before, signposted as a forest reserve.

"Didn't you see the cars in the parking lot?" I asked him doubtfully. "It looked like everyone from Lewes and Brighton had brought their kids and a picnic lunch."

But since I had no better idea to offer, we agreed to return and, if necessary, simply observe English families doing what American families do on a Sunday picnic: eat, talk, laugh, fuss, argue, throw balls or Frisbees, push strollers, pour more coffee, take a little walk, and pack up to go home.

The parking area for Friston Forest *was* crowded. Many families *were* sitting at picnic tables. Others reclined in the folding lawn chairs that seem to appear, ready for tea and a doze in the sun, from every English car trunk. I could see a sign, WOODLAND WALK, with an arrow pointing to what looked like a scrubby woods behind the picnic area. Sighing, I picked up my walking stick and headed for the marked path, prepared for a a fifteen-minute loop crowded with holidaymakers.

But the path did not loop. In a few minutes, we had left behind all sight and sound of the picnic area. We passed one cluster of children who were playing on the path and then no one. The wide path opened onto several narrower paths, but we steered forward. I glanced at my watch: fifteen minutes, then twenty. No sign yet of circling back to the parking lot. Eventually we emerged onto a wider path that ran along the edge of the woods and led, far in the distance, into another, even larger forest on the next hill.

But we had to turn around. As we retraced our steps, with the forest on our left and sheep-covered hills on our right, it would have been hard to argue that the English countryside was seriously overcrowded.

Probably the England I love is not overrun because the places James and I seek out do not attract crowds. We know enough not to try to ogle the Crown Jewels at the Tower of London, file through Canterbury Cathedral, or pass the day in Stratford-on-Avon. But even in the most visited areas of England, we often manage to find green havens of solitude. Last summer, staying two weeks just outside London, in an area close to the outstanding gardens of Kent and Sussex, we always expected a certain number of fellow garden visitors. No one can realistically hope to wander alone through the White Garden at Sissinghurst in July.

But not every garden has been discovered by tour buses. At the end of one long, meandering afternoon, we turned on a whim as we passed through the village of Lamberhurst to follow a sign that led to the Owl House Gardens. Checking my *Good Gardens Guide*, I discovered that the editors were a bit sniffy about Owl House: "not a visit for the avid plantsman," they warned, "but a pleasant place for a family walk along the woodland paths." The guide did not even give the gardens a starred rating.

Having just been properly impressed by a long visit to nearby Scotney Castle Garden (one star), lavishly set around a picturesque ruin, and the day before, glorious Sissinghurst (two stars), I might ordinarily have asked James to drive on. It was four-thirty, and time to think about a bath and dinner. But I liked the quirky sound of Owl House. And who could resist a garden located at Mount Pleasant, Lamberhurst? It was owned by Maureen, the Marchioness of Dufferin and Ava. This melodious title evoked a whimsical, King of Ruritania, Gilbert-and-Sullivan atmosphere. So we entered a long orchard-lined drive that led to the Owl House Gardens.

Tired as I was, I barely registered the medieval house, the oldest in Kent (said the guide), with the crookedest chimney. By this time of day, I had exceeded my quaintness quotient. But I did quickly notice that the grass-covered parking lot was deserted: not a single car besides ours. Consulting a brochure we'd bought at the gate from the tenant who had come out to greet us, we set out to follow its map.

Good Gardens was right: this was not a plantsman's paradise, and none of the rhododendron or azaleas were still in bloom. But what Owls House had in abundance was an unassuming charm. It radiated a sense of leisure. With no one in sight, we had the parklike garden to ourselves, and we could explore it at our own pace, unruffled by the murmurs or rustlings of passing visitors.

I was also relieved that I felt no need to *do* this garden. Before visiting Sissinghurst, I had read two books about it and several sections of memoirs involving its creator, Vita Sackville-West. Once there, I was naggingly aware of how

I should properly register design, perspectives, color harmonies, textures, and seasonal variations. Even at Scotney Castle, impressively labeled by the National Trust Guide as "one of England's most romantic garden landscapes," I had known I needed to pay attention. But here I could simply float.

At first I thought that the Owl House Gardens ended below the house. But then James pointed to two parallel lines on the map, indicating a path leading at right angles from the lawn, and passing an area enticingly labeled Bluebell Woods. It ended at Wisteria Temple. Suddenly I was no longer tired. Setting an easy rhythm with our walking sticks, we strolled down the wide path, Versailles Avenue. Despite its name, it was neither formal nor daunting, but merely a pleasant, darkly shaded, dampish lane. It was, in fact, just the sort of lane that made me think of Jane Austen and pony carts.

At Owl House, it was easy to picture carefree outings. Touches of innocent pretension merely emphasized the unassuming, domestic, and happily untidy nature of the garden. The Wisteria Temple—like Versailles Avenue, somewhat wistfully overnamed—was a battered and lopsided pergola standing in a clearing next to a sheep-filled pasture. The daisy-studded grass looked just right for a picnic—perhaps, since the house had long since vanished from view, even a little dalliance.

Since the garden closed at six, however, we did not dally. Returning on Versailles Avenue, we turned down Owl Walk—this name, like Bluebell Woods, was a modest triumph—and wound around three ponds: Maureen's Water Garden, Moomina's Water Garden, and Kling

Kling's Pond. I remembered Kling Kling. Behind Owl House, marked solemnly on the map as Dogs' Graves, were four memorial stones. Maureen, Marchioness of Dufferin and Ava, had loved Pekinese, and the inscriptions on the stones recalled each one. Kling Kling, "Heavenly Pekinese," recently departed, was the pet about whom an amusing sign at the entrance still cautioned drivers: BE-WARE! HEAVENLY PEKINESE WITH SUICIDAL TENDENCIES!

We lingered around the ponds, crossing and then re-crossing several picturesque bridges, listening to a tiny waterfall, admiring the tall primulas and a few iris. The flowers seemed to have grown almost by accident, coexisting quite contentedly with weeds and undergrowth. Nothing seemed out of place, yet nothing seemed planned. I understood the comment approvingly recorded in the Owl House brochure: "Indeed, recently one elderly garden visitor was heard to say 'When one of my grandchildren is in some kind of a mess I always say, go and visit the Owl House Gardens, for their extreme beauty and peace have great healing qualities.' "

It would be easy for a skeptic, I thought, to think of a mess not readily solved by a garden visit. Yet I was not in the mood to scoff, for beauty and peace do have healing qualities. I had felt their presence the day before in St. Mary's Church at Goudhurst, not far from Sissinghurst. This was also the day I had clipped the *Times* article about rising vandalism in rural churches. But the door to Goud-hurst Church, a lovely, light, and spacious building, was open.

While James wandered up and down the aisles, absorb-ing the architecture, I began studying monuments on the walls. Toward the end of a trip to England, I find myself unable to give full or fresh appreciation to yet another barrel vault, Tudor rood screen, or Norman font. Instead I look for stories.

In Goudhurst Church, I read about families. Certain names recurred, centuries apart. I learned about a son lost at sea, a baby daughter dead within a year, a rector who had faithfully served the church until his death at ninety-one. I stopped in front of a grandiose seventeenth-century stone tomb, complete with figures carved in relief, free-standing effigies within their own pillared space, and sur-mounted by elaborate heraldry. Not far from it, in an ornate classical niche, a marble bust crowned with a wig of tumbling stone curls celebrated an eighteenth-century parishioner.

The simplest monument provoked my strongest curios-ity. On a bare wall hung a plain stone plaque, adorned only by an inscription: "In loving memory of Mary Louisa Hinds, Mary Hinds, Jessie Maria Hinds, Sarah Alice Hinds, Lydia Croft and Arthur Hinds, Children of George and Sarah Ann Hinds, of Beechhurst, Goudhurst. For many years they gave faithful service to this church. Also of Edith Lee, youngest daughter of George and Sarah Hinds." Hinds was a name I'd seen elsewhere in the church. I wondered what kind of house Beechhurst might be; I liked its sound.

More important, what about Mary Louisa, Mary, Jessie, Sarah, and Edith? How long ago had they lived? When had each died? Of what? Had none of them ever married? Why not? And why was Edith, the youngest, added as an afterthought? Had she perhaps arranged for the plaque and tactfully left her own name till last? When James touched my shoulder, I was still inventing histories for the devoted Hinds ladies, for their brother (who must have also never left Goudhurst), and for their family home.

As we left the Goudhurst churchyard, which bordered on the A262 but also opened on its other side to a tranquil view of Kent's green tree-covered hills, I felt for a few moments a luminous sense of connection. It sometimes surprises me, that awareness of my own brief place in a long progression. But it is one of the reasons England draws me back.

Every time I return, I readjust my sense of scale. At home, I am used to looking at what Americans like to call "the big picture." We are a land of extravagance, sweeping gestures, and vast spaces. Coming from a state which once advertised itself as the Land of 10,000 Lakes, I have to remind myself in England to think small.

It is not just that the scale of English landscape is different. Any visitor quickly sees that the countryside is divided, subdivided, and divided again by hedgerows, paths, lanes, and odd-shaped fields. Although many farms have been subsumed in recent years into larger operations, much of the land is still a patchwork of small squares, each with its own terrain, trees, shrubs, and wildflowers. Ancient monuments, bits of fallen wall, hidden streams, and remnants of old forests turn each square into an individual story written in fine print.

I also notice the smaller aspects of English life, its customs, idiosyncrasies, and peculiarities. Take cat hotels, for instance. On my last trip to England, I suddenly became aware of the surprising number of signs for cat boarding, often posted on country lanes in front of handsome houses.

At home, we call such institutions "kennels," a designation that definitely lacks the allure of an establishment I glimpsed on a back road in Dorset: THE FIRS: CAT HOTEL. I especially liked the even grander name I spotted on a leafy estate in Kent: CATS HOLIDAY HOME.

The English love their pets, and a careful observer can spot many signs of the attention paid to small creatures. Driving one afternoon through Dorset's Marshwood Vale a few years ago, James and I stopped to admire Marshwood's medieval church. A hand-lettered notice on the door promised: BLESSING OF THE ANIMALS. BRING YOUR PETS TO MARSHWOOD CHURCH ON SUNDAY AT 4 P.M. I envisioned a parade not only of dogs and cats but of turtles, goldfish, hamsters, gerbils, parakeets, perhaps even a garter snake. What would be more at home in a medieval Christian church than a tame snake?

"What's a beetle drive?" I startled James by asking on another afternoon as we passed through the Dorset village of Evershot. "We just drove by a sign for one in the window of the village store. Can you turn around or back up?"

I probably already had a slight case of beetles on the brain. The day before, we'd visited Cadhay Manor near Ottery St. Mary. The elderly lady who guided us clearly loved the old house, with its polyglot architecture and dusty collections of guns and china. On a bedroom dressing table, she proudly showed us a large black beetle preserved in fossilized amber. "It's considered quite lucky, you know," she said, "to have an amber beetle." I thought for a while about that beetle. I wondered who had found it, why it was lucky, and who would really want a preserved beetle on her dressing table. I made a cryptic note in my diary that day: "Small things. Beetles."

What Evershot was promoting was not, of course, a beetle drive that involved massed villagers driving a terrified swarm of insects down the main drag and out of town. Nor was it a charity event to support the preservation of some rare English insect in danger of extinction. Nor was *beetle drive* part of the vernacular I simply didn't recognize, as *jumble sale* is English for *rummage*. What Evershot was advertising was something that sounded much more ominous than any of my fantasies: *Fete in Aid of Eradicating the Deathwatch Beetle.*

"What is a deathwatch beetle?" James asked me. I had a vague idea, I told him, that it was a plague that infested rotting old wood, something like termites, a particular menace to medieval churches, probably any very old house, and indeed any very old building, which would include most buildings in England.

"But why do you suppose they call it a deathwatch beetle?" I went on. "I don't like the sound of it. It makes me think of the Dedlocks in *Bleak House*, who could hear on cold rainy nights the footsteps of an ancestor pacing in the stone courtyard. A sign of impending doom. Remember? Just before Lady Dedlock fled and died in disgrace in that plague-ridden burial ground?"

I was much more comfortable contemplating the Mouse House at Dalemain. As we followed our guidebook through this rambling country house in the Lake District, we looked dutifully at its architecture. We watched as instructed for visible signs of the original structure, which was supposed to be a twelfth-century fortified pele-tower.

We hurried through the dark Tudor section and lingered in the light and gilt-edged Georgian rooms. In terms of scale, this was a very large house.

But what I remember most about Dalemain was the smallest structure I have ever seen in England. The guidebook warned us to keep our eyes near our feet as we descended the back stairs, past what was once the night nursery. There, carved out of the dark space between two stair treads, was a tiny electric-lit room, glassed in front and furnished like a dollhouse. It held a two-inch hand-sewn Mrs. Mouse.

Of course I have seen dollhouses, of many kinds in many places. Queen Mary's elaborate dollhouse at Windsor Castle is one of England's favorite tourist attractions. But I never would have had the imagination to think of creating one between two stairsteps. The quirkiness of the Mouse House, and its mouse-sized gray-felt occupants, seemed to me peculiarly English.

Whenever I return to England, I find myself noticing things I might not see at home, if indeed they exist there. From abbey ruins to a Mouse House, they form the various strands—sometimes slight and indescribable—that have slowly turned into a strong and tightly woven bond between England and me. "Why do you go back to England so often?" Jenny once asked. Even now, after almost finishing a book to answer her question, I am not sure I have told her why.

Perhaps I could answer her best if I could show her the images that crowd into my mind. When I think of England, I might see the Salthouse beach in Norfolk on a windy fall afternoon. A long line of muffled bird-watchers in heavy jackets sit almost motionless in a row, looking through their binoculars out to sea. The sky is gray and the waves whip about fiercely, but behind the high pebble bank, in a hummocky field protected from the wind, dozens of rabbits frolic atop a large warren. The field is surrounded by marshland, where more ducks than I can count float lazily among the reeds. As I scan the horizon, astonishingly flat for miles, it easily swallows all of us—the ducks, the rabbits, the bird-watchers, James, our friend Leonard, and me.

Impressively anachronistic in his ankle-length black cassock, the friendly young rector at Heckington in Lincolnshire shows off his church, built from 1307 to 1335. "Historians of church architecture come from all over Europe to study this church, because it's all of a piece," he says proudly. He makes sure we see all the church's treasures, including its carved stone gargoyles and fantastic ornaments. One shows a fourteenth-century marital spat: the husband pulls his wife's tongue, she yanks his beard, and a priest in the middle vainly tries to make peace. "Wonderful, isn't it? Just wonderful!" says the rector, and laughing, we agree. The rector, who used to be a music teacher, asks if we'd like to hear the church's fine pipe organ. Before rising to greet the next visitors, he sits down at the manual and plays a triumphant passage of Handel.

James and I clamber all the way to the top of Tumpa, a high hill in the Brecon Beacons, and then look down on a farming valley that seems like a faraway world of its own. Although a mist blows in wisps over the hilltop, the green fields below, turned into a jigsaw puzzle by meandering hedgerows and patches of woods, flicker in and out of sunlight.

Three old men stand at the side of a path in Deepdale,

a cleft between fells near Ullswater in the Lake District. Weather-beaten, dressed in worn dark green oilskins and wool caps, they are leaning so intently on their walking sticks that they do not notice James and me until we are just behind them. When we ask what they are looking at, they point to the opposite fell, where a fox hunt is taking place. The followers do not ride but have to run on foot after the hounds, moving black specks against the grayish green of the mountain. The fox has gone to ground in some rocks. The black specks cluster and roil around the rocks. "Oh aye, they'll never it get now," says one man, and I think he sounds glad.

Opening a door in Hammerwood Park, an almost derelict eighteenth-century mansion now being slowly restored, we almost stumble in surprise upon a room filled with whirling dancers. Turning, promenading, and bowing, they execute elaborate figures called out by a man in a white curled wig and blue satin waistcoat. Everyone is in period costume, the women in upswept hairdos and ankle-length Empire dresses, some with seed-pearl beading, hand-sewn tucks, and graceful sashes. One is a girl in her early twenties, another a white-haired woman probably seventy. The dancers all smile at one another as they do their turns. For the last number, they turn to the mesmerized onlookers and reach out for partners. Ducking toward the door, I look back to see a middle-aged foreign-looking man, definitely needing a shave, bulging out of baggy blue-striped pants and suspenders, brow furrowed as he concentrates on following the delicate steps of the dance.

After doing my marketing in Lynton, a village on the North Devon coast, I decide to wander for a while. On an impulse, I stop at the Exmoor Museum, whose signboard hangs over a somewhat dilapidated cottage. Its few rooms are jammed with dusty artifacts. Nothing seems to be sorted or in any particular order. I pass quickly by old photographs and stuffed birds, but I stop, bemused, in front of a glass jar of gooseberries, with a yellowed card dating it at 1915.

In Sidmouth, on the Devon coast, James and I are taking a walk before breakfast along the deserted Esplanade. A heavy fog hangs over the sea, blanketing the forbidding limestone cliffs. It is so chilly this early June morning that I shiver inside my wool sweater. Suddenly an old man, bent and white-haired, emerges from one of the steep wooden staircases that lead down to the beach. Wrapped in a terry-cloth robe, he carries a black wet suit over his arm and scurries across the road into a hotel.

Another fog, this one a thick white cloud, shifting, dispersing, and coalescing again, covers the tidal flats just outside Padstow, Cornwall. It is quite hot on this June morning. From my cliffside path, the sands look so inviting I scramble downward, take off my shoes, roll up my jeans, and wade into the gently swirling currents. The water around my ankles is cold but not unpleasant. As I move through the white curtain, I can only see a few feet at a time. I have disappeared into a muffled world of lapping water, flitting seabirds, and cool brown sand between my toes.

On a daylong trip from the North Norfolk coast to the Lake District, James and I wearily leave the M1 to look for a place to eat our picnic lunch. We drive a short way into Clumber Park, a large National Trust reserve of perhaps

3,500 acres. Pulling off the main road, an imposing avenue of double-planted lime trees, we park on some open ground under shady trees. No other cars appear, and we congratulate ourselves on having found such a remote and undisturbed spot.

As I am munching my sandwich, a voice suddenly says, "Excuse me." James and I both start. Outside our car window is a young man on a bicycle. He has appeared silently from nowhere. "Excuse me," he says again, "may I see your ticket?" He is from the National Trust. He checks our membership card, thanks us, and pedals away.

We have arrived too early at London's Museum of Garden History, so we head to the nearby Thames. It is a clear, cool, sunny November morning, and the great buildings of the city are sharply outlined against the sky. They are so familiar that as we stroll along I barely register them: the Tate, Big Ben, the Houses of Parliament. A few working barges are cautiously making their way up and down the working river. I study its muddy swirls. Upriver, Chelsea, Kew, and Hampton Court, I think; downriver, Greenwich, Gravesend, and the open sea. The names release their own flood of images: George Eliot's house in Cheyne Walk, Pope's couplet on His Highness's Dog at Kew, Anne Boleyn threading the political maze of Hampton Court, Sir Christopher Wren at Greenwich, and Conrad's *Heart of Darkness*, with its powerful evocation of the storied Thames. The sun glints on the river this morning, but I remember Marlow's warning: "This too has been one of the dark places of the earth."

It is darkening dusk when James noses our rented car slowly into an almost obscured drive just outside the village of Chideock in Dorset. We have been looking for a particular cottage we might want to book for a week next spring. The drive ends at a tiny medieval church—Catholic, not Anglican, a rare survival in England—in the grounds of a stately manor whose windows are now shuttered and dark. The owner, we decide, must be away. We get out of the car to look tentatively around, and from a dark cluster of trees outside the church comes an extraordinary sound, a ghostly cacophony of clucking, hooting, and fluttering. In the hushed dusk, it has an alarming effect. James, who grew up in rural western Minnesota, eventually realizes what it is: a flock of pheasants, roosting for the night.

Sailing down Oxford Street, I look complacently out the front window of a double-decker London bus at the milling shoppers and window displays. The bus inches through heavy traffic, but I am in no hurry. I am on my way to Hyde Park, where I plan a leisurely circuit ending at Harrod's Food Hall. On the seat beside me I have tucked my flowered vinyl shopper, ready for a load of cheeses, pâté, salads, and rolls, everything James and I could want for a lunch tomorrow on our way to the West Country.

On a bright, cold, and very windy September morning, James and I bundle up and head a few miles to the Cromer pier in North Norfolk. The wind is so strong that the few people on the promenade are bent double. Waves crash onto the beach below, and the water is brown with blown sand. Sometimes a particularly fierce wave splashes over the promenade itself. We walk out onto the pier and find refuge on the lee side of the main building. There it is quite sunny and warm, and we sit close together, watching the waves and feeling the pier tremble beneath us. An occasional gull unsuccessfully tries to beat its way against the wind. A party of leggy adolescent schoolgirls troops onto the pier, giggling, clutching their lunch bags, coats flying. A ship steams very slowly across the horizon. Below the pier, the nearby volunteer lifeboat station is open. Its heavy wooden rowboat hangs inside, poised to slide down the ramp into the heavy seas.

Our last night in Lynmouth, I follow James along the North Walk, a paved path carved into a cliff high above the ocean. Below the path, the cliff falls precipitously down to the water; above, it rises almost vertically to the plateau of Lynton, a neighboring village. Earlier in the day I had picked a pint of blackberries from the bushes that cling to the rocky sides of the cliff. Two wild black goats were sunning themselves on an unapproachable promontory.

Tonight, it is dark, the stars are hidden, and I think perhaps it may rain. Tired from packing, I sit on a bench and wait for James to finish the walk. No one else passes me. As I look out on the sea, I can just glimpse a few lights on the distant coast of Wales. The sky and water gradually blend together in a pale gray-blue mist. It is so peaceful I can sense my chest rise and fall with each breath. I feel I, too, am suspended in the mist.

When James returns for me, I rise and take his hand. "Promise me we can come back here," I say softly.

"I promise," he says, and puts his arms around me. We turn and walk slowly home.

About the Author

A graduate of Smith College, the University of California at Berkeley, and the University of Minnesota, where she received her Ph.D., Susan Allen Toth is an adjunct professor of English at Macalester College in St. Paul, Minnesota. She is the author of *Blooming, Ivy Days,* and *How to Prepare for Your High-School Reunion.* She is also co-editor of *Reading Rooms.* She lives in Minneapolis with her daughter, Jennifer, and her husband, James Stageberg, with whom she wrote *A House of One's Own.*